TEXANS

AT

GETTYSBURG

BLOOD AND GLORY
WITH HOOD'S
TEXAS BRIGADE

JOSEPH L. OWEN AND RANDY S. DRAIS

FONTHILL

Front Cover: *Hood's Texans* by Mark Maritato

Fonthill Media Language Policy

Fonthill Media publishes in the international English language market. One language edition is published worldwide. As there are minor differences in spelling and presentation, especially with regard to American English and British English, a policy is necessary to define which form of English to use. The Fonthill policy is to use the form of English native to the author. Joseph L. Owen and Randy S. Drais were born and educated in the United States; therefore American English has been adopted in this publication.

Fonthill Media Limited
Fonthill Media LLC
www.fonthillmedia.com
office@fonthillmedia.com

First published in the United Kingdom and the United States of America 2016

British Library Cataloguing in Publication Data:
A catalogue record for this book is available from the British Library

Typeset in 10.5pt on 13pt Sabon
Printed and bound in England by CPI Group (UK) Ltd, Croydon, CR0 4YY

'Small as the Texas Brigade is, it cannot be spared. It contains some of the best troops in the army and its loss would be severely felt.'

—General Robert E. Lee to President Jefferson Davis,
25 February 1865.

This book is dedicated to Sergeant Joseph B. Polley (1840–1918) and Colonel Harold B. Simpson, USAF Ret. (1917–1989), who were the historians of Hood's Texas Brigade and kept alive the history, heroism, and sacrifice of the soldiers and officers who fought for Texas, Arkansas, and the Confederacy from 1861 to 1865.

CONTENTS

Acknowledgements

I have always been fascinated with the Civil War—in particular the Battle of Gettysburg, and what soldiers from Texas made of fighting in such a faraway place as Pennsylvania. After reading the outstanding recollections of the veterans from both North Carolina and Georgia in Michael C. Hardy's *North Carolina Remembers Gettysburg* and J. Keith Jones's *Georgia Remembers Gettysburg,* I was inspired to gather and edit those of Hood's Texas Brigade and the other soldiers from Texas and Arkansas. I sought out both Michael's and Keith's advice on how to proceed in gathering them, and they proved invaluable.

Without the assistance, editing, and counsel of co-author Randy Drais, whose knowledge of the battle and the Texas Brigade's involvement is phenomenal, this book would not have been possible.

I would like to thank John Versluis and the staff of the Texas Heritage Museum in Hillsboro, Texas, for their assistance in providing photographs and granting access to other resources; Zack Waters, whose outstanding book *A Small but Spartan Band: The Florida Brigade in Lee's Army of Northern Virginia* also inspired me to edit *Texans at Gettysburg: Blood and Glory with Hood's Texas Brigade.* Zack's support, enthusiasm and wisdom are greatly appreciated; noted Gettysburg historian and author Scott Mingus Sr, who was also a great source of inspiration and advice; and Gettysburg Licensed Battlefield Guide David L. Richards gave invaluable advice and suggestions—our thanks go out to David.

The authors wish to thank artist Mark Maritato for his support and permission to use his outstanding paintings for the front cover and two chapter introductions in the book; Diane Kirkendall for the photograph of Hood's Texas Brigade Monument at Austin; Patricia Rich for the photographs of the Texas and Arkansas Monuments at Gettysburg; Maurine Liles and Shirley Grammer of the Wilson County Texas Historical Society for their kindness and enthusiasm; John Hoopes, who provided the memoirs and photos of his great-great-grandfather William A. Abernathy of the 17th Mississippi Infantry Regiment; Katie Hall of the Old State House Museum in Little Rock, Arkansas; the Texas State Archives and Library of Congress; Susan Chandler, Director of the Nesbit Memorial Library. Much appreciation goes to Lana Henley for her information about Lt. Col. Benjamin F. Carter, Commanding Officer of the Fourth Texas Infantry Regiment.

I would especially like to thank my wonderful wife Cathy, whose profound patience, invaluable editing, and sage advice was the major factor in the successful completion of this book.

Joseph L. Owen
Blanco, Texas, 19 December 2015

Introduction:
A Brief History of
Hood's Texas Brigade

The Texas Brigade was organized on 22 October 1861 in Richmond, Virginia, due largely to the efforts of John Allen Wilcox, a member of the First Confederate Congress from Texas. Many Texans were joining the Texas Brigade until they had formally organized into regiments in Richmond itself.[1] Often referred to as Hood's Texas Brigade, they were the only Confederate infantry troops from the Lone Star State to fight in the Eastern Theater during the Civil War.

The Texas Brigade was first led by Brigadier General Louis T. Wigfall and was initially comprised of three regiments: the 1st, 4th, and 5th Texas. The 1st was commanded by Wigfall and Lieutenant-Colonel Hugh McLeod, the 4th by Colonel John B. Hood and Lieutenant-Colonel John Marshall, and the 5th by Colonel James J. Archer and Lieutenant-Colonel Jerome B. Robertson.[2] Other troops were added to the brigade during the early years of the war: the Eighteenth Georgia Infantry Regiment (under the command of Colonel William T. Wofford) was assigned to the Texas Brigade on 20 November 1861; eight infantry companies (under the command of Lieutenant-Colonel Martin W. Gary) from Hampton's South Carolina Legion were added on 1 June 1862; and the 3rd Arkansas Infantry Regiment (commanded by Colonel Van H. Manning) was added in November 1862 during the reorganization of the Army of Northern Virginia (ANV). During this reorganization, General Hood was given command of a division and General Robertson became the commander of the Texas Brigade. It should be noted that although the 3rd Arkansas Infantry Regiment remained with the Texas Brigade until the end of the Civil War, both the other non-Texas units were reassigned during this reorganization in 1862.[3]

Brigadier General Wigfall resigned command of the brigade on 20 February 1862 after being elected to the Confederate Senate, and on 7 March 1862 Colonel Hood was promoted to Brigadier General and placed in command of the entire brigade. Because of his bold and solid leadership, the Texas Brigade soon became known as Hood's Texas Brigade or Hood's Texans, and it served valiantly in General James P. Longstreet's 1st Corps in the ANV, participating in over twenty battles in 1862 (including Gaines' Mill, Second Manassas and Antietam).[4, 5]

The Texas Brigade operated along the Blackwater River near Suffolk, Virginia, shortly after the battle of Fredericksburg, and in the spring of 1863 received new uniforms in Richmond. The Texas Brigade rejoined the Army of Northern Virginia in May 1863.[6] Although the Texas Brigade was not involved in the Battle of Chancellorsville, it played a prominent role on 2 July 1863 at the Battle of Gettysburg. When General Longstreet's 1st Corps was sent to reinforce the Army of the Tennessee, the Texas Brigade fought in September at the Battle of Chickamauga, where General Hood was wounded and forced to leave his division, ending his official connection with the brigade.[7] It later joined in the sieges of Chattanooga and Knoxville, Tennessee, in October and November.

In February of 1864, General Longstreet appointed General John Gregg as commander of the Texas Brigade. After the 1st Corps returned to the Army of Northern Virginia shortly before the Battle of the Wilderness in May 1864, General Longstreet filed court-martial charges against General Robertson's performance in Tennessee for alleged delinquency of duty in the Tennessee Campaign. Robertson was later reprimanded, replaced as commander of the Texas Brigade, and transferred to Texas, where he commanded the state's reserve forces until the end of the Civil War.[8] However, command of the Texas Brigade changed once again after General Gregg was killed at the Battle of Darbytown and New Market Roads, near Richmond, on 7 October 1864. The brigade was temporarily led by Colonel Clinton M. Winkler and then by Colonel F. S. Bass before being taken over by Colonel Robert M. Powell until the end of the war.[9]

The Battle of Gettysburg

By the time Hood's Texas Brigade reached the rolling hills near Gettysburg, it had already fashioned a reputation as perhaps the finest fighting unit in General Robert E. Lee's Army of Northern Virginia (ANV). In the 151 years since the Battle of Gettysburg, thousands of books have been written about the battle and the regiments from the Union and the Confederacy that fought from 1–3 July, 1863. It is surprising to find that there has been no 'stand-alone' book written exclusively from the Texans' recollections in Hood's Texas Brigade or other Texans that fought in the battle. Certainly, the memories of Texan soldiers have been included in many books about the battle—brief quotations from Private Joseph B. Polley and Sergeant Val Giles (both of the 4th Texas), among others. Yet there has never been a book written exclusively about the Texans' experience of Gettysburg.

Soldiers would write to their loved ones in Texas in the days and weeks after the battle. They also shared what they remembered in newspaper articles decades later. These recollections varied from several pages to just a paragraph, but all were an important piece of the story. Many Texan veterans even started recording their thoughts weeks before the battle was fought, as they marched through Virginia, Maryland, and Pennsylvania with the ANV led by General Robert E. Lee. Marching through the towns and countryside, they encountered civilians who were either silently pro-Confederate, or boastfully pro-Union. The soldiers would write home about how plentiful the harvest was, as they gathered in food and supplies confiscated from the population (paid for in Confederate currency). Their spirits were high, despite knowing that a battle loomed ahead.

The Battle of Gettysburg would begin for most of the Texans in the late afternoon of 2 July 1863, as battle lines stretched southward from the town. Union Colonel Strong Vincent's brigade was assigned to defend the hill of Little Round Top, minutes before Hood's Brigade began their advance.[10] The 1st Texas and 3rd Arkansas Infantry Regiments rushed to the western side of Houck's Ridge at Devil's Den, moving up a ramp of open acreage that came level with the top of the boulders. A Federal volley of rifles and cannon pushed them back. The 1st Texas and 3rd Arkansas mounted a series of attacks but were met by elements of Ward's Brigade, including the 4th Maine, 124th New York, 99th Pennsylvania, 86th New York Infantry Regiments and Smith's New York Light Artillery Battery.[11] The Federals were holding out until four Georgia regiments joined the battle, and fell back, except for the 4th Maine Infantry Regiment. The 1st Texas, 3rd Arkansas, and Georgia Regiments inflicted heavy casualties on the men from Maine, exceeding 50 percent.[12] They secured the area, but at a the cost of 819 of their own killed or wounded.

At the same time, the 4th and 5th Texas Infantry Regiments charged with regiments from Alabama up Little Round Top and fought against the 16th Michigan, 44th New York, 83rd Pennsylvania, and the 20th Maine. At least twice the 4th and 5th Texas charged up the hill and took heavy casualties.[13] Men who were not struck down by bullets collapsed from heat stroke and exhaustion, and they were ultimately unsuccessful in dislodging the Union regiments and capturing the summit of Little Round Top.[14]

During the late afternoon of 3 July 1863, Union cavalry regiments under Brigadier General Elon J. Farnsworth were ordered by Union Cavalry Commander Judson Kilpatrick to attack the Confederate flank after two failed mounted attacks against the skirmish line of the 1st Texas and the 47th Alabama. Kilpatrick ordered Farnsworth to lead a mounted assault with the 1st Vermont Cavalry, but the sloping ground and large boulders broke up the charge.[15] The cavalry charge was a failure, with General Farnsworth among the Union dead.

The battle would be permanently etched in Texan memory, and kept alive at the Hood's Texas Brigade Association reunions held throughout the state. The recollections and articles in this book are from the soldiers of the brigade and other Texans on either side of the battle lines. These are their stories, and it is an honor to share them. But for some minor clarifications in their grammar and punctuation, are presented as they were originally written and published. At times the soldiers relating their memoirs of the battle deviate from the present to the past tense, and vice versa, and employ language that may offend some readers; these idiosyncrasies have been preserved for sake of historical authenticity and accuracy.

First Texas Infantry Regiment

The 1st Texas Infantry Regiment, organized on 22 October 1861 and led by Brigadier General Louis T. Wigfall, was considered the 'cornerstone' regiment of Hood's Texas Brigade, and was the first to reach Virginia and fight in the Army of North Virginia (ANV).[1] It was originally conceived as an over-strength battalion with Companies A through to H. It later became a regiment, to which Companies I, K, and L were added. Company M came in July 1862, making the 1st the only twelve-company regiment in the ANV. The 1st Texas saw its first combat at Eltham's Landing on 7 May 1862 during the Peninsula Campaign. At the Battle of Antietam it charged through a cornfield to blunt the assault of Major-General Joseph Hooker's I Corps, suffering 82.3 percent of its force killed, wounded, or captured—the highest casualty rate of any unit in the Civil War.[2] It consisted of the following:

Company A—Marion Rifles (Marion County)
Company B—Livingston Guards (Livingston County)
Company C—Palmer Guards (Harris County)
Company D—Star Rifles (Marion County)
Company E—Marshall Guards (Harrison County)
Company F—Woodville Rifles (Tyler County)
Company G—Reagan Guards (Anderson County)
Company H—Texas Guards (Anderson County)
Company I—Crockett Southrons (Houston County)
Company K—Texas Invincibles (San Augustine County)
Company L—Lone Star Rifles (Galveston County)
Company M—Sumter Light Infantry (Trinity County)

Flag of the 1st Texas Infantry Regiment flown at the Battle of Gettysburg. (*Texas State Archives*)

Lieutenant-Colonel P. A. Work
First Texas Infantry

The regiment, together with the brigade having been ordered forward to the attack at about 4.00 p.m., continued to advance by the front for a distance exceeding half a mile (the 4th Texas upon the right and the 3rd Arkansas upon the left) when Company I, commanded by Lieutenant J. H. Wooters and thrown out as skirmishers, engaged the skirmishers of the enemy, driving them back upon a regiment supporting the enemy's battery, and then, aided by volunteers from [the 1st Texas] … succeeded in driving back the regiment and silencing the enemy's guns, taking and holding possession of the latter.

While this regiment was closely following our skirmishers, and had [come within] 125 yards of the enemy's artillery, the 3rd Arkansas Regiment on my left became hotly engaged with a strong force of the enemy upon its front and left, thus leaving my left flank uncovered and exposed, to protect which I halted, and threw out upon my left and rear Company G, commanded by Lieutenant B. A. Campbell (some forty men), which soon engaged the enemy and drove them from their threatening position to the left and the front of the 3rd Arkansas. It was while in the execution of this order that Lieutenant Campbell, a brave and gallant officer, fell, pierced through the heart.

Owing to the failure (as informed by Brigadier General Robertson) of the troops that were assigned to the position on the left of [Robertson's] brigade to arrive promptly, neither this nor the 3rd Arkansas was able to advance, without advancing against a vastly superior force, and with the left flank of the 3rd Arkansas (protecting my left) exposed to attack. After the lapse of several minutes, Benning's brigade made its appearance, but instead of occupying the ground to the left of Robertson's brigade, so as to enable the latter to move forward with its left flank secure from attack, it [took] the ground still occupied, by a portion at least, of this brigade, the 15th Georgia Regiment falling in and remaining with the 1st Texas Regiment. After several ineffectual efforts upon the part of both commanders of the 15th Georgia and myself to separate the men of the two regiments, we gave the order to move forward and occupied the crest of the hill, some 100 yards or more to the front, and where the enemy's artillery was stationed, where we remained until the close of the day and until two o'clock on Friday morning.

During the evening of the 2nd, an incessant fire was kept up by this regiment, and the enemy were several times repulsed in their efforts to retake the hill. My position was such that I was enabled [a deadly enfilading fire to be poured] into the enemy as they advanced through a wheat field to attack the troops in position on my left, and I have no doubt that this fire contributed greatly to the repulse of the enemy attacking our forces some 300 or 400 yards on my left.

Once during the evening, the troops on my left were driven back, and my left was exposed, when, directing Captain H. E. Moss, Company D, to take charge of the colors, and retaining them there with a few men to hold the hill until the regiment could safely retire, I ordered the regiment to fall back to a stone fence about 100 yards in my rear.

The major part of the regiment and the 15th Georgia fell back as ordered, but quite a large number, having noticed that the colors were not moving to the rear, refused to withdraw, and remaining upon the crest of the hill, succeeded in holding the enemy in check in their immediate front, and obliquely upon their front and left, until the troops upon my left had been re-formed and were again advancing, when I directed Major F. S. Bass to return to the crest of the hill with the body of the regiment, and, with Captain D. K. Rice of Company C, proceeded myself to collect together all fugitives, slightly wounded, and exhausted men, and placed them so as to protect my right and rear from an attack in that quarter, one of my advanced scouts in that directed having reported to me that a column of the enemy was moving down a ravine or hollow and threatening me in that quarter.

Having made every disposition to guard my right and rear, I placed Captain D. K. Rice in charge of such defense, and proceeded to the Third Arkansas Regiment, of which General Robertson had ordered me to take charge. After the loss of some half hour in searching for the 3rd Arkansas, I found Lieutenant-Colonel Taylor and Major Reedy, of that regiment, both alive and uninjured and in charge of the regiment, which was doing its duty nobly and well. Late in the evening a terrible fire of artillery was concentrated against the hill occupied by [the 1st Texas Regiment], many were killed and wounded, some losing their heads, and others so horribly mutilated and mangled that their identity could hardly be established; but notwithstanding this, all the men continued heroically and unflinchingly to maintain their position.

Immediately after dark, having detailed Companies E and I for the purpose, I sent three pieces of artillery captured to the rear. There were three other pieces—two at one point and one at another—that I was unable to remove, for the reason that they were located between the lines of the enemy and our own, and were so much exposed that they could not be approached except under a murderous fire.

While they could not be removed by us, neither could they be approached by the enemy, for the same fire that drove the artillerists from their guns and infantry from their support was ever in readiness to keep them in check and drive them back.

Every man of the regiment proved himself a hero. Hundreds might be mentioned, each of whom with reason and propriety might point to his gallant acts and daring deeds, and the lieutenant-colonel commanding feels that he cannot call attention to the bearing of a few, only of those, without doing some share of injustice to those not mentioned; although he is urged to mention the names of Privates W. Y. Salter of Company I, J. N. Kirksey and G. Barfield of Company B, and W. J. Barbee of Company I, for great and striking gallantry, and does mention them, he feels that he is neglecting others of equal merit. Private Barbee, though a mounted courier, acting for Major-General Hood, entered the ranks of his company, L, and fought through the engagement. At one time he mounted a rock on the highest pinnacle of the hill, and there, exposed to a raking, deadly fire of artillery and musketry, stood until he had fired twenty-five shots, when he received a minie-ball wound in the right thigh, and fell. Having exhausted their original supply of ammunition, the men supplied themselves from the cartridge boxes of their dead and disabled comrades, and from the dead and the wounded of the enemy, frequently going in front of the hill to secure a cartridge box.

Many of the officers threw aside their swords, seized a rifle, and going into the ranks, fought bravely and nobly. The regiment lost in killed 25, in wounded 48, and in missing 20, a list of the names of whom, giving the company and character of wound of those wounded, is hereto annexed as part of this report.[3]

Captain George T. Todd
First Texas Infantry

We followed the track of the routed enemy, and crossed the Potomac [River] into Maryland and Williamsport on 20 June 1863. We leisurely advanced through Maryland and camped in Chambersburg, Pa, for several days. We were well treated and well fed by the people and enjoyed our stay among them. There was absolutely no plundering or depredations committed by our army. Our advances reached Harrisburg and Carlisle. On 30 June we received rush orders to march eastwards towards Gettysburg, and we marched nearly all night of the 1st July, hearing all day the thunder

Captain George T. Todd.
(*Texas Heritage Museum*)

of the guns where Hill and Ewell were winning the first days battle near Gettysburg. We debouched on Seminary Ridge in full view of the enemy about 8.00 a.m., 2 July 1863; loaded, without capping our guns, and filed to our right taking position in reserve, on Lee's extreme right. But little, even skirmishing was doing till afternoon, and we rested till about 4.00 p.m. when Generals Hood and Longstreet rode down the lines, and we were ordered to advance with the entire division. We charged across the Emmetsburg Pike, through the famous peach orchard, driving back the enemy under General Sickles who lost a leg there. The 1st Texas and 3rd Arkansas regiments diverged to the right from the 4th and 5th Texas, and were soon climbing a steep and rocky height, 'Little Round Top' I think, where we captured a battery of four guns, and held our position under a storm of artillery and rifle fire till after dark, when we received orders to fall back to the road. Here the blood and brains of E. P. Derrick, one of my company, was scattered over my face and hat. The enemy were so close that we had to wrap blankets around the wheels of the artillery and move three pieces back with us by hand, one of the pieces had fallen into a ravine and had to be left. These were the only pieces of artillery captured by either side in the battle of the 2nd and 3rd July. (I think our forces captured some on the 1st July, but don't know number.) On the 3rd and last day of the battle our regiment was thrown on our extreme right, and were posted behind a stone fence, where we were charged by cavalry under General Farnsworth. We killed and wounded nearly all in our immediate front, but many turned our flanks on both sides, and getting in our rear were met by a number of teamsters and litter bearers, and surrendered to them. All I saw were drunk. We captured several hundred. One of my company, Bent Allen, jumped over the wall, and got General Farnsworth's epilates and spurs. He was killed in front of our company. Before the assault, which ended our part in the battle, we and Hood's whole division acted as reserve, and witnessed the charge of Picket's division on the enemy's center. We saw the position captured and the enemy's retreat, but they reinforced and we did not. Had Hood's division been supporting Picket we would surely have held the ground. As it was, we held nearly the entire field undisturbed all day of 4th July, (the fatal day of Vicksburg's (Mississippi) surrender, and during the night of 3rd and 4th, we being on our extreme right, plainly heard the artillery and ordnance wagons of General Meade leaving the field and moving to our right in order to flank us. This compelled General Lee, with over 5,000 prisoners to guard, to move to Hagerstown, where we offered battle for ten days, waiting in vain for an attack. While Gettysburg was indeed 'the high tide,' not of 'rebellion,' but of State sovereignty under the Constitution as we know it taught ... impartial history must concede that Lee's army not only held its own, but won the victory at Gettysburg. Another record must be made. Lee's army was never defeated on a single field of battle—even when 'worn to a frazzle' at Appomattox. Flanked often and compelled to fall back in retreat, yet they were never driven afoot by the greatest assaults of our powerful foe 'the Army of the Potomac.' Deny this, who can? But for the scarcity of artillery ammunition, and inconvenience of getting it, I don't think we would have left Maryland. Our regiment crossed at Falling Waters (Maryland), about 15 July, and after a short stay in the valley we marched through the Blue Ridge and were, in August, again in camp near Gordonsville and Culpeper Court House, from where we started on the Gettysburg campaign. We were soon rested and recuperated and, tho' our ranks were thinned, again ready for the fray. Our losses in killed and wounded were much less than at Sharpsburg (Antietam). A few of the regiment were captured on post. I wore a Confederate-made gray wool hat, which was sprinkled with the blood of comrade E. P. Derrick, killed at my side on 'Little Round Top.' 'Going into camps' came to be a very simple and quickly executed operation. The regiment fronted in line and broke by company front to the rear, formed line, stacked arms and broke ranks, allowing 50-feet streets between the companies, each mess erecting their dug tents or quarters in rear of the line of muskets. The field officers and commissary and guard tents were conveniently near. The authorities now thought that General Lee was strong enough to protect Richmond with two thirds of his army, and Longstreet and Hood were ordered west to help General Bragg.[4]

Captain George T. Todd
First Texas Infantry
Recollections of Gettysburg

George T. Todd, Esq., Adjutant of Marion County (Texas), No. 1265, writes from Jefferson, Texas:

The 'Reminiscences of the Battle of Gettysburg' by Colonel A. H. Bello of the 55th North Carolina Regiment, in the April *Veteran* covering the first day's victory and capture of Gettysburg, and also Major W. M. Robbin's letter, all of which was before Sterling Price Camp of Dallas, Texas, are most interesting and instructive. I have often read General Lee's report and General Longstreet's book besides many other accounts of the great battle, and was myself commander of Company A, 1st Texas Regiment.

In reading Major Robbin's vivid description of the fighting by Law's Alabama and Hood's, Wollford's, and Robertson's old Texas brigades in the evening of the second day, I find myself again on the field, charging beyond the peach orchard among the rocks and boulders of 'Devil's Den,' where we captured a battery, and held the position till after night, when we moved back to where we camped in line of battle, rolling off the captured guns with us.

I honestly believe that if Hood's Division or even Law's or Robertson's old brigades had been rushed forward en echelon to the support of General's Pickett and Heth on the third day, we would have held the crest they so gallantly won and complete victory would have been ours. But as Major Robbins told Colonel Bello: 'We were very near victory several times, but I have concluded that God almighty did not attend it.'

Major Robbins, however, does not relate the whole of the movement on 3 July to repel the cavalry charge on our extreme right. It is doubtless true that his regiment, the 4th Alabama, and perhaps the 15th was engaged in that movement, but I know that the 1st Texas, under Lieutenant-Colonel P. A. Work, was also part of it. We (1st Texans) were thrown behind a stone fence on the right of the line, and from that safe place poured a most deadly fire from our Enfield rifles upon the on-charging sweep of Kilpatrick's cavalry. General Farnsworth (believed by us to be Kilpatrick himself) fell in the left in front of our regiment, and one of the 1st Texans ran forward and got his epaulettes and spurs. He also reported that he shot himself on the account of the agony he was in. Their charging lines overlapped and outflanked our line on the right, and several hundred of them dashed to our rear. They were checked by some teamsters and litter bearers, when they galloped back to our lines with sabers extended, in token of surrender.

While so much is said and written about Pickett's charge and repulse in our center, history should not omit or overlook Kilpatrick's charge and bloody repulse on the right, which formed the final and closing scene in this greatest and bloodiest of all battle dramas.[5]

Private Henry Berryman
First Texas Infantry

Newton Monroe and Henry Waters Berryman were educated with the intention of attending the US Military Academy, as their father had, but they learned to fight in a real war, the Civil War. Both were in Hood's Brigade, First Texas Infantry, Company I. Lieutenant Newton Monroe Berryman was said to have been the bravest man in the brigade. Henry Waters Berryman was known as the best forager. The latter was wounded twice in battle, once seriously when shot in the shoulder in the Battle of the

Wilderness, and once slightly in the Battle of Gettysburg. The Yankees were about to run over his body when a boy soldier, Charlie Scully pulled him into a ditch, where he cut the bullet from his shoulder himself. After the war, the brothers headed homeward afoot. Charlie Scully was with him.[6]

Private James O. Bradfield
First Texas Infantry

Hood's division held the right flank of our army. We began forming our line of battle in a wide plateau leading back to the rear, while in front about 200 yards distant was a skirt of timber on the brow of a hill which led to the valley below. In this timber our batteries were posted, and as the Texas Brigade was forming immediately in their rear, we were in direct range of the enemy's guns on the mountain beyond. As our artillery began feeling their batteries, the answering shells struck our lines with cruel effect. The 4th Texas suffered most severely. As they were passing this zone of fire, one shell killed and wounded fifteen men. It certainly tries a man's nerve to have to stand still and receive such a fire without being able to return it.

Just here occurred one of the little incidents that, happening at times like this, are never forgotten. In our company was a tall, robust fellow named Dick Childers, who was noted for the energy and talent he displayed in procuring rations. On this occasion Dick's haversack was well stocked with nice biscuits which a kind Dutch lady had given him. As we were marching by the right flank, our left sides were turned towards the enemy. A shell from the mountain in front struck the ground near our batteries, and came bouncing across the field, and as Dick happened to be just in the line of fire, it struck him, or rather, his haversack, fairly, and scattered the biscuits all over that end of Pennsylvania. But the stranger part of it is that it did not knock the man down, but so paralyzed him that he fell, after it had passed, and lay there unable to move a muscle. The litter bearers picked him up and laid him on a stretcher, as if he had been a log. The boys all contended, however, that it was the destruction of Dick's rations, and not any shock the shell gave, that paralyzed him.

We marched onward by the right flank, about a quarter of a mile, moving parallel with the enemy's lines, and halting, left faced and formed for work. We were on the brow of a hill which sloped here quite abruptly down into the narrow valley. We could see the enemy's lines of battle—the first on the level space below us, behind a heavy rock fence; the second, at the top of the ridge a hundred or two yards further on, while still further, and entirely out of our reach, at the summit of a higher range, their batteries were posted so as to sweep the whole space over we were to advance. Their battle flags floated proudly in the breeze, above the almost perfect natural breastworks formed by the fence and the large rocks that crowned the low ridge upon which they stood. There were but two small cannons on the lower ridge, and these were captured and pulled off the hill by the 1st Texas Regiment.

About two o'clock in the afternoon, the order was given to advance all along the line. We moved quietly forward down the steep decline, gaining impetus as we reached the more level ground below. The enemy had already opened fire upon us, but we did not stop to return it. 'Forward— double quick,' rang out, and then Texas turned loose. Across the valley and over the stream that ran through it they swept, every man for himself. The first man down was my right-file man, William Langley, a noble, brave boy, with a mini-ball straight through the brain. I caught him as he fell against me, and laid him down, dead. As I straightened up to move on, that same familiar 'spat' which always means something, sounded near, and looking around I saw Bose Perry double over and catch his gun. He did not fall, however, but came on, dragging his wounded leg, and firing as he advanced. But it was getting too hot, now, to pay attention to details.

The enemy stood their ground bravely, until we were close on them, but did not wait for the bayonet. They broke away from the rock fence as we closed in with a rush and a wild rebel yell, and fell back to the top of the ridge, where they halted and formed on their second line. Having passed the rock fence, and as we were moving on up the hill, an order came to halt. No one seemed to know whence it came, nor from whom. It cost us dearly, for as we lay in close range of their now double lines, the enemy poured a hail of bullets on us, and in a few minutes a number of our men were killed or wounded. We saw that this would never do, and so, without awaiting orders, every man became his own commander and sprang toward the top of the hill at full speed.

By this time, Benning's [Georgia] brigade, which had been held in reserve, joined us and together we swept on to where the Blue Coats stood behind the sheltering rocks to receive us. Just here, and to our right, in a little cove called the 'Devil's Den,' which was covered by the 4th and 5th Texas, Law's Alabama and Anderson's Georgia brigades, occurred one of the wildest, fiercest struggles of the war—a struggle such as it is given to few men to pass through and live.

The opposing lines stood with only the sheltering rocks between them— breast to breast, and so close that the clothing of many of the enemy was set on fire by the blaze from the Confederate rifles. This continued for some time, but finally our fire grew so hot that, brave as they were, the Federals could no longer endure it, but gave way and fled down the slope, leaving us in possession of the field. The Lone Star flag crowned the hill, and Texas was there to stay. Not alone, however, for just to our right stood Benning—'Old Rock'—that peerless old hero than whom no braver man ever lived. Striding back and forth in front of his line, he was calling to his gallant Georgians: 'Give them h-ll boys, give them h-ll' and the 'boys' were giving it to them according to instructions.

On the right of Benning stood Anderson and Law, and the 4th and 5th Texas, as firm as the rocks which sheltered them. I cannot hope to describe the deeds of daring and heroism that was enacted. Beyond the valley in our front, on the summit of the practically impregnable ridge that stretched forth from Gettysburg, stood the enemy's battery, 200 guns. Of these, about forty were playing in close range upon the position we occupied. Their fire and that of our own batteries, and the constant roar and the rattle of thousands of muskets, made the earth tremble beneath our feet, while the fierce, angry shriek of shells, the strident swirl of grape and canister as they tore hurtling through the air and broke live a wave from the ocean of death upon that devoted spot, the hissing bullets, and their 'spat' as they struck rock, tree or human flesh—all this, with the shouts and imprecations, the leaping to and fro and from boulder to boulder of powder-begrimed men, seemingly gone wild with rage and excitement, created a scene of such indescribable, awe-inspiring confusion that an on-looker might well believe that a storm from the infernal regions was spending its fury in and around a spot so fitly named 'The Devil's Den.' Had it not been for the protection afforded us by the large rocks and boulders which lay scattered over the hill-top, no living thing could have remained on its summit.

The fearful artillery fire of the enemy was intended to cover the massing of their infantry, who were now to make one more grand effort to regain the ground they had lost. Our boys prepared for this by gathering up all abandoned muskets within reach, and loading them. Some of us had as many as five or six lying by us, as we awaited the attack.

We had not long to wait, for soon the long blue line came in view, moving in a gallant style up the valley. The Federals were led by splendid officers, and made a noble charge: but when they met the murderous fire from behind the rocks where we crouched, they faltered. Only for a moment though, and they came right up to the rocks. Again they faltered, for now, most of their officers were down. Again it was but for a second, and cheered on by some of the bravest men I have ever seen, they rallied in the very face of death, and charged right up to the muzzles of our guns.

There was one officer, a major, who won our admiration by his courage and gallantry. He was a very handsome man, and rode a beautiful, high-spirited gray horse. The animal seemed to partake of the spirit of the rider, and as he came on with a free, graceful stride into that hell of death and carnage, head erect and ears pointed, horse and man offered a picture such as is seldom seen. The two seemed the very impersonation of heroic courage. As the withering, scathing volleys from behind the rocks cut into the ranks of the regiment the major led, and his gallant men went down like rain before a scythe, he flowed close at their heels, and when, time and again, they stopped and would have fled the merciless fire, he rallied them as if his puissant arm alone could stay the storm. But his efforts were, in the end, unavailing; the pluck of himself and his men only made the carnage more dreadful, for the Lone Star banner and the flag of Georgia continued floating from the hill, showing who stood, defiant and unyielding beneath their folds.

In the last and most determined charge they made on us, the gallant officer made his supreme effort. Riding into our very midst, seeming to bear a charmed life, he sat proudly on the noble gray, and still cheered on his men. 'Don't shoot at him—don't kill him,' our boys shouted to each other; 'he is too brave a man to die—shoot his horse and capture the man.' But it could not be. In a second or two, horse and rider went down together, pierced by a dozen balls. Thus died a hero, one of the most gallant men that ever gave up his life on the red field of carnage. Though it was that of an enemy, we honored the dead body as if it had been that of one of our own men. Such courage belongs not to any one army or country, but to mankind.

It was about this time that a spectacular display of reckless courage was made by a young Texan, Will Barbee, of the 1st Texas. Under twenty years old, he was ordinarily a jolly, whole-souled lad, not at all given to extraordinary performances. But when a fight was going on, he went wild, seemed to have no sense of fear whatever, and was a reckless dare-devil. Although a courier for General Hood, he never failed to join his regiment, if possible, and go into battle with it. On the present occasion, when General Hood was wounded, Barbee hunted us up. It was the hottest of the fight, I heard some say, 'Here comes Barbee,' and looking down from the rock on which I was lying, I saw him coming as fast as his little sorrel could run, and waving his hat as he came. Just before reaching us, the sorrel fell, but Barbee did not stop to see what had happened to the brute. He hit the ground running, and snatching up a gun as he came, was soon in line.

About five paces to my left was a large, high rock behind which several of our wounded were sheltering themselves. To the top of that, where the very air was alive with missiles of death, Barbee sprang, and standing there, erect and fearless, began firing, the wounded men below him passed up loaded guns as fast as he emptied them. But no living being could stay unhurt long in such a fire. In a few minutes, Barbee was knocked off the rock by a ball that struck him in the right leg. Climbing instantly back, he again commenced shooting. In less than two minutes, he was tumbled off the rock by a ball in the other leg. Still unsatisfied, he crawled back a second time, but was not there more than a minute before, being wounded in the body, he again fell, this time dropping on his back between the rock that had been his perch, and that which was my shelter. Too seriously wounded this time to extricate himself from the narrow passageway, he called for help, and the last time I saw him that day, he was lying there, crying and cursing because the boys would not come to his relief and help him back onto the rock.

There were many in the regiment as brave as Barbee, but none so reckless. The best blood of Texas was there, and in the 4th and 5th Texas, and General Lee could safely place the confidence he did in Hood's Texas Brigade. But God must have ordained our defeat. As was said by one of the speakers at a reunion of the Mountain Remnant Brigade:

> At the first roll of the war drum, Texas sent forth her noblest and best. She gave the Army of Northern Virginia Hood's matchless brigade—a band of heroes who bore their country's flag to victory on every field, until God stopped them at Little Round Top.[7]

Private James O. Bradfield
First Texas Infantry
The Two Biggest 'Fools' of the Confederate Army

With a loving emphasis, instead of a sneer, upon the word 'fools,' showing his high regard for the bravery of two of the South's soldiers of the Confederacy, J. O. Bradfield, Chaplain of Hood's Brigade, detailed during the annual reunion of the organization in Bryan the story of these two men, as it occurred in the Battle of Gettysburg ... [This] was the turning point, perhaps of the war, and ended Lee's second invasion of the North, the first one having been stopped at Antietam.

General Hood, said Mr Bradfield, had a boy sergeant in his command by the name of Barbee, and when Hood was wounded that little Barbee left and came immediately to the 1st Texas Regiment. He was a courier and not supposed to carry a rifle. He came to where three of us were lying on top of a rock and firing over the edge of the rock at the enemy on the hill. Barbee picked up a gun and cartridge belt, ran up to the rock, got up on it, and standing erect began shooting. Evidently he did not like to do his fighting from ambush but wanted it right out in the open. In front of us lay the whole Federal army, and there he was, standing on that rock, firing as fast as he could reload at the enemy's lines, exposed to the fire of a multitude of guns.

It was only a few moments until one of the many bullets coming his way hit him in the leg and knocked him off the rock. That did not seem to please him for he rested a moment and then climbed back on the rock and began firing again. A little while longer and another bullet came and hit the other leg. He was knocked off the rock again. He picked himself up off the ground, recovered himself, climbed back on the rock, and with a bullet in each leg, resumed his occupation of firing at the enemy and he did not conclude until a bullet struck him in the side and he was unable to longer continue the hugely one-sided struggle against the Union army.

A few moments after the young fellow had been knocked off the rock for the last time, my two comrades were cut in two by shell fire and I was the only man left alive on the rock. So, I concluded that it was just about time for me to leave and beat a retreat for the rear where I might find some companionship.

As I was passing toward the rear he saw another man standing upon a rock, firing just as Barbee had done, this making 'the second biggest "fool" in the Confederate army.' He was up there in the thick of firing. It was too far away for me to distinguish who he was but I afterward learned that the man was from the same Texas command and that he lived through the battle and the war, escaping miraculously unhurt from his daring escapade of standing up on the rock and I also learned that this man's name was our comrade, Lawrence Daffan, father of Katie Daffan, life secretary of Hood's Texas Brigade.[8]

Private James O. Bradfield
First Texas Infantry
Wounding of General Hood

When General John Bell Hood was wounded, following his determination to disobey orders, even if he had to stand court martial for it, the Confederates lost in the Battle of Gettysburg, in the opinion of J. O. Bradfield, of Austin, life chaplain of Hood's Texas Brigade. Mr Bradfield explained his reasons for the conclusion in a story given to an *Eagle* reporter recently when attending the brigade's reunion here, as he was sitting in front of the Hotel Bryan waiting for the morning train that would bear him back to Austin where he had been attending the 55th annual reunion of Hood's Texas Brigade.

General Hood, said Mr Bradfield, had started into the line of Battle of Gettysburg to detail the 1st Texas Regiment to do to the summit of Little Round Top, which was unoccupied. General Law of Alabama and General Hood had gone to General Longstreet and asked permission to send a body of men around Little Round Top Mountain. But, finally, Jim Dearing, one of Hood's scouts reported that only one man, a Federal flag man, was on the mountain and that it could easily be occupied by the Confederates. General Hood had sufficient military knowledge to understand that this mountain was the key point in the day's strategic maneuvers and he determined to occupy the mountain, contrary to orders, despite the fact that he might have to stand court martial for disobedience ... He assumed the responsibility for the act himself.

General Hood then started into the line of battle in person and was soon in the thick of the firing. Just as he reached the heart of the heaviest firing he was shot off his horse, wounded, and carried to the rear. Thus his determination to occupy Little Round Top Mountain was never carried out.

Had General Hood been spared to have accomplished what he set out to do, I am satisfied, said Mr Bradfield, that Pickett's charge would never have been made and that the forces of General Meade would have been swept aside by the armies of the Confederacy in this battle that resulted in the turning point of Lee's second invasion of the North.

Providence intervened and it was this hand that saved the day for the Federal armies and lost the battle for the Confederates.[9]

Color Sergeant George A. Branard
First Texas Infantry
Reminiscences of the Confederacy: Tough but True

Captain George A. Branard, the gallant color bearer of the 1st Texas Regiment of Hood's famous Texas Brigade in Virginia, is as a matter of fact one of the most truthful men alive. He is a good talker, was a close observer of the stirring events in Virginia during the four years' service with his regiment there and can put more point and life in a story than anyone I know. He has the happy faculty of making even the commonplace incidents of camp life strikingly interesting and his descriptions of 'tight places' are something to make one's hair stand on end.

General J. B. Polley, who fought next-door neighbor to Captain Branard in the same brigade during the same four terrible years, knows the captain from the soles of his feet to the top of his head and loves and admires every inch of him. One of the most striking characteristics of the Captain is his absolute confidence in himself and his complete self-possession. It is impossible to 'rattle' him. General Polley says that it is not self-possession or self-confidence either, but that 'George' as he calls him is a hardened sinner and has told his stories so often that he really believes them himself. 'Why,' said the general to me lately, 'I'll be blamed if I am not beginning

Branard's Pride. (*Mark Maritato*)

to believe some of them myself. I've heard him tell them the same way so many times.'

Of course, the general never says this before strangers and I will add further, he never says it behind George's' back. The general told me the other day in Dallas that he stayed up at night and lost many hours of valuable sleep planning how to trip George up, but that his best laid plans and schemes had gone up in smoke when he tried them on George, that they failed miserably and fell harmless before his exasperating coolness (the General called it gall).

These few remarks are merely introductory to one of George's stories—a true one he swears, and one he says Dry Jones and all of the other surgeons of the 1st, 4th and 5th regiments will swear to, too.

Last spring, he, General Polley and I were together and, of course, nothing but war talk was in order. George did the talking and General Polley and I did the rest. General Polley had just explained, at George's request, how he got shot in the toe of his foot while running away from the Yankees, when George, without further preface, broke in with:

'Well, the most remarkable wound I saw during the war was at Gettysburg. I was pretty well used up myself and was waiting my turn on the field surgeon's table when they brought a fellow in who was shot right here (placing his finger about an inch below his stomach). There was a big hole in front that you could put two fingers in. The surgeons placed him on the table, pulled off his shirt and saw at a glance that he was done for. They ordered him taken away to die, for they had no time to waste on mortally wounded men. Well, they took him on one side, and placed him under a tree and after I got fixed up, I lay down near him. The next day he was alive and showed no signs of dying and all that day he seemed to be getting along all right. There he was with a great big ball of some kind inside him, for it must be inside him, for there was no hole behind it to come out. Finally, a doctor came and looked at him for his being alive since it was against the laws of medical science and he became interested. About daylight the second day, a red line formed all around his body and the line got darker and darker until it was as black as your hat. Then the mystery of his being alive was explained. The ball had not gone in at all. It had entered the skin, travelled all around his body and came out the same hole again.'

'George! George!' said General Polley. 'The Lord loveth a cheerful liar, but I fear you please him to well.'

'It's the truth and I can prove it,' said George, not the least disturbed or discountenanced by General Polley's remarks. 'Since you insist, I must believe it,' said the general, 'but will you tell us what became of the bullet after it came out?'

'Certainly,' said George. 'It went in the hole, circled all around the man's body, came out at the same hole and went right back into the gun of the Yankee who had shot the gun off. Do you want more particulars or details?'

'No,' said General Polley. 'I'll not encourage you to lose your soul further than you have lost it already.'[10]

Color Sergeant George A. Branard
First Texas Infantry
Meeting of Comrades

An interesting meeting of old comrades of the late war took place in this city this morning, the parties to it being Captain George A. Branard of this city and Captain J. W. Watts of Palestine, both members of Hood's Texas Brigade and the 1st Texas Regiment. The special complexion of this meeting arises from the fact that Captain Branard was color bearer for the regiment and Captain Watts was one of the color guard, and on the field of Gettysburg, when the former was shot down, presumably receiving a fatal wound, Captain Watts picked him up and took him to a place of safety. At the time the wound was received, they were leading a charge of the Texans on Little Round Top in the hottest part of the terrible battle, and the farthest part of the battle field reached by the Confederates.

The meeting of these two old vets was really a fraternal meeting.[11]

Color Sergeant George A. Branard
First Texas Infantry
Letter from J. H. Martin to G. A. Branard Regarding Gettysburg and Other Events

Hawkinsville, Ga, 21 March—Mr George A. Branard, GC, Polk Avenue, Houston, Tex.:

Dear Comrade—I have just returned home from a two weeks' absence and have received your letter from the 18th last, by the mail. I have not seen the article in the Confederate *Veteran* until after the reception of your letter, as I had been out of the county attending our Supreme Court.

I am glad that you concur with my recollection of the Battle of Gettysburg. The popular opinion is that Pickett's division suffered more severely at Gettysburg than any other engaged in that bloody fight, whereas the truth is there were nine Confederate divisions engaged in the Battle of Gettysburg, and Pickett's division was seventh in point of losses. The losses of the several divisions were in the following order: Heth's, Rhodes, Hood's, McLaw's, Pender's, Johnson's, Pickett's, Anderson's and Early's. You will remember that the corps of Hill and Ewell were engaged on more days than one, for they were fighting around Gettysburg the day before we arrived. The loss of Hood's division was sustained in practically one charge, and our losses were 1,947 killed and wounded, whereas Pickett's losses were 1,359. We had much more difficult ground to cover than Pickett had, and the difference was Pickett charged Cemetery Heights on comparatively good ground and Hood charged the mountains on the Federal left on the worst kind of ground and a position that was well-nigh impregnable, and Pickett failed and Hood succeeded. That was the real condition of affairs, but all the Richmond papers, the Whig, Examiner, Dispatch etc., made history during the war and always exalted even a skirmish of the Virginia troops into a wonderful battle and ignored the troops of other states, and as history and the publications since the war followed the footsteps of the Virginia papers, the glorious deeds of other troops have been minimalized, while those of Virginians have been greatly exaggerated.

The rock that you mention in your letter, I think that I recollect. It was off to the right of where I first led my company in through the mouth of the Devil's Den, and my recollection is that one of Hood's couriers dashed down to the left of the rock you mention on a white pony during the fight. I agree with you except as to the distance, which, I think, was about a 150 or 200 yards from the ravine in which I entered.

I recollect full well, too, that on the next day after our charge the Texans had moved further to the right. The next day after the charge on the evening of 2 July, I was stationed on the mountain where the Yankee battery was located and had a pretty good view of the rear, and I recollect very distinctly when the Yankee cavalry dashed through and got into a field, directly on our rear, and I thought at the time that we stood a good chance of being captured, but soon discovered that a gap had been opened by our men for the purpose of entrapping the Yankee cavalry, who were being fought by the cooking detail and teamsters of our side, and was told that not one of them ever got out. I recollect full well the incident of the cavalry Brigadier General killing himself to prevent capture, but until the reception of your letter that it was Farnsworth I could not possibly recall his name.[12]

Color Sergeant George A. Branard
First Texas Infantry

George A. Branard of Houston, secretary and treasurer of Hood's Brigade Association, has sent, being directed by the association for safe keeping only, a plate of General John B. Hood, which was formerly presented to them by J. W. Dallas of Company I, 5th Texas Regiment, the owner of the plate having been E. H. McKnight of Oklahoma. He also sent a bloodstained and bullet-riddled artillery or cavalry flag, which belonged to some Texas troops. Mr Branard was color bearer of the 1st Texas Regiment, and fell with the flag that Governor Lanham has now in his possession on the mountains of Gettysburg, remaining unconscious for some fifteen minutes. He was sent to the field hospital, and after two days again took the flag, carried it through the battle of Chickamauga, where he was again shot down, receiving two wounds in his left arm, thereby ending his career as color bearer.[13]

Career of George A. Branard

The career of George A. Branard is one of the most interesting of the entire Confederate army. 'I enlisted in Company L, First Texas Infantry, as a Fourth Corporal, and came back a disabled Color Sergeant,' is all the account which Secretary Branard has ever been willing to give of his service in Hood's Brigade. But from General J. B. Polley, who once commanded the Texas Department, United Confederate Veterans, additional details were obtained in regard to how Branard came to be a 'disabled Color Sergeant.'

'Branard's promotion from Fourth Corporal to Color Sergeant occurred at Eltham's Landing, Virginia, known to the Federals as West Point,' said General Polley. The promotion was made in 7 May 1862, and occurred this way: Thomas Nettles of Livingston, Texas, who I believe is still living, was Color Sergeant of the 1st Regiment, with a guard of eight Corporals. He became impatient at the long delay in the opening of the first battle, and evidently believed he was going to be denied the opportunity of shooting at a Yankee. During the skirmish he went down into a rifle pit to get his shooting chance. While he was shooting at the Yankees, they were also shooting at him, with the result that he received a bullet in the shoulder which made it impossible for him to carry the flag. He transferred it temporarily to Branard. In an engagement the next day, Branard—this with a twinkle in his eye—thinking he was going to the rear, got too far in front of the regiment to hear the command to halt and fall back. When someone shouted at him to fall back, he declared that the regiment could fall back if it wanted to, but he'd be d——d if he fell back. The Colonel heard the remark, and, admiring both its courage and spirit, ordered the regiment forward to form under the colors. And he then and there promoted Branard from Corporal to Color Sergeant. The Colonel was A. T. Rainey of Palestine.

That's how Branard came to be Color Sergeant. How he came to be a 'disabled' one is another story. It happened at the battle of Gettysburg. Branard had carried the colors in advance of the regiment and in the face of a shell and rifle fire which was raking the regiment in a terrific manner. Only one other color bearer, and he was with a Georgia regiment, dared advanced his colors as far afield as did Branard. As the Georgia sergeant planted his standard along that of Branard, the latter decided upon another advance. In the face of protests from every man who witnessed the act, he again advanced the Texas colors, and this time into the very teeth of the Federals. The daring act won the admiration of the enemy, and the command was passed down the line not to fire on the intrepid Texan. It was obeyed by the riflemen, but did not reach or was not heeded by the artillery. A screaming shell severed the flagstaff and a small piece of the missile struck Branard above the left eye. He still wears the scar and has never been able to use the eye since, the sight being totally destroyed. The wound did not cool Branard's fighting blood. With the shattered flagstaff still in his hand, he essayed to charge single-handed the entire Federal army, and would doubtless have done so had he not been captured by his own men and carried off the field.

Branard was once reported dead. This was at Knoxville. In bearing his colors far in advance of the regiment, he encountered an immense fallen tree, too high to jump or even to climb over. He threw his colors over and attempted to crawl beneath the tree. It had been raining at a terrific rate and Branard, covered with mud and slime, became wedged beneath the tree. In the meantime some of his men found his colors. Out of this grew the report that he was dead.[14]

Private Sam R. Burroughs
First Texas Infantry

It was the third day of the conflict, about 1 a.m. We were still in possession of the brow of Devil's Den, lying prostrate upon our rifles, intermingled with the dead, the dying, the mortally wounded; the flickering tongues of flame, springing from the ignited clothing and knapsacks of both friend and foe, and which through a painful session had stood, as so many beacons, indicating the points of greatest carnage, had been mercifully extinguished; the moon, in her glowing brightness, which had been reluctantly dividing her rays between rift and cloud, had sought and found a friendly hiding place from that cruel and ghastly spectacle, beyond the dear vapors of that western horizon; midnight darkness had taken possession of that scene of death and havoc, as if in mercy to conceal it from sweeping nature; deep silence prevailed, save an occasional cry of a wounded soldier, whose successive time had not arrived to be carried to a better and more comfortable quarters; the low, muttering, indistinct converse of the enemy, or the click of the rocks as he built his defenses. The order came! 'In silence, by the right flank, forward march!'

This movement covered the fronting space of nearly four regiments, since, in the assaulting charge, a farm house and its appearances, which stood near the enemy's line, had severed our brigade in twain, making this gap between the 1st and 2nd Texas—at the time of reaching the enemy's line. This interspace, however, was gallantly defended during the engagement the day before by General Benning and his veteran Georgia Brigade.

Private Sam R. Burroughs.
(*Texas Heritage Museum*)

Silently, cautiously, and with steady step, the column felt its way in the darkness, winding around and over the great boulders, each comrade closely following his leader until a halt was called which found us belted in a semi-circular line around Round Top Mountain, about midway between base and apex. Here our line was promptly closed in ranks and relatively adjusted as well as the inky blackness would permit. Here it was the 4th and 5th Texas did their bloody work the day before: and here it was that Companies G and H of the 1st Texas were called out instantly—the one from the left and the other from the right of the regiment—to form a skirmish line co-extensive with the front of the brigade. Lieutenant Quarles commanded the line. We were ordered to the front and center of the brigade, commanded to deploy twenty paces, advance 100 yards and halt until daylight.

The advance was made, the blackness of the night being the only visible representative of nature; each man being his own counsel, measuring his own distance, sitting in judgment upon his own action, holding in sacred trust—within the soldier's intellectual being, the true valor of that individual probity and integrity which alone inspire the patriot to cast his life upon the altar of his country.

Up the ragged heights the men ascended, over rough, huge stones, boulders of all dimensions, mid scattering mountain oaks, all unseen, but felt when human flesh came in contact with their stubborn inertia, until each for himself decided his complement of distance complete. Here each skirmisher diligently sought alone some propitious rock or sturdy oak behind where imperishable bosom he could find at least partial security from that first shot.

The unveiling of this line and its sanguinary environment by the uplifting of night's amply mantle, in response to the approach of Old Soldier in his Eastern glory, could alone reveal its regularity or irregularity. The gray dawn of that July morn, laden, as it were, with ominous, tragic, historic events, we promptly realized by rapid and continuing volleys from the enemy's line. Their soldiers were responded to with equally as rapid and effective musketry. We had orders to hold this position at any cost throughout the day, hence our men ensconced themselves into the most favorable defensive positions, in order that they might be better prepared to repulse any attack from the enemy. This engagement between the opposing skirmish lines has been characterized by a stubbornness and determination on the part of each antagonist rarely observed. To expose any part of the body, the head, the hand, the knees, the foot was to attract a shower of minies, to rise or move from cover, if but for one moment, was to carry your life into extreme jeopardy. The severity with which these leaden messengers of death sped through the atmosphere to their respective marks, sadly closed the biography of many a gallant soldier on that eventful day.

It was early discovered that one of the enemy's sharpshooters was occupying quite an elevated position, directly in our front, about 200 yards distant, and in rear of his main line of battle. From this advantageous point this expert veteran, began a most annoying and destructive fire upon the ranks of the 3rd Arkansas and 1st Texas; in fact, our entire line was equally subject to the caprice of this marksman, who, in his fancied security, felt himself master of the situation. His own skirmish line, and that of ours, were too close together and on a line with each other from his lofty position for him to interfere with our skirmishers; he therefore turned his attention to our line of battle, which was about 100 yards to our rear. Several men and horses belonging to our field officers had been killed and wounded by this single marksman, and his shots were so regular and unabated that Lieutenant Colonel P. A. Work of the 1st Texas, commanding, sent a courier to our skirmish line with an order directing that the position of 'the man with the big gun' be levelled and be dislodged if possible. Lieutenant Quarles immediately gave orders that each man should use every means to execute the command. All eyes were brought into requisition in search of that particular spot from whence those destructive missiles came. It was not long, however, until it was discovered that the report of the 'big gun' and the issue of a volume of smoke from the top of a small pine were synchronous. This fact determined the point from which our adversary delivered his fire, and led to other discoveries. There were eight or ten men who managed to get together by shrewd tacking from one rock to another, and having ensconced themselves behind a long ledge with their rifles bearing upon the spot in the pine top from whence the smoke came, patiently awaited the next shot. They did not have to wait long, for in a few moments the report of the 'big gun' and the puff of the white smoke simultaneously came, and ten minies passed through the top of the pine, but, as if afterward proved, without result. Our arms were rapidly reloaded and the tree top covered again at his own stated time, our man with his 'big gun' sent another ball crashing into our ranks, and again ten additional minies threaded the green tree top, and again without effect.

This program of firing and counter firing was repeated for many rounds, until one of our boys whose position on the line was some 30 or 40 yards to our right, and who had been taking ideal observations from his standpoint, discovered that the man in the tree was really not in the pine, but that he stood upon a large limb of a proximate oak, reached horizontally out into the pine top, and that the moment he delivered his fire he dropped back to and behind the body of the oak; hence our ineffective shots. At the next volley, our guns were made to recover all the space between the pine top and the body of the oak, and when they were discharged simultaneously, a great lump or heap of humanity was heard to strike the earth with a dull thud, and immediately our Federal foes cheered vociferously, and hollered to us saying: 'You got him at last Johnnies!' After this we were troubled no more with 'the man with the big gun.'[15]

Private Sam R. Burroughs
First Texas Infantry
The Man with the Big Gun

At the Battle of Gettysburg, on the second day, Hood's Texas Brigade was belted around Round Top Mountain, about midway between base and apex. Our skirmish line which had been deployed about twenty paces and advanced about 150 yards up the mountain at 1.00 a.m., was composed of Companies G and H of the First Texas. At the first peep of daylight one of the most stubborn and determined skirmish battles began and remained throughout the entire day, which was fought during the Confederate War. It was soon noticed that one of the enemy, from some distance in the rear of his skirmish line, was using most effectively on our main line a very large bored gun, shooting over both skirmish lines, since these were so near each other to fire on our skirmishers would be to endanger his own. Several members of the 4th and 1st Texas and the 3rd Arkansas had been killed and severely wounded by this marksman and his big gun. There were also several horses killed and wounded at brigade headquarters, which was directly in our rear, and only a few paces from our main line of battle. Lieutenant-Colonel P. A. Works, then in command of the brigade, sent orders to the skirmish line to discover the man with the big gun and, if possible, put him and his gun out of commission. To this end every eye was directed, and it was soon noticed that the big gun was discharged regularly about every three or four minutes, and that its report and smoke came from the top of a small tree standing near a large oak. About five or six of our skirmishers managed by sharp and skillful tacking to ensconce themselves behind a long ledge of rock which projected from the side of the mountain, and brought their guns to bear directly on the spot in the tree top from whence the smoke issued, and at the next puff of smoke as many minie balls passed through the tree top. However, at the regular time the puff of smoke made its appearance and the large missile of death came singing over our heads and crushing into our ranks in our rear. This performance was repeated unsuccessfully four or five times, and until one of our company, Cal Stinson of Rusk, Texas, who was about 30 or 40 yards to our right, discovered the cause of our failure; he had discovered that there was a large limb projecting from the large tree into the top of the smaller, and that at the moment of fire from the big gun its owner dropped back to and behind the body of the larger tree. With this information our guns were brought to bear on a line from whence the smoke came to the body of the big tree, and when the smoke appeared again, we fired in volley and had the pleasure of seeing the marksman fall from the tree, and hearing the Yankees holler out, 'You got him at last, Johnnies.' This was the last of 'The Big Gun,' at least for that day.[16]

Private Albert C. Sims
First Texas Infantry
Thoughts of Gettysburg

To *The News*, Jasper, Tex., 7 July:

Today our thoughts run back forty-three years to the time when the stirring scenes were being enacted around Gettysburg. This greatest of all battles is considered by all as the turning point of the Civil War and a defeat to Confederate arms, yet to the 1st Texas Regiment it was a strange kind of defeat, as it was victorious each day of the conflict. We arrived on the battlefield in the forenoon of the 2nd of July and in the evening were led into battle by General J. B. Hood in person, who was wounded early in the action. There was a battery of four guns planted upon a cragged hill which was playing upon us, which we received orders to 'charge.' We did so, driving the enemy from their guns and from behind the rocks, and successfully repelled several desperate charges made by the enemy to regain what they had lost. We were rewarded victory by a big Irishman, who came rushing into our line, hat in hand, exclaiming: 'Fourth and be jabbers and ye have gained the day!' After we had captured this position we were reinforced by the 20th Georgia of Benning's Brigade, and when darkness closed the scene and fighting had ceased they began to set up claim to the honor of capturing the battery which was disputed by the Texans, but General Benning, who was there in person, quickly silenced their caveling by saying, 'Ah boys, these Texans were in possession of this battery before you were in a quarter mile of here.'

When fighting had ceased it fell to my lot to go on picket duty and I stood that night among the Federal dead and wounded and listened to their piteous wails of the dying, where continual cry was Water! Water! And none to relieve them. The poor fellows were uncared for during that night. Surely war is cruel, and that was the place to decide when the bloody work was over. Until this day in my imagination I can hear their cries, 'Oh partner! Bring me a drink of water. I will give you a dollar for a drink of water. I will give you all the money I have for a drink of water.' There are sentences I heard while standing there which haunt me until now. But what could I do? A sentinel standing between two sleeping armies in near proximity to each other could under no circumstances leave my post and had no water to give. After standing two hours I was relieved by another and being overcome by the fatigue of battle, I lay down among the dead and slept like them until the break of day, when I was aroused by my comrades to rejoin my command, which had been removed further to the right [while] other troops had been put in our place of the previous day.

The third day we lay behind temporary breastworks made of rocks, and listened to the hissing bombs which passed back and forth harmless over our heads, except one from our own guns, which fell short of its aim, and wounded two men in Company F. In the afternoon it was learned that Federal cavalry had got in the rear and we were ordered to go in double-quick time to meet them.

The ranks of the 1st Texas at this time had been so reduced by battle and disease that they had to deploy us as a mere skirmish line in order to make a front to meet a brigade of cavalry. The enemy made a dash through our line, firing at random, and, I might say by accident, killed one man in Company A, shooting him through the head, while the steady aim of the Texans from behind trees and fence corners left seventeen empty saddles on the field including that of their leader, General Farnsworth. The enemy passed on without a halt until they met the 4th Alabama Regiment, which had been sent to our aid. A volley or two from them with a few charges of grape from Riley's battery turned the enemy back, who made their escape around the right wing of Lee's army. I am aware that the killing of General Farnsworth had been attributed to certain Alabama troops, but evidently that was a mistake. His body was left upon the field where the Texans fought and if those who came to bury the dead were not personally acquainted with him they did not know that they were burying a General, as he was left upon the field in his underwear, and the fine Morocco cavalry boots that clothed a Federal General's foot and leg in the battle of Gettysburg were worn by a Texas Captain in the Battle of Chickamauga. Not that the Captain took them off him, but he sought them of one who did, paying him $50 in Confederate money for them.

All or nearly all of the great men who directed these movements have passed on into the great beyond, while I, who was but a weakly, beardless boy, least and last of those who joined the 1st Texas Regiment, still remain, but in constant contemplation of the time when it may be said:

Soldier rest, thy warfare's over.
Sleep that sleep which knows no waking,
Dream of battlefields no more.

A. C. Sims
First Texas Confederate Volunteers[17]

Private Albert C. Sims
First Texas Infantry

We received orders on that morning of the 1st of July to get ready to march without delay. Everybody was in a stir in camp, rolling up blankets and fly tents, gathering up cooking utensils, bucking on cartridge boxes, etc. We were soon in readiness and marched back through Chalmersburg and took the road toward Gettysburg.

Tramp, Tramp, all day the boys were marching and alas: it was the last march for many of the poor fellows. We all knew we were marching to battle; as evidence I will relate one circumstance. A young man by the name of Rod Meekling of Company B, 1st Texas, was whistling gaily as we tramped along; all of a sudden he turned to his comrade and remarked with an air of seriousness, 'Boys, I have been through many hard fought battles, but if I get through this one to which we are going, I shall count myself the luckiest man in the world.' Need I tell you that he was one of the first to fall after getting to battle, killed dead on the field.

We continued our march all day under a hot July sun and until night, when we bivouacked on the roadside for the remainder of the night. We did not stack our arms as usual, for we were in the enemy's country and everyone lay with his 'trusty companion.' News came that A. P. Hill's and Ewell's corps had met the enemy and driven them back 6 miles and captured 5,000 prisoners.

Early next morning we resumed our march and ere long we began to see the bloody shirts, the men who had been wounded in the previous day's battle and who were able to travel, wending their way back to the old Virginia shores. What effect this may have had on the old soldiers, I know not, but to me, who had never seen the like, it was no pleasing sight to behold. It reminds me of one of the Scriptures which says, 'Every battle of the warrior is with confused noise and garments rolled in blood.' However, we continued our march for some time, then quitting the road we turned to the right. We soon began to cross ridges of fresh turned earth which hid the forms of those who fell in the previous days fight. Whether friends or foes we did not know; it made no difference then, for all strife had ceased with them forever.

We continued our march until we came to a wagon train drawn up in a camping position, and on the cover of each was marked in large letters, 'Ordinance,' which meant ammunition and guns, but to me it seemed death. We passed this train a little way and came to a halt and rested and ate our scant dinner, though I had no appetite for eating. The bands would try to play, but the instruments would give a plaintive sound without much music. It was indeed hours of great suspense, we whiled away there waiting for the time of action.

At last Colonel P. A. Work, commanding 1st Texas Regiment, ordered us to fall in line; we then made a right flank movement into a thick wood. We were ordered to load our guns and went a little farther. We were ordered to cap them (in those days we used cap and ball). We then moved out into a field. Riley's battery, that accompanied Hood's Brigade, was there in position ready for action. We took our position on the left and a little in the rear of the battery; the 3rd Arkansas on our left, the 4th and 5th Texas on our right in the order named.

No sooner were we in position than did our cannon open fire through a skirt of timber which lay in our front, which was eastward, to which the enemy replied promptly, knocking out a man here and there. To avoid as much danger as possible, we were ordered to lie down until all were in readiness. General J. B. Hood, as a division commander, took a position in the front of the 1st Texas Regiment; General Robertson commanding the brigade. Hood had sent Major Sellers, his aide-de-camp, to General Longstreet for orders, and on his return Hood ordered a detail to throw down a rail fence which lay just before us, and immediately ordered a forward movement, he leading the way on horseback. The whole column moved forward and with one united effort threw the fence to the ground. Hood having passed through the gap made by said detail, we emerged into the skirts of the timber; presently random firing began along the line, but I could see no enemy. Presently a full volley from the 3rd Arkansas Regiment on our left proclaimed the enemy in sight. We pressed forward to a stone fence, where I gladly would have remained for the remainder of the evening for the protection it afforded us, but not so; we must go forward, and I leaped upon the fence, the rocks giving way, and I went head forward down a little slant on the side of a branch. My file leader, seeing me fall, turned back to ask if I was badly hurt, to which I replied that I was not, and arose and soon regained my place.

We pushed forward through a field of timothy, through which the minie balls were hissing. As we came to the brow of the hill that overlooks the valley at the foot of Little Round Top, my gun was knocked from my hand and 10 or 12 feet to the rear; I did not turn back to get it, but picked up another that lay before us. I got it choked with a ball and threw it down and picked up another. As we came down a slant by the side of a wood a shell cut off a white oak tree, which made us scatter to keep it from falling on us, but we soon closed up the gap and went forward until we were in the valley where we halted, loaded and fired, the front rank on their knees and the rear standing. We only remained in this a few minutes when we again went forward; when we came to the foot of the hill on which the battery stood there was a momentary confusion. Someone ordered a retreat and we began to fall back, but the order was quickly countermanded and another forward movement.

The 3rd Arkansas Regiment, being hard pressed, began retreating. Colonel Work ordered a part of the 1st Texas to their assistance. Captain Harding, with drawn sword, urged the balance of the regiment forward. The battery had been silenced, our aim being too accurate for the gunners. At the critical moment General Benning's Brigade came upon the field. The 20th Georgia, not knowing that they were coming to our support, supposing us to be the enemy, opened fire on us; but Geo. A. Branard, being our color bearer, stepped out in an open space and waved our state flag to and fro … when they saw, [they] ceased firing until they came to us and rendered good service in aiding us to hold what we had gained, as the enemy made several assaults to retake the cannon they had lost.

Just as it began to grow dark we distinctly heard the Yankee officers give orders for another charge. General Benning, being there in person, said, 'Now, boys, hold your fire until they come right up, then pour a volley into them, and if they don't stop, run your bayonets into their bellies.' But they did not come.

When the firing ceased the Georgians began to lay claim to the honor of capturing the battery, which the Texans disputed; but Benning quieted the dispute by saying, 'Ah, boys, those Texans had captured this battery before you were in a quarter of a mile of here.'

After the battle was over and all was quiet save the cries of the wounded, there was a requisition made for men to go on picket duty and it fell to my lot to go for Company F. I stood two hours on the Vidette Post between the two armies and listened to the cries and groans of the wounded and dying, and to their pleadings for water. One man who lay just in front of me would say, 'Oh, pardner, bring me a drink of water. I'll assure you that no one will hurt you. My leg is shot off or I would come to you. I'll give you a dollar for a drink of water. I'll give you all the money I have for a drink of water.' To all of which I made no reply, as I had no water to give and could not leave my post for anything.

I was so fatigued and overcome with excitement, heat of battle, and suffocating smoke, that I had to put tobacco in my eyes to prevent myself from going to sleep on post, when I knew it was death to be found asleep at such a time. After standing for two hours I lay down among the dead and slept like them until aroused by my comrades at break of day to rejoin our command, which had been removed further to the right during the night and other troops had taken our places.

Before leaving, Captain S. A. Wilson requested of Colonel Work that he, with the help of others, be allowed to move the cannon off the field which we had captured that evening, which they did, except one which the enemy, seeing they would have to abandon, pushed off a precipice down among large rocks, so that they could not get it out.

Generals Hood and Robertson were wounded early in the fight, and General Law of Alabama succeeded Hood, and Colonel Work took command of the Texas Brigade.

On the 3rd the battle was renewed with an artillery duel, the heaviest cannonading ever heard on the American continent. The air was alive with hissing bomb-shells and the hills and mountains fairly trembled. Our battery being a considerable distance in the rear, the shots all passed harmlessly over our heads, except two or three shots from our own battery [which] fell short of their aim and wounded two men in Company F. A courier went in full speed and told our gunners to shoot further, which they did.

About the time the cannonading ceased, news came that a brigade of Yankee cavalry had gained our rear and the 1st Texas Regiment was ordered to go in double-quick time and meet them. My knee was so sore from the fall I had at the stone fence the evening before that I could not keep up with the company, and Captain Wilson told me to stop, which I did and returned to the 5th Texas Regiment. Colonel P. A. Work saw me and asked me to stay by him while he lay down to rest, and in case he should fall asleep to awaken him if any attack should be made. I had not been standing there but a few minutes when a minie ball came whistling by me, and I heard the report of a gun in the distance. Another minute and another ball struck a hickory limb close to my head, when Colonel Work said that we had better get back to the breastworks, or that a 'd——d Yankee would kill us.' From the nature of the ground in our front, the man must have been up in a tree to have seen us.

About this time the battle was raging furiously on our left and from our position we could see our men [Pickett's Division] falling back and we had to retreat to avoid being flanked by the enemy, although there was no engagement on our part of the line.

In the meantime, the 1st Texas had met the Federal Cavalry. They had to deploy as a mere skirmish line to make a front to meet a brigade of cavalry. The Yankees, seeming to be in a state of intoxication, dashed through our line firing right and left. They killed one man in Company A, shooting him through the head, while our boys from behind trees and fence corners with their well-directed aim left seventeen dead on the field, among them General Farnsworth, their leader. The 4th Alabama Regiment had been sent to aid the 1st Texas and it is claimed that some of them killed General Farnsworth, which, however, is a mistake. If there had been any honor in killing a Federal General, doubtless that honor belongs to the 1st Texas Regiment. It happened this way: General Farnsworth came dashing up to Corporal A. F. Taylor and demanded his surrender, but Taylor replied with a ball from his Enfield, which took effect in his abdomen just below his belt. The General, looking down, saw his wound, turned his pistol on himself, and shot himself four times and fell from his horse, and if those who came to bury the dead were not personally acquainted with him, they never knew they were burying a General.

If Captain Dan K. Rice is living he can tell us something about General Farnsworth's boots. He did not take them off the General, but bought them off a soldier that did, and the fine morocco leather that clothed the feet of a Federal General in the Battle of Gettysburg were worn by a Texas Captain in the Battle of Chickamauga. Captain S. A. Wilson and Private T. D. Rock of Company F, having been overcome by heat, sat down just before the regiment met the enemy and when the Yankees [attacked, they] captured them. A few volunteers from the 4th Alabama Regiment and a few grape shot from Riley's battery turned the enemy back and they made their escape around the right wing of Lee's army.

I did not rejoin my company until next morning. I was reported captured, but I was with the 5th Texas and did not learn where it was until the next day.

Our army fell back into the plain and formed a line of battle where we lay all day on the 4th awaiting the enemy's advance, but they made none. It was like a calm after a general storm, not even a picket gun broke the stillness. At night we built fires of the rails along the lines and began the retreat into Maryland.

We marched all night and next day reached Hagerstown, Md. Lee's whole army had fallen back and formed a line in a crescent shape, each wing resting on the Potomac River. His wagon train and artillery were enclosed, thereby protecting them from the enemy.

Stewart's cavalry turned to cowboys and collected large heads of beef cattle, which they brought from out of the enemy's country. I noticed while a herd was passing, two fine milk cows ran into it and were driven out. An old lady came and pleaded with the officers to save her cows, as they were her only means of living, but her entreaties were of no avail, and she fell down on the earth and wept most bitterly. Truly war is cruel.[18]

Private Leslie A. Thompson
First Texas Infantry

The *Devine News* states that Judge Thompson of that place found among his old papers the muster roll of 'The Lone Star Rifles' of Galveston, Company L, 1st Texas Infantry Regiment Volunteers, Texas Brigade, Field's Regiment, Longstreet's Corps. The roll is written on a tinted Confederate paper at Richmond and the old document is stained with the blood of Orderly Sergeant W. C. Porter, from whose body the paper was taken by Judge Thompson after the Battle of Gettysburg. 'This company left Galveston on the 1st of August 1861, with four officers and 100 men, since which time it has received eighteen or thirty recruits' is found written thereon. The judge has sent copies of the roll to the *Galveston News* and to Adjutant-General Scurry at Austin. The judge prizes the old, faded, torn document very much, as it recalls to his mind the stirring deeds and times when men's souls were tried and their courage tested.[19]

Fifth Corporal W. T. White
First Texas Infantry

I was a member of the 1st Texas Regiment, Hood's Brigade, and about two o'clock p.m. on 3 July, my regiment was sent off a mile or more from Round Top and stationed in a public road to check the advance of the cavalry, which we understood was threatening an attack on our wagon train. We had been in our position but a very short time when Kilpatrick's Brigade, under command of General Farnsworth, loomed up in our front. We had in our regiment 196 men, rank and file; the Federal cavalry was supposed to number about 1,200. Our first impression was that we were hardly equal to the task of successfully resisting such vastly superior numbers, but the men of Hood's Brigade never did learn to retreat; so as we had a stone fence about 3½ feet high in our front, our decision was to hold our position, give them a reception, and take the risk of being overpowered and captured. They formed a line of battle in plain view of us and charged. We held our fire until they were within fifty or sixty yards from us, when, taking deliberate aim, we fired on them, bringing down many men and horses. Instead of continuing the assault, which probably would have resulted in our capture, they retreated to their original starting point, reformed, and recharged, with the same result as before.

Having repulsed the second charge, we felt that we could almost whip all the cavalry the enemy had, and from that time on, for about two hours, they continued making demonstrations against us, after which they gave up the job of routing us and bore off to our left in the direction of Round Top, and may then have come in contact with the 4th or 15th Alabama, but we had almost demolished the brigade before they left us.

After the fight was over, with almost the entire Federal brigade killed, wounded, or captured, General Farnsworth, with his staff, or part of it, was returning to the Federal lines when he came upon three or four of our boys, who had been left on picket duty at the foot of Round Top, and were on their way to join us. The General and staff rushed on our boys and demanded their surrender, when one of the boys, by the name of Taylor, and belonging to Company L, of our regiment, shot the General from his horse. As he hit the ground Taylor said, 'Now, I reckon you will surrender,' whereupon Farnsworth drew his pistol and shot himself.

We regarded that as one of the best fights we put up during the war, and feel we should have credit for it.[20]

'Parker'
First Texas Infantry

Head'qrs 1st Texas Regiment, Near Culpepper, Va, Aug 3rd, 1863

Friend Sallie,

E'er this you know we have invaded the enemy's country, and fought a desperate battle on his own soil. When we first entered Penn., we found everyone in the greatest state of excitement. They were very much frightened about their private property, and gave our men everything they asked for. It seems they were informed by the authorities of the state that if we came in their country we would destroy everything we could lay our hands on. But they were soon happily disappointed, for General Lee, so soon as he entered the enemy's country, issued a very stringent order prohibiting the use or destruction of private property, and enjoined upon both officers and men the necessity of its rigid enforcement. The consequence was our men conducted themselves with the same propriety as if they had been in their own country, with the exception of stragglers and a few black sheep who took everything that was eatable within their reach, thereby faring unscruptously. Such men, when detected, were dealt with and punished according to the nature of the offence committed. I did not hear of a house being wantonly burned by our troops while in Pennsylvania or Maryland— there were some destroyed or burned in battle.

Chambersburg was the first city of any importance that we passed through in Pennsylvania. I noticed the citizens all wore an acid look—a gloom seemed to o'erspread the city, the doors and blinds were closed to us as we marched through the principal streets.

Many of the females wore small Federal flags, others red, white and blue ribbons upon their breast, in defiance to us, and emblems of their true Yankee fanatic idea of patriotism and devotion to their country, while the men stood on the sidewalks gazing on in mute amazement, with heavy hearts and heads bent and drooping in humble submission as we passed along.

The scene was uninviting and an unpleasant one to them. Of course we did not anticipate a reception as we were want to receive in our Old Dominion State. There were no bright smiling faces or delicate white handkerchiefs waving us on in triumph there. In place of these were forced upon our ears words of contempt, hatred and a wish for our defeat. But our boys were overflowing in spirit, victory and success seemed to be imprinted on every brow. Their flaunting words fell upon their undaunted spirits like oil upon the waters, only reducing their laughter and merriment into complacency and thought. Thus marched through the first city in the enemy's country 'An army that had never been beaten, and opposed to an army that had never been victorious.' On the morning after the 2nd last, about eight o'clock a.m., our division halted on an eminence overlooking the city of Gettysburg, Penn. There was heavy cannonading and skirmishing going on at 12.00 p.m. We were ordered to the front and right, moving by the right flank along the edge and through the woods about 4 miles, until we crossed a creek into an open field, where we suffered severely from shells, not so much in our regiments, [but] in other regiments belonging to the brigade. The 3rd Arkansas had twenty killed and wounded (mostly wounded), the second shell I thought passed about 5 feet from my head. I was on horseback at the time, (the troops had halted and laid down). Being rather higher in the world that was healthy at the time, I immediately dismounted; as soon as the shelling subsided we continued to move by the right a short distance, where we moved by the left flank into line of battle at three o'clock p.m. We were ordered to charge forward over a rugged open country, down a slope and up the other side. On top of this the Yankees had a battery, supported by infantry who lay behind immense rocks. We captured the battery, drove the enemy back and occupied the position on the brow of the hill which the enemy had just left. They fell back to the side of the mountain, where they were strongly entrenched—their position was invincible. Here we fought until night closed her dark mantle over us, which was a befitting mourning over the appalling scene which lay before us. The loss of the enemy was more severe than ours. The usual duties after battle having been performed (viz. collecting arms, hauling the captured artillery to the rear, etc.) I laid down on a small piece of old tent, which I picked up on the field, to sleep among the living and the dead, as they lay mingled together on the field. After a hard day's fight one can lay down in line of battle and sleep as soundly and sweetly upon the bare ground as one could at home on a nice clean bed.

The painful duty devolves upon me of recording the death of our mutual friend, J. W. Southwick. Poor Joe, he was brave to a fault; he was upon the brow of the hill before mentioned, with his head and shoulders exposed above the rock. Some of his comrades told him to squat down and load. Joe remarked, laughingly, that they could not hit him; just then he was pierced through the head by a minie ball, a little over or behind the left temple—he fell dead. Thus has been added to the register of brave men who filled an honorable and useful place in society. To the hearts torn by this sad event, we can offer no earthly consolation. Any enumeration of his virtues will but embitter the agony of the lost. But when a higher power shall have assigned their sorrow, it will be a source of melancholy consolation that he fell fighting to give liberty and freedom to his adopted land and that his friends and countrymen will treasure his memory and deplore his death.

Joe Love and Colonel Powell were severely wounded and left in the hands of the enemy.

Alas! Our sleep was short. At two o'clock a.m. (it being eleven o'clock when we lay down) we were prudent to change our position to the right. We arrived at the place designated a little before dawn. We immediately went to work piling up rocks for breastworks on our line. At eleven o'clock a.m. on the 3rd, we were moved still further to the right (and detached from the brigade), we now being on the right flank of the army, to prevent the enemy's cavalry from flanking us in that direction. We occupied an extended line along a road having a stone fence in our front, on our right in front an open field, on the left a skirt of timber. Our regiment was extended along the fence in a single line, and the men 4 or 5 feet apart, covering the quarter of a mile. We connected on the left with an Alabama regiment; upon our right there was a space of 300 yards, which was protected by artillery. At about six o'clock p.m. the enemy's cavalry charged through the lines of the Alabama regiment on the left at the same time charging our left, but our boys repulsed them. After firing our guns, not having time to load, our boys threw rocks at them and knocked some off their horses, the balance going through the gap made in the Alabama regiment. After getting through they divided, some going to the right, others to the left; the last named filed along a fence running perpendicular to our rear on the left, when they made a dash on Riley's Battery, which was a half mile in our rear. Finding it rather hot and themselves in danger of being cut off (our battery pouring grape and canister into them) by our infantry, which was moving towards them in rear of our battery, and thinking we were merely a line of skirmishers, they about-faced and came dashing across the field in our rear. We were about face to receive the charge, which brought our stone fence in our rear, and having a rail fence which was on the opposite side of the road in front. We had taken the necessary precaution before the enemy charged, to throw a rail fence across the road at either end of our regiment, thus completely barricading the road, forming an entire fence around our regiment which served a very good purpose. (I forgot to say they previously charged down the road on our left and finding it blockaded, went back through the gap into our rear.) They would only charge to the fence which rendered their sabers useless, but our boys did not wait—many of them jumped over the fence into the field and shot them from their saddles at 300 and 400 yards' distance. They were the bravest men I ever saw. After their line was broken and all was utter confusion and many of their men shot, they would advance singly, brandishing their swords. We called out for them to throw down their swords and get off their horses, but they still kept on, getting shot. I will relate one case in particular; it was that of a Yankee Captain. Captain Massey, Company K of my regiment, called on him to surrender but to no attention, but continued coming forward. Captain Massey ordered one of his men to shoot him; he did so, shooting him through the mouth. He was taken prisoner, there being no chance for a wounded man to escape (scarcely any for a well one). Captain Massey asked him why he did not surrender; his reply was that a brave soldier never surrenders. Many of his followers met with the same fate, some even worse.

There was only one outlet; that led through a gate which was about 30 yards to the right of our regiment. Our boys ran up the wood to try and head them off, but were not swift enough for their fleet horses. Only eight, however, made their escape out of 75 or 100. In the cavalry fight we only lost one killed, three wounded and eighteen prisoners. This being the first cavalry fight that our boys had ever been engaged in, they acquitted themselves with credit. For our loss in the battle of Gettysburg, I refer you to a list of casualties published in the *Galveston News*.

In the late battles suffice it to say the 'Old First' bore herself and flag through nobly, and has won fresh laurels and lasting honors for herself, capturing five guns, of which three were taken safely off the field. We drove the enemy back in our front, and held the ground until we were ordered to the right of the army, where we whipped the cavalry, almost annihilating them. The Yankees had the advantage of position over us. We had them badly whipped. They commenced retreating before we did. Our artillery ammunition was almost exhausted and we were forced to fall back towards the Potomac. We offered them battle for three days at Hagerstown, Md. On the 10th we moved 6 miles to the right of Hagerstown, where we threw up breast-works and remained four days, offering the enemy battle and awaiting the construction of a bridge across the Potomac, the river being too high from recent rains to ford. We recrossed the Potomac on the morning of the 14th, and marched from day to day until we reached our old camp on the afternoon of the 24th.

Here are we camped in the same identical spot that were encamped upon when we started upon our long and perilous journey into the enemy's country, 15 June, 1863.

Everything looks as natural and familiar as if I had been absent but a day. This the very spot where my tent was; my horse is tied to the same tree as when we were here before, and there are the charred sticks, the remnant of our camp fire that we left burning, but like all other lights and fires, have been by time put out; to use a vulgar phrase, all looks as natural as an old shoe, for there lie my old shoes that I left when we were here before. How sad to think of the many changes and losses in that short period. How many were with us when we left performing their daily duties, answering roll calls, in good spirits and apparently long lived as any of us here today; but they are absent forever; never will they answer to the roll call again. Yet all goes on the same; the world, the great mass does not seem to miss them; but their loss is felt in the home and the private circle; around the campfire each mess mate is noted and loved for some particular quality, and when he is taken away he leaves a void not easily filled or soon forgotten.

I have just heard that the Yankees are in the neighborhood of Culpepper C. H., and the citizens are flying from that place. If so, we will be on the move ere long. Culpepper is only 10 miles from this camp. The loss of Vicksburg, Port Hudson and the capture of Morgan and a portion of his command are sad reverses to us and our country. With all this I cannot look upon our cause as hopeless yet, but on the contrary, I think we will ultimately be successful, and our cause still favorable and bright. The late riots in New York and other northern cities, Valadingham's late address to his friends in Ohio (which I send you), his unanimous nomination for Governor for that state, late news from France, from which recognition is almost certain—all these speak worlds in our favor. I am satisfied that this army is in better spirits than the people at home. It is well, if these reverses were to come, that they followed so soon our own triumphs. The nation had not time to relapse so deeply into apathy as to put it beyond recovery. If it slept at all, it was on the battlefield and will meet the enemy and repulse him just when he fancies that he has again crushed the rebellion. Adversity will bring out only in bolder relief the virtues of the people of the South—the virtues of courage and faith in a just cause and a just providence.

E'er this reaches you we will have been engaged in another fearful and desperate battle, I hope God may smile upon our efforts and crown them with victory.

Present my kind regards to all your family, and believe me to remain,

Your Friend,

Parker[21]

Fourth Texas Infantry Regiment

The 4th Texas Infantry Regiment was formed in April 1861. Transferred to a camp near Harrisburg, Texas, the regiment was shipped to Virginia as a part of the Army of Northern Virginia (ANV). The regiment first saw combat at Eltham's Landing on 7 May 1862, and first went into battle at the Battle of Gaines' Mill on 27 June 1862.[1]

The regiment established their reputation for hard fighting by successfully breaking the Union line on Turkey Hill, where Union forces resisted all previous Confederate attempts to break their line.[2]

Prior to the Battle of Gettysburg, the regiment was engaged in the battles of Second Manassas, South Mountain, and Antietam where the regiment was involved in some of the stiffest fighting on the Confederate left flank and suffered its greatest number of losses for any single battle of the war, losing 210 men (57 killed, 130 wounded, and 23 captured).[3] The 4th Texas Regiment consisted of the following:

Company A—Hardeman Rifles (Gonzales County)
Company B—Tom Green Rifles (Travis County)
Company C—Robertson Five Shooters (Robertson County)
Company D—Guadalupe Rangers or Knights of Guadalupe County (Guadalupe County)
Company E—Lone Star Guards (McLennan County)
Company F—Mustang grays (Bexar County)
Company G—Grimes County grays (Grimes County)
Company H—Porter Guards (Walker County)
Company I—Navarro Rifles (Navarro County)
Company K—Sandy Point Mounted Rifles (Henderson County)[4]

Lieutenant-Colonel Benjamin F. Carter
Fourth Texas Infantry

Lt Col. Benjamin F. Carter was born in 1831 in Tennessee. He attended Columbia College, moving to Texas in the 1850s, where he became a prominent lawyer in Austin, serving as Master Mason, Austin Lodge #12 in 1856, and Mayor of Austin from 1858–59. He married Ella O. Rust and had three children. When Texas seceded, he helped form a company called the Austin City Light Infantry, which soon became Tom Green Rifles, Company B, 4th Texas Infantry, and was elected captain in July 1861. Col. Carter arrived in Virginia in October, and by then his unit had been transferred to the Army of Northern Virginia. He got the news that one of his children back home had died in September, only two months after he had left. Only three months later there was another message, which advised him that his wife, Louisa, had died in December 1861 at the age of twenty-four years. Soon thereafter he learned that a second baby had died only four months after its mother, leaving only his five-year-old daughter named Ella.

On 27 June 1862, at Gaines' Mill, near Richmond, Virginia, the 4th Texas charged and broke the Union line. Several artillery pieces were captured, including some under the command of Capt. Mark Kerns,

Lieutenant-Colonel Benjamin F. Carter. (*Austin History Center, Austin Public Library*)

Battery G, Pennsylvania Light Artillery. For his leadership in the Battle of Gaines' Mill, Capt. Carter was promoted to Major. The cost of Gaines' Mill to the 4th Texas was forty-four killed, 208 wounded, and one missing.

At the battle of Second Manassas in August 1862, the 4th Texas again engaged the Union Army and the guns of Captain Kerns. They attacked, and all the supporting infantry and artillerymen scattered except for Captain Kerns. He manned his guns alone and fired the last shot from the battery before he was wounded. Col Carter, noting the captain had little time to live, 'left his overcoat to be buried in'. Col. Carter took note of Capt. Kern's bravery, identified his parents and returned his personal property to his family in Chambersburg, Pennsylvania. The casualties at the battle of Second Manassas for the 4th Texas amounted to twenty-two killed and seventy-seven wounded.

After much hard marching, Col. Carter and the 4th Texas found itself near a creek in Washington County, Maryland, on September 17, 1862. The creek was named Antietam, the town was Sharpsburg. Before the day ended this battle would go down in history as the single bloodiest day in American history. Col. Carter led the 4th Texas to an area astride the Hagerstown Pike and the cornfield where they fought bravely and helped save Gen. Lee's army from destruction. The battle was costly again: the 4th Texas lost 54 percent of its men.

For three days in July 1863, in a small Pennsylvania town named Gettysburg, the North and South were locked in a death struggle to determine the future of the Confederate States of America. This was also the last battle for Lt Col. Benjamin F. Carter. At 2.00 a.m. on July 2, the 4th Texas was at Cashtown. By 4.00 a.m. they had marched the 8 miles to Gettysburg and were cooking breakfast along Willoughby Run. About noon the Texas Brigade was ordered to march with McLaw's brigade, and at 4.00 p.m. Gen. John Bell Hood had his brigade properly deployed for attack.

Union batteries positioned in the Peach Orchard and Devil's Den opened fire on the Texas Brigade. Fifteen men were killed or wounded awaiting time to charge when a Federal shell exploded in the midst of the 4th Texas as the order came to charge. Almost immediately Gen. Hood was seriously wounded by an exploding projectile, and had to be carried from the battlefield. The Texas brigade under the command of Gen. Evander Law advanced through heavy artillery fire until the 4th Texas plunged over Plum Run into the woods of Big Round Top.

Advancing up Big Round Top, the 4th engaged the 2nd U.S. Sharpshooters who were securely positioned behind a stone wall. While crossing this stone wall the 4th Texas took devastating flank fire. At the stone wall Col. John Key, Lt Col. Benjamin Carter, and Lt Joe Smith were shot. Lt Smith died, and Lt Col. Carter, who was severely wounded in the face, arm, and leg, lay dying at the foot of the hill. The 5th Texas and the 4th Alabama cleared the stone wall of Federals and proceeded to push on to Little Round Top where the men of the Texas brigade showed a tenacity equaled only by the famed Stonewall Brigade of Virginia.

Again, the cost was staggering: the Texas brigade lost eighty-four men killed, 393 wounded, and 120 missing. The next day, after Pickett's charge, Southern forces were defeated. It was evident that the Army of the Potomac would not be destroyed at Gettysburg. The largest battle on the American continent had 50,000 casualties. Many leaders lay dead or wounded. General Lee began evacuating the wounded early the next morning on a train which extended 17 miles of bone-jarring pain, as the wounded crossed South Mountain on the stony, rutted, rain-swept roads that led to Virginia and home. Somewhere on the train was Lt Col. Benjamin Carter.

The ride over the mountains was so difficult and Col. Carter's condition was so severe that he was left at the Jeremiah George farm near New Franklin. There he was captured by Union troops and taken to Academy Hospital in Chambersburg. Dr Abraham H. Senseney was the attending physician. It was thought that Dr Senseney was Capt. Kern's stepfather. Historical researched has determined that the confusion of the physician attending Col. Carter is explained by the fact Dr Samuel B. Fisher D.D. (Doctor of Divinity) was not a medical doctor. Mrs Naomi Fisher was the mother of Capt. Mark Kerns of Battery G, Pennsylvania Light Artillery. This couple was now entrusted with the care of the dying Col. Carter. It was a complex emotional situation for Naomi Fisher. Her son joined the Union army against her native state (Virginia), and he died at the hands of the 4th Texas assault commander who was now mortally wounded and in her care.

Dr Fisher and Naomi evidently spoke to Col. Carter, who was with them for several days. They took his dying wish to Dr Senseney, who then spoke to Col. Carter about his desire for a Christian burial. Dr Senseney was moved, but he knew it would be difficult to grant the wish. Dr Senseney and Dr Fisher knew Col. Carter was dying, but arranging a Christian burial for a Confederate officer in war-savaged Pennsylvania was not an easy thing. The provost marshals made sure that anyone rendering aid to the enemy was subject to arrest, and Col. Carter was the enemy. Dr Senseney understood this feeling of the people; however, he also knew of Col. Carter's efforts in providing Capt. Kern's service to his parents. The doctor did know an influential townsperson, one of his patients, who was a personal friend of President Lincoln. Alexander K. McClure was called to the hospital. Mr McClure personally met and conferred with Col. Carter, and at the end of their meeting Mr McClure held the trembling hand of Col. Carter and promised him, as a gentleman and as a Christian, that he would see to it that he had a Christian burial. Col. Carter died the next day.

Mr McClure went to his church with the request, and they refused to bury the Confederate soldier. He then went to several other denominations in town that also refused to grant Col. Carter's dying wish. No one wanted a Confederate officer buried in their churchyard. Mr McClure's rebuffs led to his publicly declaring that he would deed land on his on property for a grave and would see to it that this man could have that Christian burial. At some point Mr Charles Burnette gave his personal burial plot at the Methodist church on Second Street in Chambersburg for Col. Carter's burial. Col. Carter was buried because A. K. McClure kept his word.

There was an interesting relationship throughout the war between Col. Carter and a black man named Henry Johnson, who was listed as a barber for the 4th Texas Infantry. Henry Johnson stayed behind with Col. Carter when the Texas troops returned to Virginia. Mr Johnson stayed beside him until he died and was buried. Henry Johnson then disappeared from history. It is possible that Mr Johnson was a slave assigned to accompany Col. Carter when he left Austin, because his wife's family owned many slaves at this time; however, there is no verification of this.

For thirty-three years Col. Carter lay in a peaceful grave in the old Methodist church burial ground, his resting place properly marked with a granite headstone. Then the Methodist church and cemetery were sold to the Brethren Congregation, which immediately began to enlarge the church by expanding into the old burying ground. Forty-nine graves were moved to Cedar Grove Cemetery with some of the accompanying stones. Lt Col. Carter's granite stone was not moved, but it was probably used in the foundation of the new building.

A newspaper item in the *Franklin Repository* on 19 June 1896 reads:

> The work of removing the dead … is done. The bones were placed in boxes and taken to the cemetery for re-internment. Among the bones are those of a Confederate officer who died here in the hospital during the war.

A marker commemorating the move of the bodies lists forty-seven names and two that are now marked 'Unknown remains from M.E. Church'.

For 104 years, Lt Col. Carter's final resting place was unknown, although somewhere in Cedar Grove Cemetery are his remains. Despite Mr McClure's fight to honor this man's last request, uncaring hands desecrated his grave and even spurned to remember who he was.

On Saturday 10 April 2010, over 100 people—accompanied by flags, bagpipes, drums, town dignitaries, and representatives of the United Daughters of the Confederacy and Sons of Confederate Veterans— gathered in Cedar Grove Cemetery in Chambersburg, Pennsylvania, to dedicate a new stone and iron cross to honor the memory, bravery, and service of Lt Col. Benjamin F. Carter CSA. His stone was draped with a Texas flag. In a moving ceremony, soil mixed with bluebonnet seeds from the graves of his wife, his children, and grandchildren buried in Oakwood Cemetery in Austin, Texas, were sprinkled atop the Colonel's grave. Thirty yellow roses were placed on his grave accompanied by the strains of 'The Yellow Rose of Texas.' Col. Carter's dying wish for a Christian burial had been honored a second time.

On Sunday 18 April 2010, a small group gathered at the gravesites of Louisa Rust Carter, her two babies, and his daughter, Ella Carter Wooten, and two grandchildren. Soil from the gravesite of Col. Carter was blessed and sprinkled around his family's graves. A fallen Confederate officer buried among his foe in a foreign land and his family buried so far away in Dixie were finally reunited the only way possible.[5]

Major John P. Bane
Fourth Texas Infantry

About 4.30 p.m., the 2nd instant, we were ordered to advance on the enemy, who occupied the heights about 1¼ miles distant, the 5th Texas, the directing battalion, on my right, and the 1st Texas on my left. Advancing at double-quick, we soon met the enemy's skirmishers, who occupied a skirt of thick undergrowth about one quarter of a mile from the base of the cliffs, upon which the enemy had a battery playing upon us with the most deadly effect.

After a short pause, while repelling the skirmishers, I was ordered by General Robertson to move by the right flank, so as to cover all the ground between us and the directing battalion, moving about 200 yards, sheltering themselves behind rocks, from which, after a sharp contest, he was driven to the mountain … there I was pained to learn that the gallant Lieutenant-Colonel B. F. Carter was severely wounded while crossing a stone wall near the base of the mountain. I was also informed that Colonel John C. G. Key, while gallantly urging the men to the front, was severely wounded. The command then devolved upon me. Many of the officers and men had been killed and wounded by this time.

Finding it impossible to carry the heights by assault with my thinned ranks, I ordered my command to fall back to the part of timber, the position then occupied by enfiladed by the batteries on the left, and exposed to heavy fire by musketry in my immediate front. Being joined by the 5th Texas on my right, I again attempted to drive the enemy from the heights by assault, with like results. Again, being reinforced by the 48th Alabama, commanded by the gallant Colonel James L. Sheffield, and the

44th Alabama, whose commander I did not learn, we again charged their works, but were repulsed, and then, under the order of General Law, I ordered my command to fall back under cover of the timber on a slight elevation within short range of the enemy. I formed my regiment in the line of battle, leaving the battlefield contested ground.

At the dawn of day, I had a stone wall about 2 feet high thrown up, which afforded some protection to the men occupying the position from which we had driven the enemy, until sunset of the 3rd instant, at which time I was ordered to move my command, in conjunction with the remainder of the brigade, by the right flank, to occupy the ground from which we first advanced upon the enemy.

I accord to each and all of my officers and men my warmest congratulations for their continued and unceasing gallantry during the entire engagement.[6]

Captain Decimus et Ultimus Barziza
Fourth Texas Infantry

Between Chambersburg and Fayetteville we remained until the evening of the 1st of July, and after a tedious march all night arrived in the vicinity of Gettysburg at daylight on the second. It will be remembered that Ewell had attacked the enemy on the first, and had gained a decided advantage. Now the second day's contest was at hand. During the morning the troops were being put into position, and a calm, as of death, seemed to rest upon the earth, whilst the slow, ominous rumbling of artillery moving in position reminded us that the carnival was at hand. Everybody was confident and in the highest spirit of enthusiasm.

We were some hours getting into position but finally formed in an open field, under the declivity of a gradually rising hill in our front, upon the top of which the artillery was posted; all things ready, the batteries in our front opened, and we were soon hotly engaged with the enemy's guns on the opposite heights. The enemy's shells screamed and burst around us, inflicting considerable damage. It is very trying upon men to remain still and in ranks under a severe cannonading. One has time to reflect upon the danger, and there being no wild excitement as in a charge, he is more reminded of the utter helplessness of his present condition. The men are all flat on the ground, keeping their paces in ranks, and a shell is heard, generally trying to sink themselves into the earth. Nearly every face is overspread with a serious, thoughtful air; and what thoughts, vivid and burning, come trooping up from the inner chambers of memory, the soldier can only realize.

Captain Decimus et Ultimus Barziza.
(*Texas Heritage Museum*)

At any rate, the drawn cry of 'Attention!' brought everyman to his feet, and details were made to pull down the fence in our front. Everyone knew what that meant, and it was really a relief to move forward. The word 'Forward!' was given, and on we moved. So soon as we cleared the brow of the hill and became exposed to the enemy's artillery, off we went, not at an orderly double-quick, but in a wild frantic and desperate run, yelling, screaming, and shouting; over ditches, up and down hill, bursting through garden fences and shrubbery, occasionally dodging the head as a bullet whistled by the ear. Arriving in a road, we halted a minute or two, reformed and started again. On we go with the same speed, jumping over and plunging through creeks, pulling through mud, struggling through underbrush, still keeping up the loud, irregular and terrible Confederate yell. Shells and grape shot, canister and minie balls, came hurtling through our ranks, bursting, screaming, whistling still that same wild, reckless, unhesitating rush towards the enemy's guns.

Suddenly we find ourselves at the base of a range of hills, a rough, woody, rocky country. Here the great severity of the Federal Infantry stopped our progress, and then commenced a rapid, continuous and murderous musketry fight; we at the base, they on the sides and top of the hills. From behind trees and huge rocks we poured in our fiery discharges; the din was incessant and deafening. 'Keep your eyes on the colors,' we would occasionally shout and repeat; 'close to the right,' 'they are giving back,' and other similar commands and exclamations could be heard during the short intervals of firing.

During this musketry engagement we were within 25 to 50 yards of the enemy. The trees were literally barked, and thousands of bullets flew to atoms against the hard rocks. Our line was compelled finally to retire, and left me wounded in the hands of the enemy.

I tried to feign dead, but it would not answer, and sometime after I was taken to the enemy's rear. Thus ended as much as I know of the second day's fight.

During the artillery fight above mentioned, I saw General Longstreet in a small wood immediately behind our batteries, sitting on his horse like an iron man with his spy glasses to his eye, coolly watching the effect of our shots. Limbs of trees fell and crashed around him, yet he sat as unmoved as a statue. I really believe he loves the music of cannon-shot; if so, it is an affection that is not indulged by his faithful soldiers.

On passing to the rear, I saw the reinforcements of the enemy coming up and was indeed somewhat surprised at the nonchalance they exhibited in marching steadily towards the fighting.

I was taken to the Field Hospital of the 12th Army Corps, which had been established some distance at the rear of the lines. It consisted of the barn and other out-houses of a farm, sheds, etc., besides a great quantity of hospital tents, which were afterwards pitched.

About mid-day on Friday the battle of the 3rd day opened heavily; the artillery was terrific; as it progressed, great anxiety was discernable among the Federals; the surgeons ceased their operations and looked anxiously to the front; hospital flags were perched on the fences, trees and houses; soon came streams of ammunition wagons, ambulances and disabled artillery, driving frantically to the rear; thousands of soldiers rushed back, and we were driven up again to the front by cavalry in their rear; the wounded Federals, who were able to walk, were sent off hastily, and the scene was that of a routed and panic-stricken army. We, Confederates, who were at the hospital, were buoyant, and strained our eyes to see the gray backs rushing across the open field. But, alas! the storm gradually grew less violent, wavered, became more distant, and we knew the day was a bitter one for us. A little more vigor on the part of the Confederates that day would have secured the victory. Whilst the fight was raging that day, I was so confident that I remarked to the surgeon of the 12th Corps, 'General Lee would have his headquarters by tonight 10 miles on the Baltimore Pike.' 'It must be confessed,' he replied, 'that this looks somewhat like it.' During all this day hundreds of wounded, both Confederate and Federal, were brought in. Our wounded were generally well treated, and were put side by side with the enemy's. Every shelter in the neighborhood was crammed; even hay-lofts were filled with the bleeding, mangled bodies. The surgeons, with sleeves rolled up and bloody to the elbows, were continually employed in amputating limbs. The red, human blood ran in streams from under the operating tables, and huge piles of arms and legs, withered and horrible to behold, were mute evidences of the fierceness of the strife.[7]

Captain Decimus et Ultimus Barziza
Fourth Texas Infantry

We noticed the arrival home some time ago of our gallant friend, Captain D. U. Barziza of the Texas Brigade in Virginia, who was wounded and taken prisoner at Gettysburg and lay in Yankee prisons nearly a year. He has now been assigned to the command of Camp Greer near this city, and is doing his duty there accordingly. He is known as a prompt and efficient officer, and trusts he may not have to wear the Captain's bars much longer. He has earned his Majority and ought to have it.[8]

Private George Allen
Fourth Texas Infantry

Was wounded in the battle of Gettysburg, 2 July 1863, in right arm close to the shoulder, and it was amputated on 3 July. I was taken prisoner at David's Island. I was in the battles of Eltham's Landing, Va, Seven Pines, Gaines's Mill, Malvern Hill, Second Battle of Manassas, South Mountain, Sharpsburg, Fredericksburg and Gettysburg, where I was disabled for war and for life.

At the battle of Gettysburg I lost my arm, but it strengthened my faith in God and Christ and Southern rights. Thousands of men lay dead and wounded on the battlefield, but that day we built our monument and the glory of the name of the old Gettysburg leader, General Robert E. Lee, and his brave men will never die.[9]

Private J. H. Cosgrove
Fourth Texas Infantry
Grand Letter to General J. B. Polley by a Comrade on Fame's Eternal Camping Ground—Visit of a Confederate Soldier to the Battlefield

[Seldom is language more effectively used in tracing the pathetic scene of war than in the communications reproduced here:]
Petersburg, Va, 2 June 1907
To Floresville, Texas

Dear Joe,

You were right. To visit the spots where, forty and odd years ago you and I were units of a mighty force in arms that made history which will last so long as there remain recorded annals among men, is a wanton destruction of ideals in memory which had grown with us to be 'sacred sanctuaries.'

The face of all nature has changed. Even around this historic spot the scars of war—and you know how deep and distinctive they were in and about this city—have been obliterated, and the gardener's plow turns the glebe once torn by shot and shell.

They are raising turnips and 'sich,' dear Joe, on the sacred ground which, in the distant past, lapped the blood of our comrades, companions and friends—gone to fertilize truck for the New York markets are the bones of our martyrs. A thrifty soul from Pennsylvania—the immigrant the South invites—has enclosed the crater hallowed in history as a spot where Americans battled most desperately; a spot where thousands went down to immortal glory. There, dear Joe, the Pennsylvanian, the immigrant aforesaid, has fenced in and charges those who once there contended 25 cents to see a vine and weed grown 'hole in the ground.' An old ANV man of the Washington Artillery comments on this tribute as a more wanton charge than Grant made on Petersburg. The joke fell on dull, unsympathetic ears, and the reply marked the ethical standard of the modern buccaneer. 'Two bits please,' was all he said.

'Why should we complain?' as my friend from Louisiana observed. 'He is getting even for what we did to him or his in the long ago.' And from time past came that camp song of 1863 when we were floating back from Gettysburg:

> Old Bob Lee's heel is on thy shore,
> Pennsylvane, my Pennsylvane;
> His hand is at thy stable door,
> Pennsylvane, my Pennsylvane
> You won't see your old hoss no more
> We'll ride him till his back is sore,
> An' then come back an' git some more
> Pennsylvane, my Pennsylvane.

We left him, with his 'two bits, please' ringing in our ears, and I ruminated of the time when you and I and all of us helped make the hole from which modern commercialism draws its thousands.

You remember—of course you do—when we lay in line of battle not far from where these lines are penned, waiting the issue of Mahone's expulsion of the army. I can hear in memory the crash of musketry, the boom of cannon and the dear old Rebel yell which told that all was well. How grandly the Virginians and North Carolinians fought that day! Around and near us, in the houses and caves, women and old men and children, with tear-stained and pallid cheeks [and] anxious eyes, with eager expression prayed for victory, and when word came that 'God and the brave army of Northern Virginia had again triumphed,' their cheers and hand claps were mingled with our yells.

And forty and odd years after, this picture of the past, the history in the making, is rudely disturbed by the money changer's charge to see the spot we created and consecrated to the immortals!

If these things be true—and they do seem, for I saw them—'other men' should be thankful they are not as we.[10]

Second Sergeant Val C. Giles
Fourth Texas Infantry

On 26 June 1863, on our way to Gettysburg, Longstreet's Corps waded the Potomac River at Williamsport. It rained on us in Virginia, it poured on us in Maryland, and it flooded us in Pennsylvania.

When we reached the Maryland side of the Potomac we stacked arms, built fires, and prepared to cook our rations. The rain came down in waves, putting out our fires and drenching the men to the skin. It was an eventful day in the history of the Texas Brigade. Not a gun was fired, yet many of the boys were shot … in the gullet.

A gill of whiskey was issued to every man. It was chain lightening and knocked out many a valiant soldier. We never knew where General Hood got it, but every man in the Regiment was a know-nothing after he got his gill. A brilliant and eventful day in spite of the fact that it rained pitchforks the whole day long. We performed a feat never performed by any other troops during the war. We ate breakfast in the State of Virginia, dinner in the State of Maryland, supper in the State of Pennsylvania, and slept in the State of Intoxication—four states in twenty-four hours. Just before reaching the Pennsylvania state line, I stepped out of ranks and waited for Company K to come up. Captain 'Howdy' Martin was at the head of his company, his long cavalry saber thrown across his shoulder, squirrel-gun fashion.

'Captain,' I said, 'I have fallen back for reinforcements. I want you to help me capture the State of Pennsylvania.' 'All right Sonny, show me the keystone and we'll smash her into smithereens. Fall in line.'

So, arm in arm, a Captain and a Fourth Sergeant invaded the United States. In this day and time, such familiarity as that between a Captain and a Non-commissioned Officer would appear ridiculous in the eyes of strict disciplinarians, but Captain Martin was a man we all loved and could approach. When we reached the stone marker on the side of the turnpike that marked the boundary line between Pennsylvania and Maryland, we waved our hats and gave a Rebel yell that was taken up by the soldiers in the front and carried back for miles by those in the rear. Captain William H. Martin was gruff in manner, homely in appearance, a soldier from circumstance and not from choice, practice, or education—a nobleman pure and simple. 'Glorious Old Howdy' was the friend of the private soldier under any and all conditions. I am glad I did not shoot him in the dark that night when he found me up a tree on picket duty in the Chickahominy swamps! It was four o'clock in the morning when I reached my company, and the regiment was getting ready to move. I reported to Captain B. F. Carter, who told me to 'go way back, take a nap, and join the company by ten o'clock.' That was the most cheerful order I had heard for forty-eight hours, so John Griffith and I hid ourselves to some elevated ground near the railroad and slept like two babes in the woods.

'Get out of here! What are you skulking back in the brush for? Go to your regiment at once!' That was the sweet response that woke us from Nature's restorer, balmy sleep. It was a young stripling of a lieutenant who fired that remark at us as the 4th Alabama hurried past on its way to the front. The battle had begun again, and unfinished business was the first thing taken up in the morning. It is fortunate that we were gay on the way to battle, for all gaiety was replaced by grim realities and a bitter fighting on the field. One night at Gettysburg I shall never forget. A night of blood, blunders, and confusion. General Longstreet had orders to be at Gettysburg by sun-up on 2 July 1863. General Lee expected him. At sun-up … his Corps was only 8 miles away—a Corps famous in the Army of Northern Virginia for speed and endurance. To prove it, when the Battle of Chancellorsville began, Hood's Division of Longstreet's Corps was camped 7 miles south of Richmond. We had just returned from that never explained 'bacon raid' to Suffolk, in that 'low ground of sorrow' in the Blackwater and Dismal Swamp Country. At reveille that morning we received orders to cook three days' rations and be ready to move at once. At ten o'clock we passed through the city of Richmond, and that night camped at Ashland, in the Hanover Slashes, the birthplace of Henry Clay, 30 miles from our old camp south of Richmond. At Second Manassas we covered 20 miles in less than five hours, and yet at Gettysburg we were ten hours going 8 miles. It was not the fault of the rank and file. They were there—and ready. It was four thirty in the afternoon when we reached the battlefield, nearly ten and a half hours behind time. I don't know what the future historians—those fellows who are going to set everything right—will say about it, but that delay lost the Battle of Gettysburg to the Confederates, as Grouchy's failing to go to Napoleon lost the Battle of Waterloo to the French. If, as John S. C. Abbot says, 'The Battle of Waterloo changed the map of Europe,' who knows, but that the tardiness of an army corps at Gettysburg caused the map of this country to remain as it was. The loss of those ten hours gave the enemy ample time to occupy and fortify Cemetery Ridge and Little Round Top. Little Round Top was the key to the Battle of Gettysburg, and when we failed to occupy it, as General Lee expected us to do, the battle was lost. It was nearly five o'clock when we began the assault against the enemy … strongly fortified behind logs and stones on the crest a steep mountain. It was more than half a mile from our starting point to the edge of the timber at the base of the ridge, comparatively open ground all the way. We started off at quick time, the officers keeping the column in pretty good line until we passed through a blossoming peach orchard and reached the level ground beyond. We were now about 400 yards from the timber. The fire from the enemy, both artillery and musketry, was fearful. In making that long charge, our brigade got jammed. Regiments lapped over each other, and when we reached the woods and climbed the mountains as far as we could go, we were a badly mixed crowd. Confusion reigned everywhere. Nearly all our field officers were gone. Hood, our Major-General, had been shot from his horse. He lost an arm from the wound. Robertson, our Brigadier, had been carried from the field. Colonel Powell of the 5th Texas was riddled with bullets. Colonel Van Manning of the 3rd Arkansas was disabled, and Colonel B. F. Carter of my regiment lay dying at the foot of the mountain. The side of the mountain was heavily timbered and covered with great boulders that had tumbled from the cliffs above years before. These afforded great protection to the men. Every tree, rock and stump that gave any protection from the rain of minie balls that were poured down upon us from the crest above us, was soon appropriated. John Griffith and myself pre-empted a moss-covered boulder about the size of a 500-pound cotton bale. By this time order and discipline were gone. Every fellow was his own general. Private soldiers gave commands as loud as the officers. Nobody paid any attention to either. To add to this confusion, our artillery on the hill to our rear was cutting its fuse too short. Their shells were bursting behind us, in the treetops, over our heads, and all around us. Nothing demoralizes troops quicker than to be fired into by their friends. I saw it occur twice during the war. The first time we ran, but at Gettysburg we couldn't. This mistake was soon corrected and the shells burst high on the mountain or went over it.

Major Rogers, then in command of the 5th Texas Regiment mounted an old log near my boulder and began a Fourth of July speech. He was a little ahead of time, for that was about six thirty on the evening of July 2nd. Of course nobody was paying attention to the oration as he appealed to the men to 'stand fast.' He and Captain Cousins of the 4th Alabama were the only two men I saw standing. The balance of us had settled down behind rocks, logs, and trees. While the speech was going on, John Hagerty, one of Hood's couriers, then acting for General Law, dashed up the mountain, saluted the Major and said: 'General Law presents his compliments, and says hold this place at all hazards.' The Major checked up, glared down at Haggerty from his perch, and shouted: 'Compliments, hell! Who wants any compliments in such a damned place as this? Go back and ask General Law if he expects me to hold the world in check with the 5th Texas Regiment!' The Major evidently thought he had his own regiment with him, but in fact there were men from every regiment in the Texas Brigade all around him.

From behind my boulder I saw a ragged line of battle strung out along the side of Cemetery Ridge and in front of Little Round Top. Night began settling around us, but the carnage went on. There seemed to be a viciousness in the very air we breathed. Things had gone wrong all the day, and now pandemonium came with the darkness. Alexandre Dumas says the devil gets a man seven times a day, and if the average is not over seven times, he is almost a saint.

At Gettysburg that night, it was almost seven devils to each man. Officers were cross to the men, and the men were equally cross to the officers. It was the same way with our enemies. We could hear the Yankee officer on the crest of the ridge in front of us cursing the men by platoons, and the men telling him to go to a country not very far away from us just at that time. If that old satanic dragon has ever been on earth since he offered our Savior the world if he would serve him, he was certainly at Gettysburg that night. The advance lines of the two armies in many places were not more than 50 yards apart. Everything was on the shoot. No favors asked, and none offered. My gun was so dirty that the ramrod hung in the barrel, and I could neither get it down nor out. I slammed the rod against a rock a few times, and drove home ramrod, cartridge and all, laid the gun on a boulder, elevated the muzzle, ducked my head, hollered 'Look out!' and pulled the trigger. She roared like a young cannon and flew over my boulder, the barrel striking John Griffith a smart whack on the left ear. John roared too, and abused me like a pickpocket for my carelessness. It was no trouble to get another gun there. The mountain side was covered with them. Just to our left was a little fellow from the 3rd Arkansas Regiment. He was comfortably located behind a big stump, loading and firing as fast as he could. Between biting cartridges and taking aim, he was signing at the top of his voice: 'Now let the wide world wag as it will, I'll be gay and happy still.'

The world was wagging all right—no mistake about that, but I failed to see where the 'gay and happy' came in. That was a fearful night. There was no sweet music. The 'tooters' had left the shooters to fight it out, and taken 'Home, Sweet Home' and 'The Girl I Left Behind Me' with them. Our spiritual advisors, chaplains of regiments, were in the rear, caring for the wounded and dying soldiers. With seven devils to each man, it was no place for a preacher anyhow. A little red paint and a few eagle feathers were all that was necessary to make that crowd on both sides into the most veritable savages on earth. White-winged peace didn't roost at Little Round Top that night! There was not a man that cared a snap for the golden rule, or that could have remembered one line of the Lord's Prayer. Both sides were whipped, and all were furious about it. We lay along the side of Cemetery Ridge, and on the crest of the mountain lay 10,000 Yankee infantry, not 100 yards above us. That was on the morning of 3 July 1863, the day that General Pickett made his gallant, but fatal charge on our left. Our Corps, Longstreet's, had made the assault on Cemetery Ridge and Little Round Top the evening before. The Texas Brigade had butted up against a perpendicular wall of gray limestone. There lay on the night of the 2nd with the devil in command of both armies. About daylight on the morning of the 3rd old Uncle John Price (colored) brought in the rations for Company B. There were only fourteen of us present that morning under the command of Lieutenant James T. McLaurin. I felt pretty safe behind my big rock; every member of the regiment had sought protection from the storm of minie balls behind rocks or trees. The side of the mountain was covered with both. When Uncle John brought in the grub, he deposited it by a big flat rock, lay down behind another boulder, and went to sleep. Sergeant Mose Norris and Sergeant Perry Grumbles had been killed in our charge the evening before, and Sergeant Garland Colvin was wounded and missing. Somebody had to issue the grub to the men, and as an incentive to induce me to take the job, the Lieutenant raised me three points. He too was located in a bombproof position behind another big boulder just in front of me.

'Giles,' he said, 'Sergeant Norris always issued the rations to the men, but poor Mose is dead now and you must take his place. I appoint you Second Sergeant of Company B. Divide the rations into fourteen equal parts and have the men crawl up and get them.' Every time a fellow showed himself, some smart aleck of a Yankee on top of the ridge took a shot at him.

I didn't even thank the Lieutenant for the honor (or better, the lemon) that he handed me, and must admit that I undertook the job with a great deal of reluctance. A steady artillery fire was going on all along the line and a sulphuric kind of odor filled the air, caused by the great amount of black powder burned in the battle. Maybe it was the fumes of old Satan as he pulled out that morning, leaving the row to be settled by Lee and Meade. We were comparatively safe from the big guns, but it was the infantry just above us that made things unpleasant. I crawled up to the camp kettle and boiled roasting ears and meal-sack full of ironclad biscuits that Uncle John had brought in, and began dividing the grub and laying it on top of a big flat rock. The Yanks on the hill became somewhat quiet, so I got a little bolder and popped my head above the rock. They saw my old black wool hat and before you could say 'scat,' two minie balls flattened out on top of the rock, making lead prints half as big as a saucer, and smashing two rations of grub. One roasting ear was cut in two, but the old cold-water ironclad biscuits went rolling down the hill, solid as the rock from which they flew. Cuss words don't look well in print, but I don't see how a fellow can tell his personal experience in the army without letting one slip now and then. In this case I'll let it pass! When the bullets struck the lunch counter, the newly made Second Sergeant disappeared from view. The remark caused that grim old Lieutenant to laugh and say, 'Let the boys crawl up and help themselves.' The range was so close that when those bullets struck the solid rock, it flew all to pieces, a small fragment striking me on the upper lip, drawing a few drops of blood and mussing up my baby mustache. Second Sergeant was my limit in the 4th Texas Regiment.

There was a man in my company by the name of J. J. Haynes, a quiet unassuming fellow, who accepted conditions, obeyed his officers, did his duty, and never grumbled. He enlisted in Austin, Texas, in the spring of 1861, and went with us to Virginia. He carried a musket in the battle of Etham's Landing, Seven Pines, and all through the seven days' fight around Richmond. On the 20th of August 1862, a few days before the Battle of Second Manassas, he was detailed and assigned to the Brigade Litter Corps. Hays disliked to leave his old company and go with strangers, for the Litter Corps of a brigade is made up of eight or ten men from each regiment composing the brigade. However, he entered [with] no protest, gave up his gun, and shouldered a litter. At the battle of Gettysburg, nearly a year later, Longstreet's Corps was ordered to storm Cemetery Ridge. From where we started on the crest of the hill to where we halted at the base of the mountain, the ground was strewn with dying and wounded men. The Litter Corps had more than they could do, and no man worked harder or exposed himself more recklessly than Haynes. As he was crossing a low, marshy place approaching the firing line for another load, a bomb shell struck the soft earth a few yards in front of him, penetrated the ground 5 or 6 feet, and exploded with a tremendous roaring crash under his feet. Man, litter, bandages, canteens of water, old clothes and all went up in a cloud of dust and smoke. Everyone who saw it supposed that the man was literally blown to pieces, but such was not the case. When the dust, smoke, and fragments settled down, phoenix-like Haynes rose to his feet. Drawing his sleeve across his dusty brow, he faced the enemy and a frowning world, took off his old wool hat, waved it high over his head, and shouted at the top of his voice: 'Hurrah for hell! Damn you, shoot again!'

General J. B. Robertson commanded Hood's Texas Brigade at the Battle of Gettysburg, and was an eyewitness to the blowing up of Haynes. It occurred a few minutes before the old General was shot from his horse, and Haynes assisted him off the field. General Robertson always referred to Haynes as 'the bravest man in Lee's Army.' The first day of fighting, on 1 July, was in and around the little town of Gettysburg. The Confederates were commanded by Generals A. P. Hill and Ewell. The enemy was driven back and the town captured. During the first day's fighting, a majority of Longstreet's Corps was on the march between Chambersburg and Gettysburg. It was a forlorn hope to start with, and General Hood knew it. He begged General Longstreet to let him move to the right and fall on the enemy's left flank on Little Round Top. Three times Hood appealed to the Corps Commander to permit him to attack on the left, and each time received the answer, 'General Lee's orders are to attack on the Emmetsburg Road.'

That was blunder number two. The first blunder was failing to get to the battlefield at sun-up on the morning of the 2nd and taking possession of Cemetery Ridge and Little Round Top, which was not occupied by the enemy until noon that day. The Federals' success at Gettysburg was not a physical victory for Meade. The Confederates held every foot of the ground they occupied when the battle began up to the evening of the 4th, when General Lee quietly marched his men off the field. The enemy were at home on their own ground with advantage of position, while we were their unwelcome visitors far from home. If Lee was beaten and his army so completely demoralized as some Northern historians would have us believe, why didn't Meade follow up his so-called victory and capture Lee and his played-out army? Gettysburg was a drawn battle, both armies had had enough. When we pulled out from there, we made thousands of weary, worn-out Yankees supremely happy. They stood on the summit of Cemetery Ridge and Little Round Top and saw us move out in plain view, and were so glad to see us go that they forgot to shoot us in the back as we marched slowly from the field.

A farewell salute was certainly due us on our departure, for we had made it exceedingly interesting for them for three days. We took all our paraphernalia off with us that was of any value, leaving only a few broken gun carriages, and old wagons, donating the old junk as souvenirs to the enemy. We held the same position up to the evening of the 4th, receiving rations but once, which came to us at night. Fortunately, a majority of the men had their haversacks plenty well filled with good old Pennsylvania grub when we went into the fight.[11]

Second Sergeant Val C. Giles
Fourth Texas Infantry

While a small group of my old brigade were comparing recollections of the Battle of Gettysburg, a well-dressed, genteel appearing man stepped up and said: 'Excuse me gentlemen for this intrusion, but I wanted to shake hands with every one of you, for this is not the first time we met; I belonged to the Twenty Second New York Regiment and met Hood's Brigade at Gettysburg and have a small souvenir in the way of a scar that some of you boys gave me thirty-nine years ago.'

We found him to be a genial good fellow, without a drop of bitterness left in his jolly old Yankee heart.

I met a number of ex-Federal soldiers there and they appeared to be enjoying the reunion as much as the old 'Jonnies' themselves.[12]

Val C. Giles
Austin, Texas

Private J. M. Polk
Fourth Texas Infantry

I think we left Suffolk during March or April 1863, and went back to Petersburg and Richmond, and then went north and joined General Lee somewhere on the Rappahannock. Then the whole army, with Stuart's cavalry, started north. We all knew we would soon have another big killing.

Nothing of importance happened on the march; plenty of rain, creeks all up, and a hard time on the gray backs; not many young men of this generation know what a gray-back is, but if they had been in General Lee's army one month without changing their clothing they would know the meaning of the word. General Jackson had gone to his long home and General A. P. Hill took his place. We crossed the Potomac River at Williamsport, Md, on the 26th of June, 1863. Here we took a lot of government stores from the Federals, and among other things a lot of whiskey. It was rolled out on the hill, the heads knocked out of the barrels and issued to the men by the cupful. I don't suppose the oldest man living in America ever saw so many drunk men at any one time. It was all the officers could do to hold them down; they were full of new ideas. Colonel Manning of the 3rd Arkansas was very strict with his men, and he tried to carry out army regulations. 'Take that man and dip him in the creek,' he commanded. 'Now set him up on his feet and see if he can walk.' The man staggered a little and fell down. 'Dip him again.' All the other officers had all they could do to keep the men from fighting.

We traveled on and stopped at Greenmantle, Pa. General Lee issued orders to the men not to leave their commands as they were now in the enemy's country, and not to depredate on the citizens. We traveled on through Chambersburg: the houses were all closed and the women waved the Stars and Stripes at us. We moved on a short distance and then stopped and struck camp. The people here were all Dunkards. They seemed to think more of their stock then themselves; they had a very fine barn, but lived in an ordinary looking house. I was put on guard at one of these houses, and stood at the gate all day to keep the men from depredating on them. A woman called me in to dinner, which was one of the finest meals I ever sat down to. The old lady remarked: 'Oh, this cruel war! I just wish you men with your muskets could get them big fellows in a ring and stick your bayonets into them and make them fight it out. You could settle it in a few minutes.' I was young then and had never given the subject a sober thought, but since I have often thought of that old woman's remarks. Of course we all know now, for we have some experience in war, that if all the leaders and men who make war speeches and excite the people knew that in case of war they would have to pick up their gun and help fight the battles and take their chances along with the men, there would not be many wars. They would adopt Dr Franklin's plan—raise money and pay for the territory or property in question rather than go to war.

We traveled on, and soon heard cannonading and knew that the ball had opened. Late in the afternoon we heard that our column had a fight with the Federals. This was the first day's fight at Gettysburg. I always thought it was on the 2nd of July, but in order to agree with everybody else I will call it the 1st of July, 1863. By sun-up the next day we passed over the battleground and saw the dead and wounded, and we could see our artillery in front of us, all unlimbered and in battle array, flags flying and men going in every direction. About four o'clock in the afternoon, I understand we were on the right of General Lee's army; the line of battle was 7 miles long. Sam Miller and I left the ranks to get canteens of water for our company and I never saw Sam anymore until the war was over. He was captured and sent to Fort Delaware. Mat Beasly was ordered to take Captain Porter's old company, from Huntsville, into the fight. They never had gone into a fight and came out with a captain or lieutenant. We all gathered around Mat and said to him, 'Good-bye; you are gone now.'

Bob Crawford said: 'I am sorry for you, but I can't help you in anyway.' He was the only captain that came out alive with that company. Moving slowly, we entered the valley in a wheat field. We could see the Federals on the hills to our left, and the Stars and Stripes waving at us. About this time a shell from the Federal batteries came along through our lines and cut a man's head off; his name was Floyd from San Antonio. I was within about forty steps of him. Just then the command was given to 'forward!' It was about 300 or 400 yards to the foot of the hill, on which bordered a rock fence. When we were forty or fifty steps from this fence the Federal batteries on the hill turned loose in every direction. This scattered our men; many of them were killed, wounded, and captured. We were right in front of the battery. No time for shining shoes. So great was the confusion that I have no recollection of passing over the fence. I can remember when I was about halfway up the hill I stopped behind a big rock to load my gun; I could see Captain Reilly's battery a little to our right, and he was cleaning off the top of that hill. There was a solid blaze of fire in front of his battery. Right here, as well as I can remember, Bill Smith fell. He was a son of Tom I. Smith, an old pioneer, after whom Smith County, Texas, was named. He left behind his wife with her father, W. H. Mitchell, as the head of Richland and Chamber's Creek, 10 miles west of Millford, Ellis County, Texas, and never saw her anymore, and I doubt if she ever knew what became of him. When we reached the battery at the top of the hill the men had all left. Some dead were lying around, I don't remember how many. Harris in our company was in front of me. He put his hand over the cannon and was looking over the hill. The cannon was lying on a rock, I think, and the wheels behind the rock. I could hear the minie balls going over our heads. I said to him, 'Hold on Harris; we are by ourselves; wait till the balance comes up.' 'Oh, I want to see where they have gone,' replied Harris: 'they are not far off.' About that time a shell burst in front of us and a piece went through his breast, and it seemed to me that I could run my arm through that man's body. His face turned white as cotton, and strange to say, he turned around and tried to walk in that condition, but fell over and was dead in less than five minutes. His people lived somewhere in Virginia, but I don't know their address. Now, I could see the 3rd Arkansas to our left, and could hear Colonel Manning's voice; then I saw 300 or 400 Federals throw down their guns and surrender to him. I saw General Hood walking down the hill holding his arm. I understood his arm was broken above the elbow and 4 inches of the bone was taken out. By daylight the next morning we had a line of battle on top of that hill; we lay there all day. About twelve o'clock in the day I heard firing in our rear. I saw a house on fire and thought we were surrounded and would be captured, but I soon learned that a regiment of Federal cavalry was trying to destroy General Lee's ammunition train, which was protected by two regiments of infantry. The Federals succeeded until they were right in among the wagons; then the infantry closed in on them, and I don't think a man escaped. The Colonel refused to surrender and shot himself. Then commenced an artillery duel. General Lee had two 225 pieces of artillery, and he turned all of it loose on the Federal lines, and I suppose the Federals had as many or more to reply with. Just imagine what a thundering noise all those cannon made, all firing, you might say, at once, to say nothing about the loss of life and property!

I never did believe that any man knew the number of armed men engaged on both sides at the Battle of Gettysburg, but I will give it as my opinion, from what I could see or hear there must have been, all told, Federals and Confederates, at least 175,000 men and the number of killed, wounded and captured on both sides between 40,000 and 45,000 men. It has been forty years now, and I don't remember the names of my own company that were lost, much less the army. We lost our Lieutenant-Colonel, Carter of the 4th Texas, and I heard that Hood's Brigade lost 500 or 600 men. About three or four o'clock in the evening of the third day at Gettysburg we were still in line of battle on the hills; I don't know enough about the country to say whether it was Cemetery Ridge, Little Round Top, or what it was. The Federals made a charge and our left gave way. We fell back in the valley and formed in line of battle. I heard the cavalry horses and the horns. 'Look out boys!' someone shouted, 'get ready for a cavalry charge.' But for some reason they never came. I suppose their prudence and judgment got the best of them. I know nothing about the cavalry service, but I know it's a hard matter to get a lot of cavalry to charge a line of infantry. They know it's a serious matter, for many of them will go to their long homes when they try it. It began to get dark and commenced raining. The sergeant ordered me to go back on the side of the mountain on picket. Lieutenant Mills of our company was with us. Lieutenant Hugh Fuller, 5th Texas, from Houston, and I sat down on a big rock. We were compelled to keep up a strong picket line all night. Dead men were all around us, and it rained all night. It was as dark as a nigger's pocket. I was sleepy, hungry, and tired. I could feel the gray-backs moving around. I knew it would take a dose of red pepper occasionally and somebody to stick pins in me all night to keep awake, but it would not do to go to sleep here.

Between midnight and day I was nearly dead, completely exhausted. I lost all feeling of fear or duty and began to nod a little. Lieutenant Mills came along and tapped me on the shoulder and said, 'Don't go to sleep here.' But if I had known that I would be shot the next minute, it would have been all the same with me. But Mills was an old neighbor and friend, and he said nothing about it, but it would have been a serious matter with me if he had reported me. At daylight, General Lee's army moved off and left the battlefield of Gettysburg. About eight or nine o'clock he came riding along, and the men began to wave their hats and cheer him. He simply raised his hat, rode along and said nothing. He was plain, simple and unassuming in his manners and never encouraged anything of this kind. We all wanted to show him that we had not lost confidence in him. We passed through Hagerstown between midnight and day, crossed the Potomac and went down through Virginia to Richmond.[13]

Private J. M. Polk
Fourth Texas Infantry

… General Lee was a man who had but little to say to anybody. He always looked to me like he was grieving about the want of men and means to carry out his plans. Patrick Henry defines it as 'the illusions of hope.' But as our enemies would say, 'we are looking for something that we have never lost and don't expect to find.' About this time a copy of *Harper's Weekly* has a picture of General Robert E. Lee, and says that, 'although he was educated at the expense of the government he is now trying to destroy, he is looked upon by the eyes of the world as master of the arts of war,' and we might say that the name and fame of Robert E. Lee will live and command the respect of our people when most of our noted men are forgotten. Pulling back from Gettysburg, John Maley left the ranks to get some rations in a haversack but managed to get lost, and the Federal cavalry picked him up and took him to Washington City and put him in the old Capitol prison. President Lincoln came around through the prison and John walked up to him and said, 'How do you do, Mr President; my name is John Maley from Texas.' 'Glad to know you, Mr Maley.' 'Well, Mr President, I think you and me have been in all the jails and prisons in the United States.' 'Well, I don't know, I've been in this one and one in Springfield, Il, the only ones I remember now.' 'Well, I've been in all the balance, Mr President, so that makes it all right, sir.' They must have turned him out to get rid of him, for it was not long till he was back in his company, and related his interview with the President.

Another incident was of a man that belonged to some Georgia regiment. The captain came along and found him lying down on the side of the road and said, 'What are you doing here, John?' 'Captain, I'm given out, old shoes worn out and feet blistered. I can't march no further, Captain.' He knew there were some ambulances in the rear that would pick him up, so he left him. About the time he reached his company he heard firing in the rear, and looked around and John passed him making about 7 feet at a jump. 'Hello, John, I thought you couldn't march any further.' 'March, the devil, Captain, you call this marching?' Two of our men stopped beside the road to rest. An old preacher rode up and says, 'Well, young men, what regiment do you belong to?' They told him the company and regiment. 'What regiment do you belong to?' 'Well I don't belong to any particular regiment. I belong to the army of the Lord.' 'I am sorry to inform you, old man, you are a long ways from headquarters.' We passed through Hagerstown between midnight and day, crossed the Potomac and went down through Virginia to Richmond; there we shipped for Bragg's army.[14]

Quartermaster-Sergeant J. B. Polley
Fourth Texas Infantry
Gettysburg
Letter of 30 July 1863

Heretofore, Charming Nellie, it has been my privilege and delight to boast of victory—acknowledge and glorious victory. I know the Northern people claim that Lee's army met defeat at Sharpsburg-Antietam, as they call it—but the calm, unbiased judgment of the future will never sanction the claim. Considering that the Federal army outnumbered ours fully two to one, that Lee held his ground against all assaults, that he stood ready to receive an attack for one whole day, and then retired slowly, deliberately, without molestation and without additional loss, certainly only the partisan swayed and blinded by prejudice, passion, and pride can refuse to him the laurels of the victor. An army knows when it is whipped, and when, after a hard-fought battle, brave men still wear confident smiles and cheer their general as he passes—as Lee's army did him the day after its return to Virginia soil—it is because they know they have won the fight. But, alas! Sharpsburg furnishes but little of compensation for Gettysburg, for her defeat—bloody, terrible, and disastrous defeat—stared us in the face at the beginning of the conflict, and swept down on us, an overwhelming pall of gloom, at its ending. At Sharpsburg McClellan attacked, and Lee held his ground; at Gettysburg, Lee made the assault, and Meade, the successor of McClellan, held his ground. At the one place the Federals met withering, deadly repulse—at the other, the Confederates. While at Gettysburg the Confederates fought heroically; while Pickett's charge on Cemetery Heights has never been equaled in vigor, dash, and reckless daring; while every division, brigade, and regiment of the Southern army did its duty nobly and well, the odds, both in numbers and position, were against us— the God of War hostile, and inevitable, crushing defeat fell to our lot.

Sergeant J. B. Polley.
(*Texas Heritage Museum*)

Nor did it come at Gettysburg only, for on the same day Pemberton surrendered, Vicksburg fell—the news of that companion disaster reaching us almost simultaneously with the knowledge of our own misfortune. That a mistake was made at Gettysburg is admitted by all; who made it is now too late to inquire. The cavalry out of place and reach, General Lee lacked the exact information requisite to successful generalship. Fighting where we did—assaulting heights defended by superior numbers and difficult to scale even by unarmed and unopposed men—it seems now impossible to have won. Had we moved to the right across the Emmitsburg Road, and, selecting our position, awaited the attack Meade would have been compelled to make, the result might have been different, the Confederates now singing the songs of victory instead of doing their best to keep out of the slough of despond. Why we did not move to the right, General Lee only knows, and defeat—novel and humiliating as it is—has not shaken our confidence in him and his subordinate commanders. The rank and file of the army did its whole duty and absolutely refuses to admit that, either through carelessness or intention, its generals did less. We are not such hero-worshipers as to believe even Lee infallible, especially when we remember his noble and magnanimous words, 'It is all my fault men, it is all my fault.' Self-respect would have prohibited that admission had it been wholly untrue.

Butler says in *Hudibras*: 'In all the trade of war, no feat is nobler than a brave retreat.' That is biting, subtle irony in the connection in which it appears, but might be written seriously and truly of the retreat from Gettysburg—of the endurance of the Confederate army, the brave front ever turned upon the pursuing enemy, and the generalship of Lee. Beaten and crushed, decimated by death and wounds, gaunted by hunger and footsore with marching as was that army, Meade, although elated by victory, dared neither to follow it closely nor attack it when, like a lion in his path, it stood at bay; and at Hagerstown it lay in defiant but restful security long enough to build pontoon bridges, send across them its immense train of wagons, and follow at its leisure. Let the Yankees boast as much as they please over this their first success. We have met repulse, but, God willing, will yet win freedom, independence, and separate nationality. Given a fair field, our disaster will be retrieved, and the Yankee nation taught that 'one swallow does not make a summer.' I can tell you little of the battle of Gettysburg, for luckily or unluckily—just as one chooses to regard it—I was not a participant. In the attack, on 2 July, on Little Round Top the brigade was exposed to a terrific fire of shot, shell, and canister, and lost many of its best men. Among the many daring acts of which the boys speak in warm admiration is that of George Branard, color bearer of the 1st Texas, who bore his flag so far and gallantly to the front that the Yankees, in recognition of his bravery, shouted to each other, 'Don't shoot that color bearer—he is too brave!' It appears that in the unavoidable confusion [of] an attack by several brigades upon a common point, the colors of several Georgia regiments and those of the 1st Texas came so near together behind a natural breastwork of rocks that they not only drew the concentrated fire of the enemy, but made it difficult to determine which flag was farthest in advance. To settle the question beyond dispute, Branard called upon his color guard to follow him, and, mounting the rocks, dashed forward toward the Yankee lines. It was here the Federal infantry sought to spare him; their artillery, however, could not be so magnanimous, and the bursting of a shell carried away all but the lower part of the flagstaff, and laid Branard unconscious upon the ground. At first we thought he was killed, but that was a mistake. He revived in a few minutes, and, if his friends had let him, would have attempted to whip the whole Yankee nation by himself—he was so mad. It is only of the lights and lesser shadows of this cruel war I care to write; its horrors I avoid as well because, soldier-like, I try to forget them, as it is unkind to shock your womanly sensibilities with things so revolting and gruesome. But, fortunately, there are a few amusing incidents to record of the battle, and to delay saying, 'Farewell! Othello's occupation's gone.' And closing this already lengthy epistle before the boys from camp have had time to make their daily raid on the corn patch, I must perforce descend to egotism; so *'revenons a nos moutons'*—which means, translated under stress of the present emergency, let us return to our wagons. After night descended on the fourth day of July and concealed our movements from the enemy, they were loaded with those of the wounded who could stand rough transportation, and ordered across the Potomac. It rained heavily all night long, and right gladly would I have crawled beneath the sheets of a wagon and found protection from the storm. But my steed refused to lead and I was forced to take the rain and be content with such cat-naps as occasional halts permitted. Just before daylight I called at a house by the roadside, and although the sour and forbidding countenance of the proprietor indicated no anxiety to cultivate amicable relations, persuaded him to fortify my inner man with two cups of coffee and a proportional share of bread and butter. Daylight brought with it the dread fear of pursuit, and the teams were pushed rapidly on. But on arriving at Williamsport, what was our surprise and consternation to find the Potomac conspiring with the enemy, and so swollen as to be impassable in the absence of pontoons! To add to the Iliad of our woes, the Yankee cavalry came swooping down on us at noon, and the dire and deplorable misfortunes of capture and captivity stared us broadly and unwinkingly in the face. Still, just as a mouse will fight when cornered, so will commissaries, quartermasters, and their immediate subordinates, and the small cavalry force escorting the train was at once reinforced by a body of men who, however non-combatant ordinarily, on this occasion faced danger gallantly and—although sadly out of practice—used the few weapons to be had with a deadly skill that soon put the foe to flight. Fortunately, too, just when the Yankees were fairly on the run, General Imboden came creeping up with a brigade of Confederate cavalry, and, without a blow to win them, coolly appropriated all the honors of the engagement. I am glad he was so generous and considerate; the last thing the gentlemen officiating in various capacities in the quartermaster and commissary departments desire is a reputation for courage; that fastened upon them, they might have more fighting to do. While endeavoring to keep out of the reach of death-dealing missiles at Gettysburg, and at the same time watch the progress of the battle, I took advantage of a lull in the firing to ride down the main street of the little town. Discovering a lot of shoes—cloth gaiters such as ladies wear—scattered in confusion over the muddy floor of a cellar and without apparent ownership, I selected a pair of No. 3's and brought them away with me. Really, I had as little idea what I wanted them for as the soldier had with respect to the grindstone he stole. However, I soon learned there was a demand for just such articles.[15]

First Sergeant Richard Skinner
Fourth Texas Infantry
Tribute to Richard Skinner

All of the people of Corsicana remember a man who was a well-known and highly respected citizen here for a number of years, and who was known to all people as 'Uncle Dick.' A copy of the *Enterprise*, published at Hamilton, Va, under date of August 22, which was handed to the *Sun* by Mr P. H. Loggins, pays the following tribute to the memory of one who will long be remembered in Corsicana. The contributor says:

In the passing away of Richard Skinner, which occurred on the 26th of April, 1913, after a brief illness of pneumonia, there has passed one of the last male representatives of a generation which made the Virginia gentleman so widely known and admired.

Born in Middleburg, Va, January 1st, 1833, his life spanned the years well into the first quarter of the present century. In his young manhood Mr Skinner went to Texas, where for many years he was engaged in the mercantile business. There also he was married to a widow Wells, who died many years ago leaving no children.

At the outbreak of the Civil War, he enlisted in Hood's Brigade, and in the Battle of Gettysburg made for himself a lasting record as a brave soldier. Wounded, bleeding, heartsick and sore, he lay on that field of carnage for seventeen days before being removed to a hospital, where three months later he came forth weary and worn with the battle fought over again between life and death. For nearly half a century this brave old ex-Confederate carried in his lung the bullet that laid him low at Gettysburg, a memento of the days when a brave man never turned his back to the enemy.

After his recovery he went back to his regiment, the 4th Texas, Company F, Hood's Brigade, where he continued to the end. At the close of the war he again located in Texas, where he was well known and much respected for his many sterling qualities, his fidelity to principle, and his ever ready response to the call of duty.

About seven years ago he came back to his home in Loudoun, where he spent the better part of his remaining days as an invalid.

Death came and closed a useful and honorable life, at the advanced age of eighty. Many knew him to love him; all who came within the circle of his acquaintance respected him.

A brave man, generous and just, a man true to his convictions and true to his friends—such a man was Richard Skinner. A long life honorably spent, his work finished. Who can doubt his joy at the sight of the 'beautiful beckoning hands,' extended from the 'gateway' to welcome him inside the portals.[16]

Color Corporal John Stacey
Fourth Texas Infantry
To Attend Reunion

Uncle John Stacey left today for Rockdale where he goes to attend a reunion of the survivors of Hood's Brigade. Uncle John is one of the seventy-five survivors of this company who fought at in the battle of Gettysburg and is the only member left in Brazos County. He is getting rather feeble but his mind is still clear and he can relate some very interesting stories. Before leaving today he said that if our president called men to arms to take charge of Carranza he stood ready to go and believes that he can show some younger bunch how to fight.[17]

Private John C. West
Fourth Texas Infantry

Chambersburg, Pa, 9 June 1863

My Precious Wife,
I had not intended to write until the 9th of July, or until a battle occurred, but the reception of your most welcome letter on the date May 11th and 13th, together with the fact that I have a prospect of a day's rest, have made me conclude to try the experiment of sending a few lines from Richmond. If I were certain this would reach you I could make it very interesting to you, for I have endured and passed through a great deal which no one can dream of, or picture, except those who have passed through the same trials.

Newspaper writers and correspondents cannot convey the idea of the hardships of a soldier's life when on a march. I wrote to your sister, Decca, from Millwood, 20 miles west of Harper's Ferry, and gave her quite a succinct account of my trials and marches for ten or twelve days previous, and since that time I have a repetition of the same. I have told her to write to you every two or three weeks, and have written to Miss Nannie Norton, making the same request of her, so that if you do not hear from me, or one of them, you must take it for granted that the letters do not get through the lines, and not think that anything is wrong with me, for I will be preserved safe from all harm. Nothing but a special providence could have saved me in perfect health and strength thus far.

Private John C. West.
(*Texas Heritage Museum*)

We have marched in heat until stalwart men, apparently much stronger than myself, have fallen dead by the roadside. We have crossed and recrossed streams, waist deep, with water cold and chilling. We have passed four or five nights and days without changing clothes, which were soaking wet during the entire time. Billy Dunkin, Billy Robinson and myself slept one night together at the very top of the Blue Ridge Mountains under a single blanket. It rained and blew furiously during the whole night, and we got up in the morning with our feet and hands shriveled just as you frequently see from remaining too long in the water. On several occasions we have waded streams just at sundown and slept in wet clothes, or sit up naked while our clothes were drying, with a prospect of being ordered to march between midnight and day. A soldier's motto is to sleep at all hazards whenever he has a chance, for it never comes amiss. We crossed the Potomac, at Williamsport, on the 26th of June, and have since marched through Greencastle and on to this place, passing through the most beautiful country I ever beheld, increasing in its charms ever since we left Culpepper. We are now between the Blue Ridge and the Alleghany; the entire landscape covered with the most magnificent farms, orchards, and gardens, for miles along the road. The most neat and elegant residences and barns; positively more tastily built than two thirds of the houses in

Waco, and as fine as the dwelling houses anywhere. I have not seen a barn in the last three days that was not more substantially and carefully built and fitted out than any house I have ever seen in the country in Texas.

Wheat is the staple product in this portion of Pennsylvania, and the crops are splendid; just ready to cut. The apple trees are loaded and the cherries delicious. I enclose two varieties of cherry seed, and will endeavor to bring some if I ever get back. The people here have quite a chagrined and subdued look as we march through these towns and villages. A lady encouraged some little girls to sing the 'Red, White and Blue' as we passed through Chambersburg. She remarked as I passed, 'Thank God, you will never come back alive.' I replied, 'No, as we intend to go to Cincinnati by way of New York.'

My impression is that we will have a desperate battle in a few days, but I cannot tell, as a soldier who minds his own business knows less than an outsider. I would not have missed this campaign for $500. I believe that if successful it will do a great deal towards bringing about a peace or our recognition by foreign powers. All of our company are doing well. Allen Killingsworth is below Richmond on a furlough. Burwell Aycock is nursing his wounds at Chattanooga. Jim Manahan is quite sick today, and has not been well for several days. I think he had sunstroke on one of those fearfully hot days. John Harrington has not been with the company for three months. He is at Richmond. I am rejoiced at your progress in Latin, and in your music, and think that if anything could make me love you more, or cause to us live more happily together, if possible, it will be the consciousness of having the most accomplished wife, as well as the most charming in other respects, in the whole country. I am glad the little boys are with you, and trust they will give you no trouble. It strengthens and encourages me to know that you are cultivating and improving yourself, instead of sitting down listlessly, dipping snuff 'for company,' or gossiping idly. Guard against the last especially. Tell Stark and Mary not to forget their lessons or me, and that I will come back some of these days and hear them. You ought to have no difficulty about the war tax. If the tax collector is a man of sense he can give you all the assistance you require, except the money to pay the tax. As far as my salary is concerned, you will have nothing to do with that. You had better send Dr Combs his money as soon as you can spare it. I have paid all the debts I contracted on the way except $75 to Major Holman. I have $50 bounty and $30 pay due me in the course of a week, and as there may be a battle soon I will not draw it, but will leave it in the hands of somebody so that you can get it, as I do not wish a Yankee to make anything by rifling my pockets on the battlefield. I intended to finish this sheet but it has commenced to rain and I must bid you good bye and get under my blanket.

May God preserve you and our little darlings until we meet again—be it soon or late. Love to our friends.

Your husband, faithfully ever,
John C. West

Hagerstown, Md, 8 July 1863
To Master Stark West, four years old

My Dear Little Man,

I wrote to mamma from our camp near Chambersburg, Pennsylvania, and as tomorrow is your birthday, and you are getting to be a big boy, I thought you would like for papa to write you a letter and tell you something about the war and the poor soldiers.

God has been very good to me since I wrote to mamma. He has saved my life when many thousands of good men have been slain all around me. On the 1st, 2nd and 3rd of July a very terrible battle was fought near Gettysburg. We marched all night, leaving camp at two o'clock in the afternoon in order to reach the battlefield in time. There had been some fighting on the 1st and we passed a hospital where I saw a great many wounded soldiers, who were mangled and bruised in every possible way, some with their eyes shot out, some with their arms, or hands, or fingers, or feet or legs shot off, and all seeming to suffer a great deal. About 2 miles farther on I found a great many soldiers drawn up in a line, ready to meet the Yankees, who formed another line a mile or two in front of them. These lines were 3 or 4 miles long, and at different places on the hills were the batteries of artillery.

These, you know, are cannons, which shoot large shells, and iron balls a long distance. We kept in this line so long, and I was so tired, I went to sleep and dreamed about you and mamma and little sister, and I asked God to take care of you if I am taken away from you. After a while we were marched off in a great hurry towards the left of the Yankee line of battle, which is called the left wing, and was opposite to our right wing, which was composed principally of Hood's division. Our brigade was ordered to charge upon one of the Yankee batteries, which was posted on a mountain as high as Mount Bonnell, with another battery on a still higher mountain, just back of it, to support it. We were standing in an open field, under the shot and shell of these batteries, for half an hour, before we moved forward, and a good many soldiers were killed all around me. One poor fellow had his head knocked off in a few feet of me, and I felt all the time as if I would never see you and little sister again. When the command was given to charge we moved forward as fast as we could towards the battery.

It was between a half and three quarters of a mile across an open field, over a marshy branch, over a stone fence, and up a very rugged and rocky hill, while Yankee sharpshooters were on the higher mountains, so as to have fairer shots at our officers. On we went yelling and whooping, and soon drove the Yankees from the first battery, but were too much worn out and exhausted to climb to the second, besides a great many of our men were killed, and minie bullets and grape shot were as thick as hail, and we were compelled to get behind the rocks and trees to save ourselves.

We renewed the charge several times, but the slaughter of our men was so great that after four or five efforts to advance we retired about sunset and slept behind the rocks. I had thrown away my blanket and everything except my musket and cartridge box in the fight, and so spent a very uncomfortable night. We remained at the same place all the next day, and every now and then Yankee bullets would come pretty thick amongst us. One bullet went through my beard and struck a rock half an inch from my head, and a piece of the bullet hit me on the lip and brought the blood.

Lieutenant Joe Smith, of McLennan County, was killed 10 feet in front of me, and John Terry and Tom Mullens were both wounded in the shoulders. I wanted to write my little man a letter, which he could read when he was a big boy, but it has been raining and the ground is very wet and everything so uncomfortable that I cannot enjoy it.

Tell mamma she had better put off her visit to South Carolina until the war is over, as she seems to be doing very well, and it will be better for her.

Your father, truly,
John C. West

Camp near Hagerstown, Md, 9 July 1863

My Precious Wife,

On yesterday I wrote a bungling letter to my 'little man' intending it for his birthday, as I feared we would be ordered off today, and sure enough I have just learned we are to leave directly. God has mercifully preserved me through the terrible Battle of Gettysburg, though my escape was as narrow as possible. I cannot attempt an account of the battle as a private only knows what occurred in his immediate presence. Our regiment went into the fight with 350 and lost 150 in killed, wounded and missing. Lieutenant Joe Smith, son of Captain Jack Smith, on Hog Creek, was killed. We had just climbed the stone fence and crossed a branch and a little marsh. Lieutenant Smith had wet his handkerchief in the branch and tied it around his head. It was extremely hot. It was about three o'clock in the afternoon, and we had double-quicked across an open field for nearly 500 yards. He was killed in 20 feet of me, just after we crossed the branch—shot through the head, the bullet passing through the folds of his handkerchief on both sides. He was a splendid officer and we miss him very much.

From the 1st to the 6th of July I never took off my accouterments night or day. I marked in my Bible the Psalm which I read while in the line of battle among the rocks on the third of July. We were somewhat in advance of our main line and held our place, but could drive the enemy no further—neither could they dislodge us. We remained there until the close of battle. I have requested my friends to save my Bible and the little tin cup, which baby gave me for you in case of any fall. I threw away my blankets and all of my extra clothing when we went into the battle, but picked up a blanket on coming out. You need not trouble yourself about my wants, as it is impossible to make a soldier comfortable. I was soaking wet from the 2nd to the 6th of July, without meat and with little bread, and have been for some time; so you see if I had all the comforts you might fix for me, I would have to throw them away on a long, wet march. It is impossible to carry them. I started from Texas to find a fight, and I have made a success of it. I am much delighted and gratified at the way you seem to be spending your time.

With kisses for the little ones, I am,
Your husband, faithfully ever,
John C. West

Camp near Culpepper, C. H., 27 July 1863
To Major Charles S. West, Judge Advocate General of
Trans-Mississippi Department

Dear Brother,

I would have attempted a letter to you long ago, but the difficulties presented to a private on a regular march unfit him for anything like recreation, and the uncertainty of getting a letter across the Mississippi disinclined me to make an attempt amid the confusion of camp life. If I were seated in a comfortable chair instead of having my naked buttocks upon the sand (for my last article of underwear is in the wash and the seat of my pants in Pennsylvania.)

I could give you a succinct account of the campaign into the enemy's country; whereas you must be satisfied with this hurried and meagre history which Captain W. H. Hammon, our quartermaster, has promised me to mail across the river. We left camp from which I now write on the 15th day of June, under a burning sun and a brazen sky. The march was conducted by that unmerciful driver, our beloved General Hood, who simply strikes a trot and is satisfied that the Texas Brigade at least will camp with him at nightfall. We moved 24 miles on that day, camping near Gaines's Crossroads, with the loss of 200 men from sunstroke.

The road for the last 10 miles was literally lined with soldiers fallen from exhaustion. We were required to wade Hazelrun, two branches of the Rappahannock, the Shenandoah and other minor streams, under positive orders not to stop to pull off or roll up. We crossed the last named on the afternoon of the 18th, and camped about a mile from it.

On the 19th we marched down the river and recrossed at Snigger's Gap on the summit of the Blue Ridge. At those last two camps we were drenched in the hardest rains I ever saw, pouring down during the entire night. On the 20th, in the morning, we built a rock fence half a mile long and made all necessary arrangements to defend the Gap if required. On the afternoon of the same day we re-crossed the river and camped on the north side, 4 miles from Berryville. On the 21st marched 10 miles down the river and 3 miles out from it through Millwood, and camped 2 miles from it and within 4 miles of Berryville on the regular turnpike, which passes through Martinsburg, Smithfield and several other smaller places.

At this camp it was formally announced that 'we are about to go into the enemy's country, that private property should be respected, that all pillaging and private foraging should be abstained from as the troops would be subsisted upon the very best the enemy's country afforded.' This amounted to an official falsehood or mistake, as the sequel showed. We trudged on, and nothing occurring worthy of record until the 26th, on which we took breakfast in Virginia, dragged through the mud and rain to the Potomac, crossed it at Williamsport, and were halted 2 miles beyond with the promise of rations and of time to cook them. Our wood was gathered, fires kindled, a stiff drink of whiskey issued to each man (about one third got pretty tight), and the order to march was given. We dragged— many slipped down and literally rolled over in the mud (for it rained all the time), and among the most conspicuous was Captain M. of the Texas, one of your legislative brethren; and finally, about dusk we reached the Pennsylvania line and took supper in the United States. A brilliant and eventful day! Breakfast in Virginia, whiskey in Maryland, and supper in Pennsylvania. The portions of the two last mention states through which we passed are the most thoroughly improved which I ever saw. There was not a foot of surplus or waste territory. All had been made to answer the demands of the consumer. Wheat, corn, clover, a half dozen varieties of grass, rye, barley—all in full growth and approaching maturity—met the eye at every turn, all enclosed in rock or strongly and closely built wooden fences. Apples, cherries, currants, pears, quinces, etc., in the utmost profusion, and bee hives *ad infinitum*. The barns were, however, the most striking feature of the landscape, for it was one bright panorama for miles. They invariably occupied the most select building site on the tract, and were equal in size, elegance and finish, and superior in arrangement and adaptation to this purpose to three fourths of the dwellings in Texas. On the other hand, the dwellings, though neat and comfortable, were secreted in some nook or corner, as if there had been a close calculation that a horse or an ox being the larger animal, required a more spacious residence than a human being. I think the class or position in society must depend somewhat on the size and elegance of the barn.

The springs and milk houses and dairies were also a noted feature of the country. I think I have seen more than fifty springs equal to those of Barton, San Antonio, San Marcos and Salado. But the most singular phenomenon which impressed me was the scarcity of visible inhabitants, in this apparently densely populated region. Women and children were seen peeping about but as shy as partridges, but in the towns and villages men, women and children thronged by hundreds. I believe two brigades of able men under thirty years of age could have been raised in Chambersburg alone. We were, of course, coldly received everywhere.

Our camp was not more than 2 miles beyond Chambersburg on the night of June 27. On the 29th we moved 10 or 12 miles to Fayetteville and were encamped there until the evening of the 1st of July, the day on which the fight at Gettysburg was opened. About dusk we started for the battlefield, Hill and Ewell having driven the enemy 4 miles back on that day. General Lee, it was said among the men, was opposed to giving battle at that point, and in favor of giving the enemy the slip (I don't know how), and marching straight for Baltimore. It was found that this would be impracticable, owing to the difficulty of protecting 20 or 25 miles of train from Yankee cavalry. It was then suggested to burn one half the train. It was opposed by the argument that the subsistence would not be sufficient and the consequent risk of demoralization for want of food. General Lee then said to fight was the only chance, and he was fully satisfied of a complete victory.

Generals Longstreet and Hood were opposed to attacking the enemy in a position of their own choosing. I am unable without a map to describe the locality of the forces or the face of the country along the entire line, but can give you a faint idea of affairs on the right wing. Hood's division occupied this, and our brigade was the last but one on the extreme right of the division. The line must have been 5 or 6 miles long. We were put into the fight at about three o'clock in the afternoon of the 2nd, having marched all night on the 1st and laid in line of battle all the morning of the 2nd, and my first lesson as a recruit was to lie for about half an hour under what the most experienced soldiers called the worst shelling they ever witnessed. Several were killed and many wounded in a few feet of me, and the infernal machines came tearing and whirring through the ranks with a most demoralizing tendency. This, however, was soon over. Our line was formed, and with a voice that Stentor might have envied, General Hood gave the command: 'Forward—steady!—Forward!' (He was on horseback, on the left of a line from our brigade to the battery playing upon us, and about 300 yards from me.) And forward we went. The word was passed down the line, 'Quick, but not double quick,' but we moved as fast as we could. Off went blankets, knapsacks and all surplus baggage, and yelling and screaming as we rushed on the batteries—one on a lofty eminence beyond a rock fence and a small branch, the other back of it on quite a mountain about 300 yards farther off and a little to the right—were full three quarters of a mile from us when the word 'forward' was given. The result was the line became broken and confused and the men exhausted (having marched all of the previous night) by the time they reached the foot of the hill. Nevertheless, the first battery was taken, and after rallying in the best manner possible, several desperate efforts were made to charge the second, but courage and even desperation was useless. There were places full 10 or 15 feet perpendicular around which we were compelled to go, and the entire ascent would have been difficult to a man entirely divested of gun and accouterments. It was a mass of rock and boulders amid which a mountain goat would have reveled, and being subjected to a fire on our left flank, made it a most dangerous and unsafe place for a soldier, and many a fellow reminded me of the alliteration, 'Round the rude rock the rascal ran.'

Our assault, with short intervals, was kept up until dark, when we rested on our arms and spent an uneasy night amid the crags. Our position was now rather in advance of the troops on our left. All day on the 3rd we held our ground, making unsuccessful sallies, checking skirmishers and passing shots with sharpshooters, one of whom, secreted in a tree on the side of the mountain, put a bullet in an inch of my head as I leaned against a rock, part of the bullet flying into my lip.

About four o'clock in the afternoon cannonading was opened along the entire line, and such a thundering and crashing and roaring surely was never heard. An eagle in the very midst of a tremendous thunderstorm might possibly have experienced such confusion. All agreed that Sharpsburg and Second Manassas was not a priming to it. Milton's account of the great battle between the combined forces of good and evil, which originated in this same question of secession, gives some faint idea of this artillery duel.

Later in the afternoon we heard a terrible musketry on our left and yells and huzzahs swaying alternately back and forth as the line gave way, first one side and then the other. We could not see through the timber, but the location of the final huzzahs satisfied us that our center was giving way. This compelled us to withdraw down the mountain and out in the open field to prevent being flanked, which we accomplished with the loss of a few men. The fighting here ceased, darkness preventing either party from making any important move. We threw up breastworks on the 4th, with the hope that the enemy would leave his position in the mountains and attack us on the open plain, where we could have routed him and kept him in such confusion that a rally would have been impossible.

I believe the wounding of General Hood early in the action was the greatest misfortune of the day. Our position could have been held by very few men, and if a considerable force had been thrown around the mountain to our right the enemy would have been routed in half an hour. I think many of the Federal army would have deserted, being in easy reach of home. Baltimore would have been ours and the New York riots would have been as famous as the Battle of Bunker Hill.

As it is, let us who will say, to the contrary, we made Manassas time from Pennsylvania. It is unnecessary to give any detailed account of myself. Suffice it to say I have endured more than I believed myself capable of. I have been through a campaign and participated in a furious and terrible battle. I am satisfied that I am not afraid to go into another, though, since the fall of Vicksburg, I prefer to be west of the Mississippi, closer to Texas and closer to my family. I would like to have a long talk with you and hope for better days when we can enjoy it. Write to my wife and let her know that you have received this letter. I had intended to allude to that 'official falsehood' referred to above, but let it pass. Suffice it to say that if we had depended on our commissaries, we would have suffered seriously for food.

Your brother, truly,
John C. West

Camp near Culpepper, Va, 27 July 1863

My Precious Wife,

I wrote to you quite a full letter yesterday and sent it to the 4th Texas Department at Richmond, the agent for which is very particular in seeking opportunities to send you letters across the river, but still it may not reach you, so I have determined to try another channel which I have found today. Captain Hammon, quartermaster of our regiment, will start for Texas tomorrow and has kindly consented to take this for me. You see by the caption that I am back at our old camp, which I am beginning to regard as home. I am sitting near the same spot from which I wrote you more than a month ago, and my surroundings pretty much the same, except the absence of our Lieutenant Joe Smith, who was killed at Gettysburg.

He was a very talented and excellent officer, enjoying, perhaps, more than any officer in the regiment, the confidence and trust of headquarters. His loss is a very serious blow to the company. By the goodness of God I came safely through, though many were killed around me. One bullet passed through my beard, grazed my ear and struck a rock about an inch from my head. A piece of the lead flew into my upper lip, but caused no interruption or serious inconvenience. Our move to Pennsylvania was a failure, and I think General Lee never would have attacked the enemy in their position on the mountainside except for the splendid condition of his army, and his confidence in its ability to accomplish anything he chose to attempt. Our division was on the right of the entire line and our brigade the last but one on the extreme right of the division, and just opposite to one of the strongest positions of the enemy, which was on a high mountain and defended by batteries on mountains still higher. We took and held the lower heights long enough to capture the batteries, but were unable after several charges to scale the higher ones, being subjected to a fire on our left flank and in front while attempting to climb over the rocks and gorges, which would have delighted a mountain goat.

On the third day, late in the evening, our center gave way, and we were compelled to retire down this mountain and take our position in the open field, where we threw up breast works and awaited the advance of the enemy. We remained here during the entire fourth day of July, and such another fourth I never expect to spend. We had no meat and very little bread for two days. Had not taken off our accouterments during the time, and the rain poured incessantly, so that the water on the level plain was 2 or 3 inches deep. On the following evening we discovered that the enemy was satisfied and were moving off. We were in no condition to follow. We remained on the battlefield until two o'clock at night, during which time I snatched a nap or two by lying on three rails, which kept me above water. In the battle I threw away my haversack and contents, except a flannel shirt and a pair of socks, which I tucked under my belt. I lost the socks and have been for several days without any, but have not experienced the inconvenience I expected, except in having my ankles considerably lacerated by briers in marching across the fields. I have had no change of clothing since, and hence have been compelled to throw away my undershirt, which had become a harbor for *innumerable body lice*. Don't blush or become shocked; no true soldier is free from them, and I will scrub well before I come home. I am having my only underwear washed today, and owing to a large rent in my pants, would be subject to arrest in any well managed city, for improper exposure of my person in a public place. However, these are small matters, and we will smile over them in the better days to come. You must not try to send me anything, or trouble yourself in the least degree about me, unless you choose to send me some token by someone who will deliver it to the agent of the Fourth Texas Department at Richmond. I have left you to take care of yourself, and you must not be disturbed about me. God will take charge of both of us. I have experienced no inconvenience in health for want of clothing. Since I have been here Allen Killingsworth has given me a pair of socks, and while I write this sentence Charley Darby sends me another pair; so I have two pair, and feel flush on socks. I have a good pair of pants in Richmond, and another for winter in Columbia, so don't trouble yourself by thinking of me or my misfortunes, but smile, chat and keep well. Attend to your music, your Latin and the improvement of the children. Watch your chickens and turkeys as if you expected me home to eat them as soon as they are grown. I wrote to you and Stark on the 8th and 9th from Hagerstown, and this is the second letter since then.

I have no idea that you will ever get the others, but some hope that this will reach you. All the Waco boys are well and at their posts now, except Herrington, Clark and Majors. Herrington is in the hospital on account of his eyes, Majors is on the way to us now and Clark is at Sulphur Springs. Since Vicksburg has fallen I think you had better not attempt to go to South Carolina. You are safer in Texas. Our cause looks a little gloomy now, but I have no fears in the final result. I believe the war has been prolonged by the late success of the enemy, and perhaps it would be better if I were on your side of the Mississippi. I said in my letter yesterday that we would have another great battle in twenty days, but I hear now that it is the opinion of our generals that there will be no considerable engagement for several weeks, though nothing is certain.

I wrote to the Attorney General of the Confederacy yesterday that I had left my office in Texas and gone into the army, and saying that I would return to Texas if he thought it desirable or necessary, but I believe I am where I ought to be and I think he will sanction my course. Every able-bodied man ought to be where he can strike the hardest blow for his country.

I received a letter from Decca Stark of June 23rd. Lamar, Douglass and sister Mac are in Columbia. I doubt not we will have a reunion after a while. You and the friends whom I have named must still offer your prayers for me, and I shall fear no harm, for nothing but the special favor of God has preserved me thus far. Tell Stark and Mary to obey you and get their lessons, and when I come home I will take one on each knee and tell them about the soldiers. Remember me to the servants. May God and the good angels guard you and the little darlings. I had had but one letter from you.

Your husband, faithfully ever,
John C. West

Camp near Fredericksburg, Va, 7 August 1863

My Precious Wife,

We have just heard of the death of Colonel B. H. Carter. He was wounded at Gettysburg—twice in the leg, and one in the face, and left in the hands of the enemy. I wrote you not more than a week ago quite a long letter by Captain Hammon, telling you all about my Pennsylvania trip, a full narrative of which could be made quite readable, but I am not conveniently situated for thinking or writing, so as to render the undertaking feasible. I am having a pretty hard time of it, but heaven is blessing me continually with good health, and I believe will save me to the end.

You must not be uneasy about me when you do not hear from me. I have received but one letter from you since I left home, yet I am satisfied that all is well, and strange to say, I have no desire to return home while the war lasts. I believe this disposition has been especially vouchsafed me in order that I may be fully prepared for all the hardships that befall me. Since the fall of Vicksburg I have not had much hope of hearing from you, though, to our surprise, yesterday Coella and Macon Mullens received letters of the 5th and 6th of July. This has encouraged me to hope for one from you. I have written you a great many letters from different points. You must not be uneasy if you hear of me being destitute or in need of anything. A soldier cannot carry enough with him on a march to make him comfortable. Another hope and desire you must give up; it is almost impracticable and hopeless to attempt to recover the body of a private soldier killed in battle, so don't think about this; I can rest one place as well as another. All the Waco boys are writing today, as notice has been given that a Mr Parsons will take them to Texas. Do all you can to keep your mind employed and your face in smiles. All will yet be well for us. Pray for me, and if I am taken from you, it will be all right. I trust in God. Kisses for the children.[18]

Your husband, faithfully ever,
John C. West

Private John C. West
Fourth Texas Infantry, Company E
Incidents at Gettysburg—Recollections of a
Soldier Who Fought with Hood in this Battle

Judge John C. West of Waco, who served in Company E, Fourth Texas, is the author of this story, which he read by request at the closing session of Hood's Brigade yesterday:

This was my first experience in a general engagement, and though we had marched all night of 1 July, reaching the battlefield about ten o'clock a.m. on the 2nd, the interest and excitement and novelty of the occasion kept me up with my eyes and ears wide open. Our brigade was on the extreme right of the Confederate line, with perhaps one other brigade on our right. We marched and countermarched and rested until about three o'clock in the afternoon when we came into line in the edge of timber opposite Little Round Top and Devil's Den. I could see the Federal batteries, or rather, the location of them, by the smoke of discharge. They were about half a mile or more from us. This was the first actual contact and full view of our enemy. We stood in column of fours, with our faces towards our right, for some time, during which the batteries commenced to play on us, and the first shot—which I recognized—seemed to be a solid shot, which struck the ground about 50 or 60 feet from the line and passed by a bound over us, scattering dust and dirt over our company. The next shot passed about an equal distance beyond us, tearing up the earth. The third shot hit our line about 8 feet in front of me, knocking off one soldier's head and cutting another in two, bespattering us with blood.

Just then we fronted to the left, facing the battery. There was a short pause. I saw General Hood on horseback about 300 or 400 yards obliquely to my left just out of direct range of the battery fire, in the edge of the timber. He took his hat, held it above him in his right hand, rose to his full height in his stirrups, and shouted in a stentorian voice, 'Forward! Steady; forward!' We started across the open field. As we moved on I heard the word passing down the line, 'Quick, but not double quick!' We went in pretty fair order across the field. As we entered the timber and brush our line was more broken. We soon struck a stone fence; then came a branch. Lieutenant Joe Smith, Company E, wet his handkerchief, wrung it out and tied it around his head as he moved up the slope, which we had now reached. Bullets and grape shot were coming thick and fast. A bullet passed through his head; examination afterwards showed eleven holes through the folded handkerchief. I think it was a white mark for a sharpshooter. As we advanced up the steep side of the mountain we encountered boulders from the size of a hog's head to the size of a small house. Our line at times could hardly be called a line at all. The battery was taken. The 1st Texas suffered the brunt of the battle. After we were up on the first ridge the ground was so rough and broken that it was impossible to form a straight line, but it was quite evident to me from the sounds of our left that we were in advance of our center. From this position we made sallies to our front, over rocks and boulders and timber. It was impossible to make a united charge. The enemy were pretty thick and well concealed. It was more like Indian fighting than anything I experienced in the war. They had sharpshooters in trees and on high places that made it exceedingly dangerous to appear in any open place. One bullet passed through my beard and grazed my left ear. Another missed the top of my head about an inch. Both struck the rock against which I was sitting. I abandoned the position instantly. Just in front of us, perhaps 50 yards, was a comparatively open space on rising ground, very small in extent. It seemed almost certain death to attempt to pass it. Singly and in squads we made several experiments to test the presence of the enemy beyond, and every time, night or day, a shower of bullets greeted us. About ten o'clock on the night of the 2nd, Goldsticker of Company A ventured out. He was mortally wounded, and lay there many hours calling for help. I can hear his plaintive cry: 'Water! Water! Great God, bring me water!' but there was no truce. Death released him before the dawn. Poor Goldsticker! He was a gambler, a German and a Jew, but he died at the front!

We held our position among the rocks all night and until about five o'clock in the afternoon of the 3rd. Colonel Carter of the 4th was severely wounded, afterwards captured, and died in the Federal hospital. Major Winkler was also wounded. Private Champ Fitzhugh of my company was captured, and I saw him no more, until by a strange coincidence I met him in May, 1864, at twelve o'clock at night in the swamp of the Mississippi River, each of us attempting to cross the river. We crossed together in a canoe (with Yankee gunboats above and below us). This by way of parenthesis.

From three to five o'clock on the afternoon of the 3rd the battle raged in the center on the left of our brigade. We had received notice that the artillery on the whole line would open about two o'clock, and upon cessation of the artillery fire the entire line would move forward. This order was carried out, and when our artillery opened the enemy answered as promptly as if a telephone message had said, 'Shoot now.'

This cannonade was the greatest and most sublime circumstance I ever saw or heard. I can conceive of nothing grander, more portentous, or awful. An earthquake, a cyclone, a thunderstorm, a hurricane all in one could not be more terrific. It sounded veritably as if hell had broken loose and the unchained demons and furies were shrieking in the air. It was grand, sublime and glorious. The anticipation of the assault which was impending at the close of this fearful storm inspired the hearts of men with the joy of battle, which so filled us that there was no room for fear. While the earth quivered the storm ceased, and the forward movement began. Our end of the line, crooked and curved by the broken condition of the ground, made no progress. We were already in advance of the troops on our left. When the contest seemed hot on our left and towards the center we moved to the front, hoping to find a weak place or an opening for flank movement, but the enemy evidently recognized the importance of that position, and we could gain no advantage there; but the fight grew fast and furious on our left. We could see nothing, but the Confederate yell and the Yankee huzzah alternated back and forth with such regularity for near an hour to satisfy us that a critical moment was approaching at the point and that we were in danger of being flanked. Soon the 'huzzah' advanced so far as to create uneasiness in our part of the line, and directly notice came from our left to 'get out of here as quickly as you can.' We did not consider the order of our going, but rushed down the slope with better speed than we had been able to make coming in. As we obliqued to the right coming up the mountain, and now obliqued to the left coming out, we struck the open field several hundred yards to the right of the stone fence and branch which we had crossed, and looking to our right, saw the Yanks in full line in the open field. We went across the field under fire without regard to tactics. Bullets were pretty thick and hit about us with that peculiar searching 'zip-zip' which suggests rapid locomotion.

Mr H. Van Dusen of Company C, 4th Texas, was just in front of me about 10 feet. I heard a bullet hit him and saw him tumble over. I thought he was dead and I so reported when our regiment got together after dark. Some men said, 'No; he is over there by a tree.' I went to the place and found Van Dusen with head bound with a white cloth. The bullet had struck him in the head, but failed to penetrate. He went to the field hospital, was afterwards captured and got among Dutch kinsfolk in Pennsylvania. It was said that they offered him every inducement to abandon the Confederacy, which he declined, went to prison and afterwards exchanged. He survived the war and returned to Texas. The heroism of Confederate prisoners in Federal prisons would furnish a splendid subject for the pen of a competent historian. The fearful and untold sufferings of these brave men, their faithful resistance of the blandishments and rewards offered in exchange for their fidelity to the Confederate cause, when hope had fled and certain death seemed imminent, have never been half revealed, and places them side by side with the noblest martyrs of the ages.[19]

Fifth Texas Infantry Regiment

The 5th Texas Infantry Regiment was organized in Richmond, Virginia, on September 30, 1861.[1] During the winter of 1861–62, the regiment had been camped across the river from the 5th New York Infantry, 'Duryée's Zouaves', and each regiment taunted each other and boasted what they would do to one another if and when they met at battle.[2] At the Battle of Second Manassas (Bull Run) the regiments ran into each other and settled old scores. The Texans drove off the 10th New York Infantry Regiment, then emerged from the woods and faced the 5th New York which was on a higher ground. The 5th New York's first volley was high, while the Texans' shots were not. And yet, the Texans destroyed the New Yorkers and there were not fifty unwounded men left after the battle.[3] In his official report, General John Bell Hood stated that the 5th Texas had 'slipped the bridle' and earned the name 'The Bloody Fifth.'[4] The 5th Texas Infantry Regiment consisted of the following:

Company A—The Bayou City Guards (Harris County)
Company B—No company name (Colorado County)
Company C—The Leon Hunters (Leon County)
Company D—The Waverly Confederates (Waverly, Walker, and Montgomery Counties)
Company E—The Dixie Blues (Washington County)
Company F—The Company Invincibles (Washington, Jefferson, and Liberty Counties)
Company G—Milam County grays (Milam County)
Company H—Texas Polk Rifles (Washington County)
Company K—The Polk County Flying Artillery (Polk and Liberty Counties)

Flag of the 5th Texas Infantry Regiment flown at the Battle of Gettysburg. (*Texas State Archives*)

Colonel Robert M. Powell
Fifth Texas Infantry

Just Before the Battle

While the troops were enjoying this novel situation of being in an enemy's country, without seeing an armed foe, charged with the duty of protecting everything animate or inanimate in the line of its promenade, the General was filled with anxiety and perplexity. Stuart, commanding the eyes and ears of the army and who had been sent out to hear and see, had failed to report to his chief. The whereabouts and movements of the Federal army were unknown. On the 28th A. P. Hill was moving towards Gettysburg and Ewell ordered to stay his march on Harrisburg. On the 1st of July Hill's advance encountered the enemy at Gettysburg, and the two armies were about to confront each other. The guns of Hill called Gordon, who was soon thundering on his left, and the whole Confederate army quickened to participate in the impending struggle. Orators, writers and glowing

Colonel Robert M. Powell.
(*Texas Heritage Museum*)

canvass have described and illustrated this, the grandest of battles. This paper is only intended to describe and recite the unwritten incidents which only have interest as a part of the great conflict—the pathetic, comic and ludicrous, which play their little parts even when kingdoms are at stakes, and have no place on the stage when heroes are the actors and the world constitutes the audience. This is only a narration of what I saw and a part of which I was.

The March to the Field

Longstreet's command had just gone out on dress parade a little before sundown on the afternoon of the 1st of July, when orders were received to march immediately. Every man was in his marching and fighting attire and as quickly as the order could be given, 'right face, forward, march!' we were on the way to the general meeting of the armies. There was not so much hilarity as usual on this night's march; an occasional report of a bushwhacker's rifle, the rattling and jarring of artillery and the measured tramp of infantry were the only sounds presaging the purposes of tomorrow. At four o'clock a.m. we halted for rest and to close up the ranks. At daylight we were again in motion. We had reached the scene of the first day's conflict, and the melancholy evidences of its results were not calculated to evoke cheerful reflections or give assurance to those about to participate in the same kind of entertainment. To the right and to the left among the wounded and dead we recognized comrades with whom we had exchanged greetings two days before. By seven o'clock we had reached a point from which could be seen the field, already quick with events which were to give it historical interest and value when the actors were forgotten. Coming over the mountains, moving along the valleys, deploying on the plains with flying banners and glittering arms, music calling from every crest and hilltop, an echo to swell the chorus, was the grand pageant of gathering armies.

Up the Little Round Top

About four o'clock p.m. on the 2nd of July, the preparations were complete. The decision had been made to deliver battle. Staff officers were riding in hot haste to the commanders of divisions and brigades, bearing the compliments of the General and with courteous salute delivering orders to attack the enemy at the signal. Captain Gorce, of Longstreet's staff, after communicating orders to General Hood, rode down the line and remarked that the possession of Little Round Top—pointing to its rugged heights—was necessary. The Texans were expected to take it. 'We'll do it!' was the reply. The signal was given and a sheet of flame sprang among the enemy's lines, hurling defiance at the advancing Confederates. Smoke from either side rolled in billows, meeting and writhing in conflict in the valley midway the engaging armies. Soon the artillery duel ceased and rattling musketry announced that the serious work had begun.

Up the Rocky Slope

On rushed the Texans, sweeping from their path cavalry which met them on the Emmitsburg pike, on through the 'Devil's Den', blazing with infernal fire, crushing and destroying opposing forces at the foot of the mountain, onward and upward they struggled over precipitous rocks, where the enemy, lying in ambush, was surprised. The ascent was so difficult as to forbid the use of arms. At last, weary and almost exhausted, we reached the topmost defenses of the enemy. Now the conflict raged with wild ferocity. We were caught in a cul de sac or depressed basin, surrounded on three sides by projecting or shelving rocks surmounted by a stone fence. Captain Cleveland, with a voice heard above the din of battle, offered a purse to the first man over the works. Sergeant Ross sprang forward to earn the reward when Cleveland ordered him back to his post, remarking:

File closers not included.
Swing up the left, Major Rogers.
I'll do it Colonel, by jingo.

Just at the moment of these utterances there was a sudden cessation of firing, and the last words, 'by jingo', were distinct and sounded so ludicrous as to excite laughter.

A Devil's Carnival

The scene was strikingly like a devil's carnival. Another yell and desperate charge followed, succeeded by a sudden and an awful hush, just as if everyone had been stricken instantly with death. I raised my head from the ground, where I lay prostrated by a wound. The only moving man I saw was Sergeant Ross. He leisurely approached the enemy's lines and taking his ramrod, which had been left leaning against a rock, he walked deliberately to the rear. I could see men lying around in every direction and in all attitudes. This desolate silence continued at least thirty minutes; to me it seemed like thirty hours. The twilight was fading into night before the victors came to gather spoils and take charge of the wounded. To their regret the wounded were the only ones who had crossed the enemy's works.

In Union Clutches

The slightly wounded were the most earnest in their appeals to be left to die where they lay, insisted that it was wanton cruelty to subject dying men to the unnecessary torture of removal and so on. They hoped to be able to escape under cover of darkness and be ready to fight another day. When first taken over the lines I was temporarily placed near a Captain White, a Union officer, posted in our front. During the fight, he had held a flag near or on the works and one of the Texans seeing him, determined to have that flag. He got it, but the Captain held on to the staff, although he seemed to be stuck full of holes by a bayonet; his hands and arms were literally torn to pieces. I think he was the maddest man I ever saw and said he would have given a hundred lives rather than have lost that flag. The Captain and myself were informed by the surgeon that we were mortally wounded. We have met since and fought that battle o'er. The wounded prisoners were gathered together in the rear of the Federal lines and spread out on the ground in an open field. There we lay, forlorn, wretched, ragged and battered, shivering in the rain. We, however, were critically observant of all our surroundings. We had an agreeable visit from some cavalry officers. A colonel who said he was from Rochester, New York, and was known as

'Dare-Devil Dick,' gave us substantial and invigorating comfort which he carried in a flask. I have forgotten his name but not his kindness.[5]

Lieutenant-Colonel King Bryan
Fifth Texas Infantry

Colonel R. M. Powell having fallen into the hands of the enemy, it devolves upon me as Lieutenant-Colonel of the regiment to report the part taken by it as far as came under my observation in the action of July 2 and 3, near Gettysburg, Pennsylvania.

About four p.m. on the 2nd instant, General Hood's division was drawn up in the line of battle, fronting the heights occupied by the enemy. The 5th Texas Regiment occupied the right of the brigade, resting on General Law's left, whose brigade was the one of direction. At the word 'forward,' the regiment moved forward in good order. The enemy had a line of sharpshooters at the foot of the first height, behind a stone fence about three fourths of a mile from our starting point, which distance was passed over by our line at a double-quick and a run.

At our approach, the enemy retired to the top of the first height, protected by a ledge of rocks. A short halt was made at the stone fence, to enable those who had fallen behind to regain their places. When the command 'forward' again fell from the lips of our gallant Colonel, every man leaped the fence and advanced rapidly up the hill-side. The enemy again fled at our approach, sheltering himself behind his fortified position on the top of the second height, about 200 yards distant from the first.

From this position we failed to drive them. Our failure was owing to the rocky nature of the ground over which we had to pass, the huge rocks forming defiles through which not more than three or four men could pass abreast, thus breaking up our alignment and rendering its reformation impossible. Notwithstanding the difficulties to overcome, the men pressed on to the pass of the precipitous stronghold, forcing and securing the enemy's second position, many of our officers and men falling in passing the open space between the heights. Here we halted, there being small clusters of rocks far below the elevated position of the enemy, which gave us partial protection. From this position we were enabled to deliver our fire for the first time with accuracy.

Seeing that the men were in the best obtainable position, and deeming a further advance without reinforcements impracticable (a great many of the regiment having been already disabled) I looked for Colonel Powell, to know his next order. Failing to see him I concluded at once that he, like many of his gallant officers and men, had fallen a victim to the deadly missiles of the enemy, which were being showered like hail upon us. I moved toward the center, passing many officers and men who had fallen, having discharged their whole duty as true soldiers. I had not proceeded far when I discovered the prostate form of our noble colonel, who had fallen at his post, his face to the foe. I hastened toward him, when I received a wound in my left arm. On reaching the Colonel, I found that he was not dead; but seeing the rent in his coat where the ball had passed out, my fears were excited that his wound would prove mortal. The hemorrhage from my own wound forced me from the field, leaving the command upon Major Rogers.

The officers and men of my wing of the regiment continued to discharge their duties in a manner worthy of our cause so long as I remained upon the field, and from their conduct heretofore I would not hesitate to vouch for them during the remainder of the battle.[6]

Major J. C. Rogers
Fifth Texas Infantry

I have the honor to forward a continuation of the report of the part taken by the 5th Texas Regiment in the action of the 2nd and 3rd instant after the wounding of Colonels Powell and Bryan, when the command devolved upon me, the regiment still holding the position as left by Colonel Bryan, firing with accuracy and deadly effect.

The order to fall back came from some unknown source, and, finding that the regiments follow on our right and left had retired, it became necessary to follow. I therefore gave the order for the regiment to about face and retire to the rear, which they did in good order until they reached the position mentioned in Colonel Bryan's report as the second position of the enemy, and here they were halted and re-formed, in connection with the other regiments. From the exhausted condition of the men, it was deemed necessary to remain here for a few moments.

The regiments were again ordered forward, and obeyed in the most gallant manner, and regained their first position, which they held as long as it was tenable; and a further advance being impracticable, owing to the nature of the ground as expressed in Colonel Bryan's report, they again retired in good order to an open space about 50 yards in the rear, when here it was discovered for the first time that nearly two thirds of our officers and men had been killed and wounded.

Only a few moments were here consumed to allow the men to recover their breath, when, in obedience to orders, I again moved the regiment forward to attack the enemy in their impregnable position. The coolness and determination of the men and officers were equal to the occasion. They advanced boldly over the ground strewn with the bodies of their dead and dying comrades to the base of what they knew to be an impregnable fortification. We held this position until it was discovered that we had no supports either on the right or left and were about to be flanked, and therefore were again compelled to retire, which the regiment did in good order, to the point mentioned in Colonel Bryan's report as the second position of the enemy, which place we were ordered to hold at all hazards, which we did.

Just before day on the morning of the 3rd, orders reached me that breastworks must be thrown up, and the position held. The order was obeyed. During the day, constant skirmishing was kept up with the enemy, which resulted in the loss to us of many of our best scouts. Late in the evening, in obedience to orders, I about-faced my regiment, and marched three quarters of a mile to the crest of the ridge from which the charge of the day previous commenced. Here we threw up breastworks, behind which we remained during the night.

I would respectfully beg leave to call attention to the valuable assistance I received from Colonel John S. Cleveland in the management of the right wing of my regiment, and Captain T. T. Clay on the left; also the heroic conduct of T. W. Fitzgerald, of Company A, who was Color Bearer. He pressed gallantly forward, and was badly wounded far in front. J. A. Howard of Company B, Color Corporal, then took the flag, and remained firmly at his post. He was almost instantly killed. The colors were then taken by Sergeant W. S. Evans, of Company F, who flaunted them defiantly in the face of the foe during the remainder of the fight, always advancing promptly to the front when the order was given.

The general conduct of officers and men was beyond all praise.[7]

Captain J. D. Roberdeau
Fifth Texas Infantry
Personal Recollection of the Battle of Gettysburg

Austin, Tex.—March 25—Val C. Giles, Esq.

Dear Sir and Comrade:

Replying to your request for my personal recollection of the Battle of Gettysburg, I would say that *The Galveston News* has been selected as the medium through which to comply. This is for others of the brigade, to review and offer their contributions to the laudable enterprise you have engaged in [of] preserving the history of our old brigade during the four years of the war in which it was a conspicuous participant. In doing so, I shall confine myself strictly to that which was under my personal observation; nor indulge in hearsay or speculation; and think if others intending to write upon the subject would adopt that plan upon review and comparison by the historian, a better deduction of the battle could be presented. Camp scenes and incidents of the march are retired.

1 July 1863 found Hood's Division composed of General G. T. Anderson's and H. L. Benning's Georgia Brigades; E. M. Law's Alabama Brigade, and Hood's Texas Brigade, commanded by General J. B. Robertson and consisting of the 1st, 4th, and 5th Texas and 3rd Arkansas Regiments, the [whole] division numbering about 8,200 bivouacked at Chambersburg, Pa. It had arrived several days previous and had employed the time in resting and recuperating from the effects of the march leading there, and was protecting private property and cooking the usual three days' rations. During the day rumors of the enemy's advance were rife and late in the evening the command was ordered to fall in and move to the front. About sunset, the division was moved on the Cashtown Road for Gettysburg, marching all night and arriving in the sight of and near the town about sunrise of the 2nd day of July. Here the division remained until about one p.m., when it was put in motion and moved to the right of the town toward Little Round Top in view, meeting McLaw's Division, withdrawn from the extreme right of Longstreet's Corps, Hood's Division being substituted with Hood's Texas Brigade on the right. Halting, Law's Brigade, by virtue of seniority of rank of its commander, paused and took position to the right of the Texas Brigade and extreme right of the division and corps. Benning's and Anderson's Brigades forming on our left in the order named. The formation of the division occurred on a high ridge nearly equal in altitude to Little Round Top. Between the two points lay a wheat field and wooded valley, much of the latter being covered by rock. The 5th Texas Regiment occupied the right of the brigade, and my Company B the left center of the regiment. While occupying the edge and forming lines of battle, we were heavily shelled from Round Top, many casualties occurring, among the Captain J. C. Farmer and Sergeant Ham Settle of Company A, 5th Texas, severely wounded. While at a halt and before the order to prepare for action was given, Colonel Fairfax of General Longstreet's staff rode up to General Hood, who was sitting up on his horse immediately to the front of and near my company, and addressed him thus: 'General, it is the order of General Longstreet that you advance up on the enemy from your present position.' Replying, General Hood said he had just received information from General Law, and his own observation assured him, that by moving to the right one half mile he

could flank the enemy's position, and should be pleased if he would ask General Longstreet's permission to do so.

To this Colonel Fairfax replied that the order was imperative, and he would be pleased to report the order would be executed. General Hood replied that he could so report at the sacrifice of the best division of the army, the latter part of the sentence being prompted at the moment by reason of a partiality, the result of long association.

Immediately 'attention' was called and fences in front thrown down, battery station lumbered up and fire opened up on Round Top. This was about four p.m., when we moved on Little Round Top, [and] with what results is too well known. Since the war General Hood and I have compared notes upon the subject, and he substantially accords with the above statement. At our reunion in Houston, a few years since, I met General Law, who likewise concurred, and in addition said that after General Hood was wounded and he assumed command and the battle was on, the charge to the right could have been affected with the result indicated by General Hood; but there was the imperative order, nor could General Longstreet have been found to obtained permission. Much criticism has been indulged in with regard to the battle, especially directed against General Longstreet for his failure to move sooner. Of this I have no statement to make, since my limited military experience permits me only to say that a line officer who properly discharges his duty has little opportunity to acquaint himself with the errors and echelons occurring upon a distant portion of the field, much less what bay be transpiring at headquarters, and merely add that upon arrival at the base of Little Round Top, it was apparent to all that a move to the right would have flanked the position.

The position occupied by the 5th Texas is known in history as the 'Slaughter Pen'—crescent-shaped with a battery on the extreme left point supported by infantry—while all in front and to the right were similarly equipped, permitting the enemy to deliver a front and left and right flank fire. They availed themselves of the opportunity as evidenced by our losses. Since the war, I met with the Federal Captain commanding the battery to our front and left, who said his battery was silenced by every member of the company being killed or wounded. The 5th Texas Regiment numbered about 250 rifles, my own Company B, 29 in all, as follows: Commissioned Officers, 4; Non-commissioned Officers, 5; and Privates, 20—total, 29.

Casualties: Commissioned Officers killed, 1; Commissioned Officers wounded, 1; Commissioned Officers captured, 2; total, 3. Non-commissioned Officers killed, 3; Non-commissioned Officers wounded and captured, 1; total, 4. Privates killed, 6; Privates wounded and captured, 1; Privates wounded, 3; Privates captured, 4; total, 14. Total casualties, 21. Aggregate percent loss, 72 percent. The other companies of the regiment and of the other regiments doubtless suffered equally, from which may be gleaned or estimated the division's loss.

The division was in superb physical condition, buoyant and confident, and doubtless, under different conditions, would have accomplished all expected of it. That it was a forlorn hope was apparent when too late: someone blundered, but not that division, nor was it demoralized.

Since early September of that year, when a crisis in military affairs was present, especially in the West and at Chickamauga on the 26th of the same month, suffering from the sorry incident to and memory of Gettysburg, had the proud distinction of breaking the lines of the heretofore invincible enemy.

It may not be amiss to add that as commander of the troops sent west, General Longstreet was chosen to lead them, endearing the confidence of his government. And it remains an undisputed fact that whatever advantage was gained in the battle was due to his genius and the troops under his command. Endowed with good perception of sight and sound he usually directed his forces where the most fighting was going on and when he got there, his presence was recognized by those opposing. Notably at the Wilderness, on the 6th of May 1864, when at the supreme moment, the heart of this great chief beat[ing] quick with anxiety, he arrived with the 'old reliable' and changed the scene from defeat to victory. It was here he was maimed for life.

Trusting that others better qualified may aid you in your undertaking and that you will send down the lines the truths of history, I am, your friend and comrade,

J. D. Roberdeau

General Longstreet
Headquarters, Chickamauga, 21 Sept. 1863
General Braxton Bragg

General:

I respectfully recommend General J. B. Hood for promotion to the rank of Lieutenant General for distinguished conduct and ability in the battle of the 20th instant. General Hood handled his troops with coolness and ability that I have rarely known by any officer on any field, and had the misfortune, after winning the battle, to lose one of his limbs. I remain sir, very respectfully, your obedient servant.[8]

J. Longstreet
Lieutenant General

Fifth Sergeant R. A. Brantley
Fifth Texas Infantry
To General Samuel Cooper,
Adjutant and Inspector General

A Confederate

At Gettysburg on Round Top Mountain I stand,
View the majestic hill and flowery land
Just where I stood more than twenty years ago
When all earth convulsed and man lay his gore
Can it be? Mighty cannon shook this very rock
Where I stood, gun to check and hand on lock,
Daring the defying Federals to strike,
To take heart's blood and such like.
There stood a small tree, now a majestic oak,
Its branches many I see still shattered and broke;
Old Rocks, changed from want to lay,
Huge cannon balls moved them away
Just over there Federals line stood
Firm to a man, popping all they could—
Cutting away almost every living creature
Leaving bare rocks and withered nature.
Here my heart throbbed with emotion grand,
Before defying Federal and all his might band;
While musket and cannon ball did play
Around my head with a whizzing mighty sway,
Whiz! Whee! Bullets by we would pass,
Scaling rocks and cutting hero and grass;
So you wicked, whizzing wretch, I could cry—
For my country, I stand, I live or die,
How I stood here I no cannot tell,
For six noble comrades by my side fell;
But left me like a statue all alone
This terrible story to write and own.
Fifth Sergeant R. A. Brantley
Fifth Texas Infantry[9]

Capt. R. A. Brantley Dead[10]
Another of Hood's Men Has Bivouacked on Fame's Eternal Camping Ground

General H. B. Stoddard has received a telegram yesterday afternoon informing him of the death of Captain R. A. Brantley which occurred yesterday morning at his home in Somerville. The news of his death will bring profound sorrow to the hearts of many old and true friends in Bryan and Brazos County.

Captain Brantley was about seventy years of age and was for many years a resident of Bryan. All the older citizens here well remember 'Bob' Brantley, the whole-souled, big-hearted friend, citizen and neighbor.

Captain Brantley in the early days lived in Millican and when the war came on enlisted in the army from that place and was assigned to duty in Hood's famous Texas Brigade. No braver soldier ever fought in defense of the South than 'Bob' Brantley, and as Color Bearer was exposed to the very greatest danger on many a hard fought field. At Gettysburg, he raised the flag of his regiment after three men had fallen under it in quick succession and though his clothing was riddled with bullets, he escaped uninjured. This flag has been in the possession of Hood's Brigade Association, and at their annual reunions it was always Captain Brantley's proud privilege to carry it in the parade when he was able to be present.

Now he, too, has answered the last roll call and gone on to join his old comrades. God rest him in peace. [11]

Orderly Sergeant B. C. Simpson
Fifth Texas Infantry

We have had the pleasure of meeting with Mr Simpson of the Bayou City Guards, Orderly Sergeant of that old company in 1863. He was captured at the Battle of Gettysburg, and taken by the Yankees to Fort Delaware. He was confined at that fort till October 1863, when, being sent on a burying detail, he managed to slip off and lose himself. He made his way at once to New York, where his relatives and friends resided. To their entreaties and persuasions to stay with them and desert his adopted country, he replied that his country was the Confederacy, and there his duty would take him. He worked his way thence to Canada, and engaged there for a time in his business as engineer, waiting for a chance to come South.

Last summer Captain Sterritt arrived in Canada to buy a steamer, and Sergeant Simpson at once sought him out, and engaged to ship with him for Texas as an engineer on his vessel. In this way he reached our coast on the *Acadia*.

Sergeant Simpson was one of the best soldiers of the old Bayou City Guards, and like all of that company, stands true to the colors of his country. He has come back like a true man, to do his duty in the war, and he will do it wherever he is placed.[12]

Second Corporal John W. Stevens
Fifth Texas Infantry

It was about the 26th of June that we left Chambersburg and marched toward Gettysburg. (Longstreet's Corps) we stopped at Fayetteville, only 5 or 6 miles from Chambersburg about 10.00 a.m. Now we could have gone on to Gettysburg that day, but General Lee was misled by Stewart's failure to report Meade's movements. It was Lee's purpose in due time to take position on the Gettysburg height, and thus force Meade to attack him, but to General Lee's astonishment, when we started to the heights, he found Mead already there. I expect this is about the only instance in which Lee was ever misled during his command of the army. I have heard General Lee severely censured by men that know nothing about the facts, or had never read carefully General Lee's report to his government, for not having moved quick enough and letting Meade outgeneral him in getting position at Gettysburg.

Private John Stevens.
(*Texas Heritage Museum*)

Now the facts are General Lee sent Stewart to find Meade and keep him (Lee) posted as to Meade's movements, and failing to hear from Stewart for some days, he naturally concluded Stewart had nothing to report, while the facts are, General Stewart was down in Maryland at a place called Rockville with a portable telegraphy battery, which he always carried with him, playing pranks on the Washington government by sending in orders for 200 extra new wagons and teams, with four mules to each wagon, and signed Meade's or some other Federal general's name to it, or perhaps the name of Meade's chief quarter-master. This prank was so cleverly done as to completely mislead General Meigs, who rushed the wagons and teams off. Of course Stewart 'took them in out of the wet,' to use an army phrase, and turned them over to our chief quarter-master. Most of the drivers were Negroes, and you may judge we took them in, too. Now, when Stewart reported to Lee, it was too late. General Stewart could beat the world at such pranks as this on the Yankees, but they were seldom of any real benefit to our army, especially when done at the expense of more important work. The result of this prank was to give Meade the advantage of us in position. But I am getting ahead of my story. I must go back a little.

When the army halted at Fayetteville, this writer and six other men were detailed to guard the house of an old man—a typical Pennsylvania Dutchman—who lived about half a mile north of town, the object for this guard for private property was to prevent any depredation on property, as was set out in general order No. 89, read to us at Green Castle. Now this guarding private houses is one of the nicest things that falls to the lot of a soldier in war times. The family guarded always fed the guard, so you see we enjoyed the prospect of rations for the time very different from our soldier bill of fare. Lieutenant J. M. Alexander of my company was Brigade Officer of the day house, pointing to it, 'I feel good all over in spots as large as a soldier's blanket.' As soon as we got our orders, away we marched to the house indicated. The approach to the house was by a line, parallel with the front porch. The family in sight consisted of the old man, his wife and three grown daughters, all showing the regular Pennsylvania Dutch character. Good people, as green as green could be. As we approached one house they were all standing on the porch looking at the army as it was going to camp half a mile away. They had not even heard we were coming: in fact, they had only a vague idea of the rebel army. They had doubtless conceived the idea that we were a set of cut-throats. They had not noticed us—the guard—until we were at the gate in front of the house. As soon as the family saw us the three girls ran into the house, the old man was so overcome with fear that his legs refused to support his ponderous body and the old lady began to wring her hands and cry. I approached him with all the dignity of my position as Commander-in-Chief of the squad, and seeing his inexpressible fear so manifest by his and his family's actions, I spoke to him so softly and kindly as possible, assuring him that he need have no fire of mistreatment: that we were there to protect him and his premises from any depredations by any of our men who might try to injure any of his property. At first he thought I was tantalizing him, but he soon became assured that we were all right and that he had nothing to fear, and in a few moments we had put two men on guard and the balance of us were sitting in the house in pleasant conversation with him and his family, who were now looking upon us as their friends and protectors, instead of enemies to be dreaded. I then, in the most affable and delicate manner possible, informed him that the party whose property was guarded had to feed the guard. They tumbled to the racket in a moment, and in the shortest possible time seven hungry rebels were seated to one of the finest old Pennsylvania Dutch dinners you ever saw, and the three young ladies were skipping around waiting upon us, and by the time we were done eating nearly every one of the boys were making love to the girls, which, in a very dignified way (in pleasantry, of course) was duly reciprocated.

We did all we could to make them feel easy and they fully appreciated it. At milking time, in the evening, the boys assisted the girls at the cow-pen and helped them to do up the chores about the place, and I don't think I am over-stating the facts when I say the girls got badly stuck on some of the boys, who promised to return and see them just as soon as the 'cruel war was over.' Now, I do not wish to be understood, in giving this minute detail as in any way reflecting on the character of those girls—they had seen but little of this world—possibly never 10 miles from home, and it was natural, after they recovered from their fright, for their regard for the boys to go to the other extreme. We remained there about two days, as I know remember.

On the first day of July, late in the evening, we were again in motion toward Gettysburg. All night long we march until about an hour or two before daylight, we stop and snatch a few hours' sleep and eat our breakfast. We are now in the vicinity of the battlefield. Hood's division is held in suspense nearly all day as a sort of reserve, moved from place to place. Finally, about 4.00 p.m., or a little before, as we are moving, southeast along Emmetsburg Road, and while the enemy's artillery is plowing through our ranks, we are halted on this road and formed in line of battle. I very well remember that as we were forming Generals Longstreet, Hood and Picket were all sitting on their horses just in front of us. Riley's battery had just unlimbered and was firing very rapidly upon the enemy. These Generals were directing the fire of Riley's guns all of which lead our men to the conclusion that we are very near to the enemy's infantry line, though we knew where their artillery was, for we could located that by belching smoke of their guns on Little Round Top Mountain. Just as we were ordered forward a fragment of a shell (from the guns that were playing on Riley) struck Hood and broke his arm. This occurred just as we passed him going into battle. Of course we were deprived of the benefits of his commanding presence. General Law was too far away to the right, and we were now moving into battle virtually without a leader and wholly ignorant of where the enemy was; had Hood not been wounded it would have been very different. We moved into battle at a very lively step and in a short time we were in full charge. There was a stone fence 500 or 600 yards in our front, behind which we expected to find the enemy. Onto it we rushed—no Yankees there. Then 400 or 500 yards further there is a rail fence, just in the edge of the timber. We expect to find the enemy there. Onto it we move on a charge, but no Yankee there. Over the fence we go, and through this timber, 200 or 300 yards, and we come to the foot of the mountain. All through this timber the ground is covered with large boulders, from the size of a wash pot to that of a wagon bed, so to preserve anything like line of battle is impossible, but we do the best we can. We are without a leader and ignorant of where the enemy is, but we push forward, now almost out of breath, and the weather is as hot as a furnace.

As we start up the mountain we get a plunging volley from the enemy, who are posted behind the rocks on the crest. They are not more than 25 or 30 steps away and well protected behind the rocks, while we are exposed to their fire. Their first volley is most destructive to our line. Every line officer of my regiment is shot down except one man—the major. Now, for the first time in the history of the war, our men begin to waver. We are suffering terribly. Finally they begin to go back. Their idea is to fall back, reform and come back again. Just at this juncture Captain Hubert calls out for Company K to stand fast. Only eleven men stand their ground—three officers and eight men—but there we stand and fight for life. The balls are whizzing so thick around us that it looks like a man can hold out a hat and catch it full. There were two twin brothers belonging to Company C, of my regiment, that got separated from their own company. They came up to where I was standing and commenced firing. In a moment one of them is shot down by my side. The other brother caught hold of him as he fell and gently laid him down on the ground, and as he did so he also received a death shot. This was a very affecting scene—those two boys were twin brothers, so much alike that you could hardly tell them apart. They were always together—where you saw one you saw the other. They had passed safely through all the previous battles unhurt—now they die together. Another young man by the name of Fitzgerald (I had known him from his cradle) walked up to where I was standing. He also was shot dead, and, as I now remember, about six men who had become separated from their own commands walked up to where I was standing and began firing and the entire six were left dead at my feet. As I now remember the only fear I felt was that our other men whom we expected to reform, and come back again, might begin firing too soon and shoot us in the back. Somehow I never thought of being hit by the enemy in front, yet they were not over 25 or 30 paces from us and the balls were flying as thick as hail (apparently). This thing continued until we had fired some 10 or 12 rounds—the roar of artillery and the din of small arms was so deafening that we could not hear each other in an ordinary tone of command. It had never occurred to me that there was any danger of being captured, or that we would not whip the fight, as soon as the retreating line reformed and come again, just then a slap on my back with a sword, and an order to throw down my gun and behave myself, came like a sudden clap of thunder. As I looked around the woods behind me were full of Yankees. My own fragment of our company were already disarmed and had a guard around them. Realizing the fact that I was a prisoner, I took out an old knife and cut my cartridge box off. We are moved rapidly through the Yankee lines to the rear, and to our astonishment they have but one line of battle.

The close of my last chapter details to you the battle and the capture of myself and a part of my company. As we are marching up the mountain through the line of battle—that a moment before we have been fighting so hard—we learn to our great chagrin that the enemy had only one line of battle in front of us, and 50 yards behind that line there was a line of cavalry deployed every 50 yards to keep the infantry from breaking when we charged them, and 500 yards behind this line was their whole supply train of some 4,000 wagons, closely parked. Then we realized what we had lost. Had General Hood not been wounded and had we been properly led into this battle, we would have gone through this line like a deer in a walk, and right into their wagon train, as we had so often before—but, 'of all the sad words, of tongue or pen, the saddest are these: It might have been.'

I think this is the proper place for me to refer to a matter that history does not make plain, and yet it is referred to by some writers in a manner that may lead some to conclude that General Lee possibly made a mistake in his plan of Battle at Gettysburg. In the account given by the general history of this battle, you remember that General Lee says in his report to the government that he was misled as to General Meade's movements, by reason of the fact that he had not heard from General Stewart, the cavalry commander, who was supposed to be between Lee and Meade, and should have kept Lee posted in regard to the movements of Meade. As I now remember, Lee says in his report that he had not heard from Stewart for about three days—at least that is the fact—and failing to hear from him, Lee naturally concluded that Steward had nothing to report, hence a stop of one day at Chambersburg and two days or more at Fayetteville, when Lee could just as well have gone on to Gettysburg from Chambersburg and occupied the heights of Gettysburg, which was his original plan of battle, but Stewart's failure to report misled Lee and thus enabled Meade to get there and occupy the heights in advance of Lee. All this time Steward is in between Meade and Washington, about Rockville, in Maryland, with a portable telegraph battery attached to the wires leading into Washington, and playing pranks on the Yankee government, which, while very successful, really was of no benefit to our cause. Now, General Stewart was a great man, a great General, and we must conclude that he thought he was acting for the best, but his blunder here, coupled with Longstreet's tardiness in attacking earlier on July 2nd, as he was directed to do by Lee, in my judgment led to our defeat at Gettysburg.

As stated in the former chapter, we left Fayetteville on the evening of July 1st, moving in the direction of Gettysburg, some 20 or 25 miles east. We marched nearly all night, reaching the vicinity of Gettysburg some time in the latter part of the night, where we halted for a few hours' rest and refreshments. That Longstreet was ordered to attack in the early part of the day is an established fact, and that he failed to attack until four o'clock in the evening is a fact well known to all of us who were in his corps. All this time Meade is moving up his army at double quick and occupying the heights that Lee intended to occupy. Notwithstanding Stewart's blunder, had Longstreet attacked earlier in the day, as Lee ordered, we could have carried the position and thus been master of the situation. We can only speculate as to what might have been the final results had we defeated Meade at Gettysburg. I can only fall back on my unfailing faith in an all wise God, who, in his love for the American people, ordered things for our best interest and his glory.

Now to return to the first paragraph of this chapter, we were huddled together that night I suppose about 1 mile in the rear of the Federal battle line and a strong guard placed around us. Soon we are closely questioned by Federal officers for the purpose of gaining all the information possible, as to our different regiments, brigades, etc., all of which is carefully noted. The men have all a ration of meat and bread issued to them about dark. This writer was too sick to want anything to eat. Next morning, July 3rd, we (about 500) were started to West Minister Station, about 20 miles away, under a guard of the 5th New York Cavalry. Our commander on this march was a captain. I wish I could remember his name, but I have forgotten it; but I well remember that he was a 'soldier,' a gentleman, and was as kind to us as he could be. He conducted the march on army regulation style, (i.e. march fifty minutes and rest ten). While we were resting the captain talked to us freely and pleasantly and seemed to sympathize with us in our hard luck. I remember very distinctly many of his remarks. On one occasion after we had rested, as we got up to form our marching order he pleasantly remarked to us: 'Gentlemen, if you had on the proper uniform and had been organized into a regiment and I had commanded you, I should feel that I was in command of a body of men that I could depend upon anywhere.' On another occasion while we were resting, a supply train drove up just as we stopped, in charge of a commissary sergeant. The Sergeant threw himself from his horse and stretched himself out on the ground and began to try to guy us, saying such things as 'What are you men doing here? You can't fight worth a d—n.' and such talk as would naturally accompany such remarks. Our men began to hurl 'cuss' words at him, and offered then and there to test the question as to whether they could and would fight or not, whereupon he hurdled back some very salty 'cuss' words at the boys. This attracted the attention of the Captain … whereupon he walked up to where the colloquy was going on and as soon as he caught on to the trend of the commissary's remarks, he administered to him the severest possible rebuke. Said he, in the most withering tone, 'You shut up and let these men alone; they are prisoners of war, unarmed and under guard, and you shan't insult or tantalize them; and if you don't think they can or will fight, d—n you, get a gun and go front yonder and you'll find all the fighting you want to do, and doubtless a little more.' Then came our time; we yelled and guyed him to our hearts content, much to the amusement of the Captain.

We are now 10 or 12 miles away from the battlefield. The roar of artillery in the celebrated charge of Pickett's division is just now opening up. About 150 to 175 pieces of artillery on each side are belching forth their streams of death and destruction just as fast as they can be worked. The roar is so loud that the fire of one gun cannot be distinguished—just a continuous roar. We halt to take our ten minutes' rest, and though we are 10 or 15 miles away, the jar of the earth is very sensibly felt. Directly a courier dashes up to the commander and says a few words to him and then moves on at a gallop. The captain calls back to us: 'Men, move on as fast as you can. They are having h—l back yonder, and if your folks break our lines we will have to hustle you very fast to keep you from being recaptured.' If I ever prayed earnestly in my life it was that day that his fears might be realized. In forming us into line for this march we were formed in two ranks. The tallest men were put first at the head of the column. This arrangement put this writer as No. 1 and my file mate was Lieutenant-Colonel B. F. Luce, of the 18th Mississippi Regiment, we being the two tallest men in the squad. I then measured 6 feet and 2 inches, weighed 222 pounds, was thirty-one years old, and I don't think there was a man in that squad of 500 men who was physically my superior, and my muscles were as hard as hard service could make them.

About the middle of the evening we reached our point of destination, which was their base of supplies. When we arrived there I suppose there was at least 1,000 wagons loaded and teams hitched, drivers mounted and all standing still. We learned that they were expecting Lee to break Meade's lines, in which event the retreat movement would begin. We watched to see if they would start to move, but at dark they were still standing there. As night closed down we were placed in some box cars, where we remained until about daylight, when an engine was hitched on and we were run into Baltimore, arriving there about 8.00 or 9.00 a.m., on the fourth day of July, 1863.[13]

Private John T. Allison
Fifth Texas Infantry

From Suffolk we went to Petersburg, then to Richmond, then on north to the Potomac and crossed over into Pennsylvania, where we rested for a few days. Then we crossed the mountains to Gettysburg. There had been a fight at Gettysburg the day before we got there. My brigade was on the right of Lee's army. We soon formed and rushed into the thick of the fight. Here we lost several of our men, and several of the boys were taken prisoners. I have heard it said that there were 400 pieces of artillery in this fight. The battlefield was something awful to look upon. And the roar of the artillery was indeed something dreadful. The cannon we heard 125 miles from the battle grounds.[14]

Private James Taylor Booth
Fifth Texas Infantry

Letter from James Taylor Booth to his mother Elizabeth White Booth (oldest daughter of James Taylor White I). J. T. Booth was in Company F.

Richmond, Virginia
22 July 1863
Mrs E. Cotton

Dear Mother,

As I have an opportunity of sending a letter to you that I am pretty certain you will receive as it comes by hand, I take pleasure in sitting down to the table to write it. I am now staying at the Texas Hospital, where I expect to remain a month yet before I will be able to join my regiment. I receive[d] a wound through the fleshy part of my thigh on the second of this month at the Battle of Gettysburg in Pennsylvania but it is nothing serious. I am able with the use of one crutch to walk about very well but it keeps me out of service a month or six weeks longer yet. The Texas Hospital is got up purposely for the Texans in Virginia. It is kept very nice and clean and we have excellent doctors and nurses and it almost seems like home to us Texans when we get sick or wounded. We lost more than two thirds of our regiment in the battle and, what was worse still, very near all of our wounded fell into the hands of the Yankees. There was one killed and twelve wounded in my company and there was only myself and another, a little Frenchman, but what fell into the hands of the enemy. Our army had a splendid time over in Yankeedom. We just took whatever we needed from the people in the way of staples. But we did not treat them half as bad as they deserve to be treated or we would have burnt their houses over their heads. That is the way they treat the people here in Virginia and I think we ought to treat them equally as bad. Gettysburg was one of the hardest fought battles of the war. We gained decidedly the advantage there although it was a drown fight. General Lee has re-crossed the Potomac and is in Virginia again. I am very sorry that Vicksburg has fallen but we must expect reverses sometime.

Well, Mother, I have to close this abruptly as the man who is going to take it is ready to start. Give my love to Josephine, Lou, Mary, Cora Ade, and my respect to Mr Cotton and Alph.

Write often, dear Mother, to your affectionate son.

J. T. Booth[15]

Private Arthur H. Edey
Fifth Texas Infantry

Editor, *Telegraph*: It will gratify the many friends in Texas of Arthur H. Edey of Company A (Bayou City Guards), 5th Texas, Hood's old brigade, severely wounded in the thigh in the sanguinary Battle of Gettysburg, Pa, to learn that his wound is rapidly healing, and that he will soon be ready for exchange. The writer has recently seen a letter from Mr E., dated from an island in Long Island Sound, some 15 miles east of New York, the place of his imprisonment, in which he speaks of many interesting incidents. Mr E., as is well known to many, was, a short time before the war, a citizen, and I believe, a native of New York, where his mother and other relatives reside. Since his imprisonment the most feeling and ardent appeals have been made to him to abandon his allegiance to the cause he has espoused.

He has had to resist an aged and much loved mother's tears, and his sense of the most sacredly tender obligations have been invoked, but in vain. This, the friends of Mr E., had a right to expect. His adhesion to our cause had its foundation in principle, and that he had fortified by a solemn oath. Had the last been the only tie, Mr E.'s standard of religious piety would have precluded him from ever forgetting or disregarding its obligation.

The son of a writer, a comrade of Mr E., writing from the camp near Fredericksburg, Aug. 25th, says in his letter, 'Our friend Mr Edey is a prisoner in Yankeedom, shot through the thigh. The boys say he acted like a true soldier at Gettysburg. When shot down, the boys fell back. Edey took off his hat, waved it, calling on them to "Come on, come on, boys, come on!"' It affords the writer great pleasure to note the gallantry and patriotism of this gentleman, who, at one time some persons were disposed to look upon greater affection for the land of his nativity, than his adoption.[16]

Privates Arthur H. Edey and Ed Collier
Fifth Texas Infantry

Two gallant members of the Texas Brigade in Virginia parted on the field at Gettysburg: the one wounded was captured, and held in Federal prisons till near the close of the war; the other escaped that day, to be severely wounded afterwards, and a cripple for life. They met by accident for the first time since Gettysburg in our office, on Saturday. The one was Arthur H. Edey, now doing a thriving commission business in Galveston. The other was Ed Collier Esq., now a lawyer in Columbus. Both, we were glad to learn, are now doing well.[17]

Private W. A. Fletcher
Fifth Texas Infantry
Battle of Gettysburg, Pennsylvania

In the course of time we were thrown into line of battle near Gettysburg, and as our brigade ranks were well depleted, we did not make a very long battle line. We were said to be near our right; and in front, less than a mile off, the country looked well elevated and from barren spots I took it to be rocky. While laying in position one of Company A privates, and I think of Galveston, stepped to the front and started to offer prayer, something that I had never heard of in our part of the line under like conditions. He was ordered back into line and just then a bursting shell wounded three of his company this happened only a few feet to my right, before going

Private William Fletcher.
(*Texas Transportation Archives*)

into battle. In times of battle there are generally what are called color companies. I suppose they are called so by their position in regimental line with colors and special color guard also. I was, on this occasion, color guard with small detail with A and F color companies. The sergeant ordered me to colors. I protested, saying I was not the man he had often heard me express myself. He said: 'Go ahead.' We were soon forward and near on the opposite side of the valley. We routed pickets and sealed rock fences, and worked our way to the front rapidly, with pickets giving away before us, firing but little.

We soon struck the foot of the hill, and found it rough and rocky, with large boulders now and then, so our lines were not at all times well closed. We soon were near enough the enemy's line for them to open fire. We had but poor chance to retaliate with much effect. Our men near me commenced falling rapidly, and especially color bearers if I remember correctly; I saw the colors fall five times, the last time in the hands of the sergeant who had ordered me to act as color guard. In falling, the flag staff struck my head in the front of my face. As it went down my forward motion cause my feet to become somewhat tangled. I gave a kick and said a curse word, and passed on. This happened near the end of our journey, and I know not who picked up the colors, but I have often thought: 'Did the sergeant see all the color guards cut down; and, thinking I was going to carry out my oft repeated declaration, pick it up in my stead?'

We stopped advancing, without orders as far as I was concerned, as I heard none. Another man and I were well to the front behind rock; the enemy was only a short distance up and so near over us that with good aim we could have near been shot in the top of the head, either standing or kneeling. At this point a field officer a-foot passed just to our rear and stopped a moment and looked up and said: 'Boys, aim well.' I said: 'Cousins, move on; you are drawing the fire our way.' He started with a determined look; and I thought and think yet, that was the bravest act I ever saw—a man inspecting a shattered battle line, with the enemy holding a position at such great odds leaning over their protection to shoot to hit our position. We did not attempt to scale the hill, for it would have been a good job on some parts for one used to mountain climbing stripped for the business. This hill may be erroneously drawn, but it was well photographed on my memory as I have stated.

We did not hold this position long before the order was passed on the line to 'Fall back.' I had no fear of the enemy charging and capturing the retreating forces, for they had ample dead and wounded to satisfy them, if all parts of our line were as baldy butchered as at the point I went in and out. I learned some time afterwards that the peak was called 'Round Top' or 'Heights'. Have never learned whether it was named before or after the battle. When we were in a scattered condition and had gotten out of danger and rather under the brow of the first elevation which we struck as we were going in, we were halted and lined and ordered in again. We advanced this time, knowing what was ahead of us if we went far, for the acts of men soon showed we all were of one mind. We forwarded without a murmur, until we struck the danger point. The men about-faced near as if ordered and marched back. The command, 'Halt!' was not heeded. Just as we wheeled I heard some fellow squeal for dear life. I looked and saw it was a lieutenant hopping, with a big toe shot off, and with his good-sized and stout lungs he made more racket than I ever heard from one wounded man.

We were stopped before we went far, and were about-faced and ordered 'Forward!' We made a few steps to the front and again without orders about-faced and marched back to protection under the brow of a hill and were halted. There was quite a lot of censure for the last two forward movements by the men. We were held in position until dark and went forward on rising ground and put up a line of rock protection. When day dawned, we could see or hear little of our helpless wounded, the great mass of them being well to the front and out of sight. We were not bothered by firing from the line as we were out of sight, but the enemy had few sharpshooters who were posted on the hillside that had favorable points of opening through timber, and when one would get a few yards to the front, before these openings, they would hurriedly get back. There was some attention to dislodge the sharpshooters but [this] failed. We lay in this position all night and most of the next day.

To our left during the day there was a charge made by what was said to be Pickett's Division. There was sure noise enough, from the roar of guns and bursting of shells, to have moved the Yanks when the Rebs charged, if they had been moveable; but they were like those in front of Hood—had a good thing and knew it, so the right of Lee's army had battled hard and met defeat at each attempt to turn the enemy's left. After all of this happening, as a participant the first day and partly in sight of the butchery the second day, it was, as far as I was concerned, discouraging; and it looked as though our officers were blind, in so far as that part of the front was concerned. It looked to me that a flank move would have dislodged the enemy, or at least, battled near equal positions. While lying in the position, one felt reasonably safe, provided he kept behind rock piles so the sound of battle was plain enough to satisfy that there was but very little changing of position; and as we were the advancing army the reading of the different parts of the line added nothing to relieve one's mind who had been through the experience the evening before and knowing just to our front lay the unfortunate Reb who was wounded and suffering.

So, taking conditions as they were, I was at the time on the dark side of life's thoughts or, in other words, hope in a depressed condition. While behind the rock protection in the evening of the second day, word was passed along the line to get ready to charge the front. The order shocked me, and my feelings were indescribable; in fact, I had a bad case of cowardly horror. I felt sure if I retraced my steps of the evening before, it would be the ending of me. I could see no object in the move, only to sacrifice the extreme left to save the army on retreat, as I felt we had gotten a good whipping all along the line and I was considering which was preferable—disgrace or death—for I felt as one feels when fright and disgrace at one and the same time has possession. I tried to force manhood to the front, but fright would drive it back with a shudder. I was in this state of torture for at least fifteen minutes. I was lying behind a rock protection and dropped asleep with fear and disgrace to be my portion. I had slept but a few minutes when our batteries behind opened fire on the enemy's supposed line, to confuse, and then we would be ordered to charge. The guns were not elevated enough and were doing fine work on our position. The bursting and flying pieces of shell and rock put us in a panic condition—we could not drop to the front and protect ourselves, for we would be exposed to the enemy. Our field officers just to our rear were dismounted and had great trouble to mount.

They soon got a few mounted by giving help, and ran to the rear and stopped the firing. All were confusion, but we soon got back into line and orders countermanding the charge were passed down the line. When I awoke my fears had gone and when I heard the countermanding order I had a feeling of regret, thinking what a great relief we could be to our wounded by dropping our water canteen by their sides as we went forward; and possibly through some unforeseen condition we might be able to remove them to the rear. I think my feeling about the necessity of aid was felt as much as those who needed it, and I have often thought: 'What is mind, and what causes its changes?' For, in this instance when the order was received for the forward move, I at once was a transformed being; feeling all the pangs of horror that one could have flash over him, feeling as I once had great pride, knowing that I had done my duty under any and all conditions to the best of my ability, and now all was lost, if I did not go into the charge and be shot down to avoid disgrace; for I knew I had been as far to the front the day before as any one I could see to my right or left, and I well knew that the enemy had the night previous to arrange or strengthen their position if such was needed; but this was not needed, for nature had long ages since done the work, and knowing the great disadvantage that was to our front caused the thought: 'Where is our boasted Lee? Why is this ignorance?' As for Longstreet, he was excusable, as far as I was concerned; for I always thought he was on the wrong side for we had no men to spare in a bull dog fight, for even with victory we were the losers. He was kind and courageous and by nature was a fighter, but not a tactician, and when he was assigned near an impregnable position that was made so by nature, with an insufficiency of men and a short time limit, what more could have been expected? In my opinion, if he was in the battle line as ordered, with instructions to force the front, there was none better capacitated to have made a success, if such was possible, with the means at hand.

I have heard since the war some censure cast at General Longstreet for Lee's defeat at Gettysburg, but heard nothing of the kind from the battling soldier who was a participant in the great struggle. Records of his orders could be the only proof that would satisfy my mind that he was at fault— so I have always thought how cruel to idolize without fault, and sweep errors aside and heap them on others. I will always censure some officer, but not knowing who cannot specify to my satisfaction the individual blame. Why were we fighting an impregnable position—was it ignorance? I guess so. It was a very unfortunate condition for the right of an army with true and tried men being shot down like dogs.

We moved to the rear some distance, just as dark was near, and the enemy did not follow closely. On our way to the rear, and a few hundred yards in front of where our men were halted and remained for the night and part of the next day, I was left at a rock pile and from what I could see the next morning, I was the extreme right outpost of infantry. My position was on the brow of an open elevation and narrow open valley in front, with woods on the opposite side, when I was left and told that I would be relieved in due time—which time did not arrive, however, until the next day, when I was called in. When our line marched out I asked no questions, but supposed I was either forgotten or the place could not have easily been found; or would have put the relief, crawling in, subject to fire from foe or friend. The rock pile gave me protection, either lying down or sitting in a stooping position. I was not on the outpost long before the enemy, or at least dark objects were seen in front. I knew there was no stock at large, and if a Reb was there, he was out of place, so I challenged none and got in several shots during the night and my aim or the report of my gun had the effect of at least moving the object. To my left some 200 yards I would now and then hear gun reports, so I felt safe on the left, as in the twilight the enemy would hardly attempt crawling through. But to my right it was different, for I heard no shooting and during the night at two different times I let the man crawl well up on the elevation, about 75 yards to the right, before I notified him of his mistake.

So I passed what seemed to be an unusually long night all alone, with eyes to the front, rear and flank. Fortunately, I was well supplied with tobacco and one who has never used it does not fully appreciate its comforting effects under similar conditions. When daylight came I could see my surroundings and the troops to the rear. I could easily be seen from our front, but saw no effort being made to relieve me. I had not unrolled blankets from my shoulder to keep off the cold morning air; therefore, being more confined as day approached caused a somewhat chilly satisfaction, but I dare not expose for exercise, for the Yanks on the opposite side of the valley in the woods did too close practice at the rock pile for comfort, whether they saw my head or not.

As the day wore on, I got very sleepy and with all the force I could bring to bear it was almost impossible to keep awake. I had heard of the use of tobacco amber or spit in similar cases, so I have ... several times used it liberally on my eyes, and it sure will keep one awake so long as the pain is greater than the desire to sleep; but I guess after a few applications, if one could see himself in a mirror, there would be a dirty pair of red eyes showing; so, with burning eyes and a great desire to sleep, my lot was a hard one. As I have stated, I was in sight of our line, and one of my mess companions, a Beaumont boy by the name of Taylor, got permission to relieve me, which he did by crawling part of the way. A few shots near him as he crawled in did not deter him. When he reached me he said: 'Bill, go to sleep, I have come to relieve you, and will call if the Yanks start to advance.' I guess the sound of his voice had no more than ceased before I was sleeping. I slept nearly two hours, he said, when he woke me and said they had called for us to come in, so we started in a stooping zig-zag run with a few bullets to enliven our efforts.

When we reached the command it was in readiness to move, but before we did, there appeared to our rear quite a force of the enemy's cavalry. They were lined up about one fourth of a mile away and had the appearance of forming for a charge. There were, a short distance to our rear, some residence buildings and they were soon burning to clear the rear which would have been front, if the charge had been made. The sight of a long line of mounted enemy and the roaring and hissing of the fire and a threatened front, made the position one of awe. Our cavalry soon put in their appearance and had a brush with the enemy's cavalry and they dropped out of sight.

While on the outpost during the night I could hear the rumbling of the enemy's artillery and wagon train going to our right. When we moved out and were marching to the rear, I was still sleepy, and at the first halt I was down on one side in the mud and getting the much needed sleep. I was told that I had caught up twenty minutes of lost sleep. When a person is in this condition, they are not very choice of pallets. I have seen men fall and not wake. I have curled up in the corner of a rail fence and slept more than once, to keep out of mud and water. I have often heard the remark 'dead asleep,' and in such an instance it is near a fact. When night came we were allowed to unsaddle, as it were, by stripping off our accoutrements and spreading blankets, if we had one. We continued this weary march for some days and stopped a short time near the Potomac River.[18]

Private William Henry Matthews
Fifth Texas Infantry

At the Battle of Gettysburg on 3 July 1863, our Texas Brigade charged the heights of Little Round Top and as we were advancing up the side of the mountain, it was very steep and rocky from our starting point, and the distance so great and the heat so excessive, that when we reached the enemy's line we were all exhausted, and could go no further.

We advanced to within 50 yards of their line and fell behind large rocks. I fell behind a rock about 18 inches high and fired one shot and began to reload lying down, and while holding up my gun for powder to fall to the bottom was shot in the arm, but I am thankful to say, that it was not broken. Our Captain, R. W. Hubert, with seventeen others was made prisoner at this place. Small things will decide the result of a battle. Private as I was, I could see it in this one. Our brigade, as I have been told, was ordered to fall back, but had we been supported at the right time we would have captured or disposed of their line of battle, and would have gained the day at Gettysburg.

After being captured, I was, with a large number of others, sent to Ft Delaware where my brother was killed, and where we remained for twenty-three months. This guard that killed my brother at Ft Delaware prison was what we called a galvanized Yank. He first enlisted in our army and later joined the Federals. This man's name was Smith, from Flint Hill, Mo. I feel that I can never forgive him. As to our treatment in prison they gave us only three ordinary crackers per day, with a small piece of beef or bacon about the size of an egg.[19]

Private W. A. Nabours
Fifth Texas Infantry

Active Service of a Texas Command

We marched across the Blue Ridge Mountains into the Shenandoah Valley and to the Potomac crossing into Maryland early in the morning. We marched entirely across the state in one day and camped in Pennsylvania that night. General Hood had his tent erected near a fine farmhouse. Some of our soldiers caught some chickens, and the lady complained to General Hood, who replied, 'You would not complain if you could see how your soldiers have done in over in Virginia. You cannot find a fowl or a hog in traveling 50 miles where your soldiers have been.' As our soldiers were marching along the near this camp an old lady hailed one and asked him where he got his knapsack. The soldier told her that he took it from a dead Yankee at Chancellorsville. On the side of the knapsack was the name of its former owner, regiment and company in large letters. The old lady replied: 'That was my son.' The soldier stopped at once, took his own things out, and gave it to the lady, who seemed to appreciate it very much.

Our return from Gettysburg was by moderate marches and without any special trouble from the enemy. We re-crossed the Potomac into Virginia and finally arrived near Fredericksburg, where we enjoyed a much needed rest.[20]

Houston, 5 March 1865

Mr Cushing: I had the pleasure of seeing a beautiful 'battle flag' intended for the 'Terry Rangers', and can well say that it is deserved and merited by that brave and gallant regiment. While admiring this banner, which is yet to float upon future bloody fields, the thought occurred to me, cannot the noble ladies of Houston, in like manner, attest their appreciation of the services rendered by the 'Bloody Fifth' of Hood's Texas Brigade. Over three years ago, the 'soldier's friend', Mrs Jane Young, sent us a most beautiful banner. That banner we carried at Gaines's Mill, Gettysburg, and many other bloody fields, and a few months since we returned it by Captain Farmer, of the Bayou City Guards, to Mrs Young, feeling that the bloodstained and bullet-rent flag of the 5th Texas would be appreciated by her.

Should the patriotic ladies of Houston deem us worthy of their confidence, let them send on a battle flag by Captain Farmer on his return to Virginia. The present battle flag of the regiment is one issued by the government, and, though it will ever be defended by our life's blood, yet the same importance and appreciation is not attached to it as one coming from the fair ladies of our own state.

Remember those who for nearly four years have been battling for Texas on the sacred soil of the 'Old Dominion.'[21]

'ONE OF THE FIFTH'

Private J. P. O'Rear
Fifth Texas Infantry

In the spring of 1863, General Lee reorganized his army and we went to Culpepper Court House, where we had a general review and inspection and then to Gettysburg, crossing the Potomac River at Williamsport. As there was no bridge or ferry we had to wade the river, which was about 300 yards wide. We reached Gettysburg on the first of July and lines were formed and the battle began about 1.00 p.m., continuing till about 4.00 p.m. Here was some of the hardest fighting which I saw or was in during the war. I visited one of the hospitals where the sick and wounded were being taken care of. It was a horrible sight. Men were wounded in every conceivable way and the intensity of their suffering was heartrending.

We marched from here to Hagerstown where we formed a line of battle, but the enemy would not attack us and we crossed the Potomac River at Falling Water. We retreated back to Virginia and established picket lines along the Rappahannock River till in September, when Longstreet's Corps (our Corps) was ordered to Georgia to support General Bragg.[22]

Private John Roberts
Fifth Texas Infantry

The Texas Brigade fought in the Battle of Gettysburg. At the Battle of Gettysburg John Roberts was severely wounded in both legs and taken prisoner. He crawled behind a large rock to protect himself from being shot again. Six Union soldiers found Roberts lying behind the rock and asked him if he had any tobacco. He gave them all he had; they took it all and left, thinking Roberts would die, but he did not.

He lay on the field a day and a night without any medical attention. The Yankees then moved him to Little Round Top Mountain. They were being fired at by General Pickett's troops. The wounded received no medical attention while the battle was raging. After the battle, however, the Federals established a field hospital. Surgeons operated on the wounded, frequently amputating legs, arms, and fingers.

While John was still in the hospital, a woman stopped by his cot and began talking to him. She asked whether or not he were ashamed to be fighting against the Stars and Stripes and many other questions such as that. John, hardly nineteen years of age, replied saying, 'I certainly am not ashamed. If I was, I would not be in the Confederate army, because when a soldier deserts his country, he loses his honor and is an outcast from virtue, peace, and fame.'

The men spent four months as prisoners at the Federal hospital, after which they were moved to Baltimore and were placed in a large brick building. John thought of this place as a hell-hole of tyranny and starvation. The temperature dropped to zero, and many of the men lacked sufficient clothing and blankets.[23]

Private John Marquis 'Mark' Smither
Fifth Texas Infantry
Camp 5th Texas Volunteers

Culpepper C. House
29 July 1863

Dear Mother,

Not having any idea that this letter will reach you but thinking there would be no harm in trying and that probably it might go through, I write. I remember rightly the last letter I wrote to you while we were at Chambersburg, Pa, giving you a detail on our adventure so far as that place. I will try and continue my little sketch of travel from there. The great and sanguinary contest at Gettysburg, Pa, down to our arrival at this place on the 24th inst.

Well! We left Chambersburg on the 30th of June and took up our line of march on the Baltimore Pike; we arrived at the little town Fayetteville on the evening of the same day. We staid over there until the next evening

when we made a forced march all night across the mountains and came up
the town of Gettysburg about nine o'clock the next morning. On arriving,
we learned that the advance of our army composed of one division each
from Hill, and Ewell's Corps had met the enemy 5 miles from the town
the day before, and after a severe struggle of several hours had succeeded
in driving them clear back through the town, capturing 6,000 prisoners;
night put an end to the conflict. The next morning it was discovered that
the enemy had taken position on an extensive range of mountains about 1½
miles from Gettysburg. Our troops by this time having all come up, General
Lee, knowing the enemy would not be routed unless they were driven from
this place, gave the order for the heights to be stormed. It was about three
one-half o'clock before our troops could be put in position. Longstreet's
Corps took position on the extreme right, Ewell on the left and A. P. Hill
in the center. Our division had to take the place of McLaws having refused
to advance on the place with his division. In front of our division lines and
opposing us was a very high and steep mountain about 2 miles high on
which the enemy had entrenched themselves very strongly. Their works were
built on a ledge of rock about 25 feet high and all the spaces in the ledge
were filled up with stone. General Hood, on being ordered to take the place,
protested, saying he could take the place very easily by flanking around the
mountain. But no, Bullheaded Longstreet ordered him to go straight forward
and forward we went. We advanced through a field about half a mile before
we reached the timber at the foot of the mountain. Our men tumbling out of
ranks at every step, knocked over by the enemy's sharpshooters who lined
the side of the mountain. On arriving within 250 yards of the timber their
batteries opened on us, with grape and canister mowing down the grass all
around our feet, but the distance being most[ly] too great they did us but
little damage. After getting within the timber we encountered the skirmishers
and sharpshooters posted behind a stone wall, but we soon had them flying
up the side of the mountain. It was here that Jas. A. McDade of Company
'D' was killed. He was a noble boy. After a time we succeeded in working
our way up the steep side of the mountain and arrived within sight of the
formidable works our Enemies had prepared for us. Nothing daunted at
the sight our boys pushed on through the brush and over the rocks until
they had arrived within 25 steps of the works. On finding that the plan
of scaling the heights was impossible for we could hardly have gone over
them if there had been no Yankees there, our side immediately took shelter,
Indian fashion, behind rocks and trees and commenced popping away at the
Yankees whenever they showed their heads. The Yankees, seeing that we had
stopped, commenced firing as fast as they could, pouring volley after volley
down on us with frightful effect. It was at this critical juncture that Colonel
Powell was mortally wounded. He was waving his sword and cheering on

the men when Lieutenant Harper was shot down at his side and the Colonel caught him as he was staggering and helped him down and he had hardly got straight himself before he was struck in the left side the bullet passing out at his backbone. He was falling when I ran to him and caught him in my arms and laid him down behind a rock. This was all in plain view of the Yankees and they were raining the bullets around us. Lieutenant-Colonel Bryan came up the line about this time; when I called his attention to Colonel Powell he came up to where we were and reached his hand out to examine him, when he was struck receiving a severe flesh wound in the arm. The command then devolved to Major J. C. Rogers. After a desperate battle of two or three hours … perceiving ourselves flanked on the right, for Law's Brigade on the right of our Regiment had fallen back, [we] received orders to fall back, which we did in good order, retreating about 200 yards were we waited and formed our line. General Law coming up at this time, General Hood being wounded gave orders to advance on the place. Now it was expected that our men, having tried it and seeing the impossibility of taking the place, would have refused to have gone in again. But no, they tried it a second and a third time and formed to go in a fourth time when night came on [and] forced us to abandon the fight. We laid on our arms all night and before daylight rose up and made a breastwork of rock. The Yanks also worked all night on their walls. We had no general engagement on our part of the line the next day, nor the next, but on that night we marched back beyond the town of Gettysburg.

The Yanks [had] withdrawn their pickets with the intention of cutting off our retreat, it was supposed. We marched very leisurely down to Hagerstown, Maryland. When finding the Potomac too high to cross we easily reformed our line and stayed about a week and then crossed the river over into Virginia. The loss in our regiment was about 215 out of 342. The 4th lost about 105, the 1st about 85 or 90, Company 'D' went into the fight with 50 and lost 32. She was ahead as usual. It is a given up fact that it is the best fighting, the best looking, and [has] more gentlemen in it than any other company in the Regiment. Captain Hill was severely wounded in the foot, Campbell Wood also. We are looking every day for Jim Hunter in camp. He is in Richmond. I saw Cousin Charlie about a week ago. He belongs to the 19th Miss. in Hill's Corps. Gabe belongs to the 11th Miss. in the same corps. The 11th had about 40 men in it. Both of them are well. Give my love to all and write every opportunity.[24]

Your Affectionate Son
Mark

P. S. Do you remember this day! Today, two years ago you gave me your blessing and told me to go and serve my country!

Unknown Private in Company H
Fifth Texas Infantry

Pickett's and Hood's Charges at Gettysburg

The following is an account of the charge of Hood's Division over the same ground, the day before Pickett led his division up the fatal heights. It is given by a participant who (perhaps justly) complains that not sufficient account has been taken of Hood's equally brave effort to capture the breastworks on Cemetery Hill:

I belonged to Company 'H', 5th Texas, Hood's old Texas Brigade, attached to Longstreet's Corps.

On Monday night, July 2nd, we moved from our camp which was on the same creek, and marched to Stone Bridge, 6 miles in rear of the battlefield. At daylight, we moved to our position in line in front of Sugar Loaf Mountain. My division was on the right of Longstreet's Corps, and my regiment was on the right of Hood's Division. Near me before the charge, Generals Longstreet, Hood, and Robertson were sitting on their horses; I heard Hood say to Longstreet three times: 'Let me take my division to the right and flank that mountain.' Longstreet replied, 'You must obey orders.' Hood, knowing the destruction which would follow, was moved even to tears. Our position at that time was a little in the rear of the crest of a hill upon which stood our batteries. When the order to charge was given the whole line moved forward, passing by the guns and descending the hill on the other side. We struck the enemy just in a meadow situated in the valley, and drove them across the Emmettsburg Road, along which was a stone fence. They attempted to rally behind this barrier, but we never stopped, and, with a rush, pressed them onward till we came to a stake-and-rider fence at the foot of Sugar Loaf Mountain, beyond which was heavy timber and rocks. Right there a funny thing occurred. Captain Cleveland said: 'Ten dollars to the first man who gets over that fence.' Privates Stones and Settler were the first to get over. Afterward, they claimed the ten dollars, but I don't know whether they got it or not.

Over the fence once we crept on up the mountain, climbing with great difficulty, occasionally pulling each other up on account of the rocks. The enemy retreated to the top of the mountain and took position behind their breastworks. Three times we charge up the mountain side to within 40 yards of the breastworks, but were each time compelled to retire by the heavy volleys from the fortified enemy. During these charges among fallen trees and giant rocks there was necessarily much confusion. Besides the musketry fire from the front there was an enfilading fire from Federal batteries, which swept the face of the mountain, doing much damage. After the third charge we fell back about 400 yards, about half way between the fence and the works, and there we stayed, though still somewhat exposed to the artillery fire of the foe. I wish to state that during the charges a portion of the 4th Alabama, Law's Brigade, somehow or other overlapped our line, and getting to the right of my regiment, swung around the enemy's works and flanking the foe, got up on top of the hill in the Federal wagon camp.

I was badly wounded in the arm the first charge, and left on the field within 40 yards of the breastworks. As our men retired, the enemy's skirmish line followed them and passed me. The thought of a prison nerved me to try to rejoin my comrades. With great difficulty I descended the mountain, passed through the Federal skirmish line, and met my command as they were returning to the second charge.

Our loss was very heavy, especially in officers of the line. I did not get off the mountainside till after my regiment had made the third charge. During the night I made my way back to the hospital situated just in the rear of our first position. My wounds were not attended to till the next day, and I was lying under an apple tree when Pickett's Division passed me in their famous charge. What happened after this I don't know, except that I saw Pickett's broken columns retiring sometime during the day. Pickett passed near me and was crying. I do not remember anything he said. I have told this to show that Hood's Division did some hard fighting at Gettysburg, and as far as I have been informed they have not received the honorable mention they deserve.[25]

Gettysburg Flag of Hood's Brigade is Given to Veterans Two-Day Meet at Bryan Ends; to Place Table on 'Last Stronghold' of Famous Fighting Unit

The fifty-fourth annual reunion of Hood's Texas Brigade closed at noon Saturday, after a two days' session in Bryan, its permanent meeting place. The election of officers for the coming year resulted as follows: Captain J. C. Roberts, Arcadia, Texas, President; J. J. Hall, Corsicana, Vice President; Miss Katie Dafan, Ennis, Life Secretary, re-elected; Dr S O. Young, Houston, Historian; J. O. Bradfield, Austin, Chaplain.

The address of the morning was made by Hon. F. L. Henderson of Bryan, his subject being 'the Confederate Soldier's Place in American History.'

To Place Tablet

J. O. Bradfield of Austin, chaplain of the brigade, made the motion, and it was unanimously carried that Hood's Brigade purchase, and have engraved, a table of stone to be placed in the walls of the Bryan public library, and to bear the following inscription: 'Bryan—The Last Home of Hood's Texas Brigade, and This Building Its Last Stronghold.'

This memorial and historical table will be laced at the next meeting of the brigade in Bryan 26 and 27 June 1926.

A touching part of the program of the morning was the presentation to Hood's Brigade from Mr Chew of Houston, through Dr S. O. Young, the brigade historian, of the original battle flag of the 5th Texas Regiment, which was made the official flag of the regiment at Gettysburg. The flag was made by Mrs M. J. Young, mother of Dr S. O. Young of Houston, and presented to the 5th Texas Regiment in 1862. The sacred, blood-stained, bullet-riddled flag was securely encased in a cedar chest, presented by Mrs Norton B. Wellborn of Somerville, in honor of her father, 'Robert A. Brantley Sr, who bore the flag into its baptism of fire at Gaines Mill.'[26]

Official Flag of Hood's Fifth Texas Brigade on Display at Office of Commissioner Smith

Lon A. Smith, railroad commissioner, has on display in his office at the capital the flag of the 5th Texas Regiment of Infantry, Hood's Brigade, Army of Northern Virginia. This flag, Commissioner Smith stated, is a contribution from the survivors of this famous brigade. The flag, worn and battle-scarred, reposes in a new cedar chest bearing this inscription: 'This case is given in memory of Robert A. Brantley, Sr, who bore this flag into the baptism of fire at Gaines Mill.'

First at Gaines Mill

Commissioner Smith gives this brief history of the flag: This flag was made by Mrs M. J. Young of Houston, May 1862, and sent to the 5th Texas by Bob Campbell, one of the first volunteers, Company A, 5th Texas. The flag saw the first service at Gaines Mill, June 1862. George Onderdonk, Company A, was the first flag-bearer. At the beginning of the famous charge of Hood's Brigade at Gaines Mill, Onderdonk was wounded and Bob Brantley seized the flag without permitting it to touch the ground and bore it gallantly throughout the charge. The flag was born in twenty-seven pitched battles; sometimes in defeat, sometimes in victory, from Gaines Mill to Appomattox.

Official Brigade Flag

At Gettysburg, Hood designated this as the official flag of his brigade. It withstood fire of shot and shell at Little Round Top. Fourteen men were killed while upholding it, and forty-seven were shot down beneath its folds.

It saw service for the last time at Derbytown, 7 October 1864, witnessing the closing chapter of Grant's 'on to Richmond campaign.'

This flag was presented to Hood's Texas Brigade at their annual meeting here last June by Dr S. O. Young of Houston, historian of the brigade. Dr Young's mother was maker of the flag. Since that time it has been in Bryan in custody of the Chamber of Commerce, and on Thursday was sent to Austin in charge of M. L. Parker, who left it with Lon A. Smith to be placed in the Texas Confederate Museum, Mrs Forest H. Farley, regent.[27]

4

Third Arkansas Infantry Regiment

The 3rd Arkansas Infantry Regiment was organized in the spring of 1861 by regimental Captain (and later Colonel of the regiment) Van H. Manning's and Lieutenant-Colonel William H. Tebbs's companies. In January 1862, the regiment was the sole representative from the state of Arkansas that was part of the Army of Northern Virginia. It was well known for its fierce fighting spirit and tenacity in battle. In November 1862, the 3rd Arkansas Infantry joined Hood's Texas Brigade, where it remained until the end of the Civil War. The regiment consisted of ten companies.[1] These were:

Company A—The Arkansas Travelers (Ashley County)
Company B—The Berlin Guards (Ashley County)
Company C—The Confederate Stars (Drew County)
Company D—The Selma Rifles (Drew County)
Company E—The Champagnolle Guards (Union County)
Company F—The Hot Springs Hornets (Hot Springs County)
Company G—The Three Creeks Rifles (Union County)
Company H—The Orphan Company (a mixed Arkansas/Kentucky company)
Company I—The Tulip Rifles (Dallas County)
Company K—The Ashley Volunteers (Ashley County)
Company L—The Rust Guards (Latonia, Ashley County later consolidate with Company A)[2]

Flag flown by the 3rd Arkansas Infantry Regiment flown at the Battle of Gettysburg. (*Old State House Museum, Little Rock, Arkansas*)

Colonel Van H. Manning
Third Arkansas Infantry

About four o'clock on the evening of 2 July, I was ordered to move against the enemy, keeping my right well connected with the left of the 1st Texas Regiment, and hold my left on the Emmitsburg Road, then some 200 yards in my front and out of view.

Upon reaching this road, I discovered, from the direction the directing regiment was taking, that I could not with the length of my line carry out the latter order; hence I decided to keep my line on a prolongation of the line formed by the troops on my right. After marching in line of battle at a brisk gait (part of the way at double-quick) for about 100 yards, all the time exposed to a destructive fire from artillery, we engaged the enemy at short range, strongly posted behind a rock fence at the edge of

Colonel Van H. Manning. (*Texas Heritage Museum*)

the woods. We drove him back with but a little loss, for a distance of 150 yards, when I ascertained that I was suffering from a fire to my left and rear. Thereupon, I ordered a change of front and rear on the first company, but the noise consequent upon the heavy firing then going on swallowed up my command, and I contented myself with the irregular drawing back of the left wing, giving it an excellent fire … [This] pressed the enemy back in a very short while, whereupon the whole line advanced, the enemy fighting stubbornly, but retiring.

Soon I was again admonished that my left was seriously threatened, when I ordered the command back 50 to 70 five yards, to meet this contingency. He was again driven back, and I stretched out my front to twice its legitimate length, guarding well my left, and advanced to the ledge of rocks from which we had previously been dislodged by the enemy's movement on my flank. I experienced some annoyance from the exposure of this flank up to this moment, when the 11th Georgia Regiment joined to my left. The 59th Georgia Regiment, coming also at this time, occupied the line with my command. Some little time later after this I was disabled by concussion and wound on my nose and forehead. The command then devolved on Lieutenant-Colonel Taylor, who will report his operations subsequent to this time.

It would be invidious to make special mention of gallantry in either officers or men when all did so well, fighting greatly superior numbers and at great disadvantage. I might safely assume that the bearing of the entire command was of the highest creditable character.

No guns or colors were captured and but few (some twenty-five) prisoners, a number of whom were sent to the rear with wounded men.

No report by Colonel Taylor is to be found.[3]

Captain A. C. Jones
Third Arkansas Infantry
Longstreet at Gettysburg

I was most pleased with the very able article on the number of the *Veteran* by Mr O. G. Thompson of Laurens, SC, in defense of our old commander, General Longstreet. It is my intention to supplement this article by a brief relation of the events as they occurred under my own eye and observation on the second day at Gettysburg, when Longstreet's Corps attacked the enemy's left at Little Round Top.

In the June number of the *Veteran* W. H. Thompson fully demonstrated his abilities as a brilliant writer, and I wish to think him for his magnificent summing up of the achievements of the Army of Northern Virginia; but in his efforts to make a case against General Longstreet his facts are sadly at fault. After briefly describing the first day's fight, Mr Thompson says:

> Lee acted with great energy. Ewell was ordered to attack Culp's Hill and the north end of Cemetery Ridge at dawn of 2 July. Longstreet, whose veterans were fresh and eager for the fight, was ordered to crush Meade's left flank, which, of course, carried with it the duty either to seize or to carry Round Top in the alternative of finding it unoccupied or in the possession of the Federals.

Now, it is well known that the battle fought on the evening of the 1st was an accidental fight. Two divisions of A. P. Hill's Corps, marching toward Gettysburg, came suddenly in contact with two divisions under General Reynolds, marching in an opposite direction and a battle was precipitated, lasting till late in the night. In this fight our side won a complete victory, capturing over four thousand prisoners, killing General Reynolds, and driving the remnant of his command through the town. The question is, where were the two armies when this battle was fought? The answer is marching on the various roads converging upon Gettysburg.

Hancock's Corps, on the enemy's side, arrived first early in the night and occupied the heights of Gettysburg. Longstreet's Corps was 25 miles off; Hood's Division had marched from Chambersburg on the morning of the 1st, arriving late in the afternoon in a little place called Cashtown. Here we were halted and went into camp, presumably for the night, and rations of flour were issued. The hungry men immediately set work to cook bread. They had scarcely prepared the raw dough when suddenly the long roll beat, and orderlies came in, rushing through them with the familiar cry: 'Fall in! Fall in!'

In less than fifteen minutes we were on the march. We marched all night long, our progress being much obstructed by wagon trains and artillery. The head of our column arrived at a point 3 miles from the town at a little after sunrise on the morning of the 2nd. Here we [heard] the first account of the battle of the evening before from some wounded soldiers bathing their wounds in a little stream that ran across the road. Here we were halted and the men allowed to prepare food and take a few hours' rest. Mr Thompson says that Lee ordered Ewell to attack Culp's Hill on the enemy's right and Longstreet on the enemy's left, positions at least 3 miles apart, at dawn. How could this possibly be? General Lee himself was not present at the battle of the evening before; he could not have arrived till a late hour of the night. How could he have known anything of the locality and the position and strength of the enemy so as to issue orders to attack at dawn, at which time Longstreet's men were still on the march at least 6 miles from the position he was ordered either to 'seize' or 'carry?' Longstreet's critic says that his men were 'fresh and eager for the fight.' It is very true that these men were tried and seasoned soldiers with powers of endurance equal to any, yet they were not made of iron, and there is a limit to all human endeavor. Consider the fact that they made a continuous march of over 40 miles without food for twenty-four hours, not to speak of the loss of sleep.

General Hood, under Longstreet's orders, commenced his movement on the enemy's left about noon. The march was slow, as an effort was made by following the hollows to conceal his movement from the enemy; but that was impossible, for as we advanced in that direction the two elevations called Little and Big Round Top, which were the objective points of the march, were the most conspicuous objects in the landscape. And here I assert that at no time during the day could troops have been moved in that direction without being discovered by the enemy in ample time to occupy the point of danger, as the enemy's lookouts on Round Top commanded a view of the entire surrounding country.

Now we approach the crucial point of the whole controversy in which Mr Thompson is fatally in error. He contends that Hood's assault was not upon Round Top, but upon Sickle's Corps at some other point; while Round Top, the strategic point, the key to the whole situation, the possession of which at any time would have compelled Meade's whole army to retreat, remained entirely unoccupied, and Longstreet had only to take position without firing a gun; that both Generals Lee and Hood entered their protest against such folly. If this were true, General Longstreet would have proved himself to be a military imbecile or else a traitor.

Mr Thompson evidently confuses Little Round Top with Big Round Top. The one was not a mountain, but only a hill at the foot of Big Round Top, which was quite a mountain, too lofty and its slopes too precipitous to be available for military purposes except as a look out. Both Generals Hood and Law well understood that the attack was to be on Little Round Top, at the time occupied in full force by the enemy under General Warren. They regarded the position [as] too strong to be taken by a front attack, and they asked permission to move to the right, pass around Big Round Top, and take position in flank. General Longstreet did not consider this movement practicable and so ordered the front attack. General Warren is quoted to prove that Little Round Top was unoccupied.

Some years ago I read General Warren's report of the Battle of Gettysburg. I distinctly remember that he said when he arrived at the summit of Little Round Top, about three o'clock, the position was not occupied, but that, discovering the movement of Longstreet's forces, he immediately took steps to move a large force upon it. Upon the very boulder on the summit of Little Round Top from which Warren took observation of Longstreet's movements there stands today the statue erected in his honor ... If there was no fighting on Little Round Top, why is his statue there?

Resuming the narrative of Hood's advance, the head of his column, the Texas Brigade leading, reached a point about half a mile from Little Round Top about four o'clock. The 3rd Arkansas Regiment (to which I belonged), being in front, formed the basis of the alignment, the order being 'on the left by file into line.' As it took at least half an hour to complete the line of battle, I had ample time to view the surroundings. To our right and about 150 yards in front there was a small grove of trees, perhaps 2 acres in extent, but from our positions there was an unobstructed view of Little Round Top. As I looked the whole face of the hill appeared to be swarming with men; in fact, most of our attack, several batteries of artillery taking their places on the summit. Ten minutes later these batteries opened upon us in point-blank range. The effect of this fire was terrific. In the twenty minutes we had to withstand this ordeal we must have lost a great many men. Within twenty steps of where I stood a shell exploded in the midst of the line, killing four men and wounding two others.

It was while in this condition that quite a dramatic scene occurred. General Longstreet rode up and, passing through the line, took position about 50 yards in front. A few minutes afterwards General Hood came down from the right and a short colloquy ensued. It was too far for us to hear what passed, but the single staff officer present afterwards reported the exact language. General Hood called Longstreet's attention to the strength of the enemy's position and asked permission to move his command to the right and take the enemy in the flank, as his scouts had reported the plan feasible. Longstreet's reply was somewhat curt: 'Hood, go where you are ordered. General Lee directs me to attack here.'

As he turned off General Hood said: 'Very well, General, but I'll get all my people killed.' He then rode a little nearer to the line and standing in his stirrups and lifting his hat, gave the command, 'Forward!' As the line swept forward Longstreet reigned in his horse and let it pass, but Hood continued to lead the advance until, a few minutes later, he was shot from his horse.

I feel myself wholly inadequate to a description of the struggle that followed. After passing the grove mentioned, the ground slopes gently for about a quarter of a mile to the foot of the hill. In passing over this ground our loss was fearful. We encountered the first line of infantry, posted behind a stone fence, near the foot of the hill. We drove this line and fought our way step by step up the slope. Halfway up a good position was secured behind a ledge of rocks, when we had a brief breathing spell and were slightly reinforced, then we again charged, driving the last line and capturing two pieces of artillery on the summit. But the end was not yet. Just as we had taken possession with our thin and shattered line there came a storm of bullets from an advancing line of the enemy, which, luckily, passed over our heads. But we were compelled to fall back for a short distance, when, being reinforced by Benning's Brigade, we again captured the heights. By this time night had closed in, and darkness [had put] a stop to all operations. We lay upon our arms that night and held every foot of ground we had gained till the following afternoon, when we were withdrawn by General Lee's order.

Reverting to the disagreement between Generals Hood and Longstreet as to the feasibility of flanking Little Round Top, my own opinion is that it would have been exceedingly hazardous, as Hood's command would have been isolated and his flank exposed to attack; and yet the problem belongs to the 'might have been,' which no human foresight could fathom.

Mr Thompson's claim that Hood's Division attacked Sickle's Corps is another error. McLaw's Division fought Sickles and gave a good account of itself.

The failure at Gettysburg is no mystery, and we might as well accept the facts as they exist. And there is no necessity for making a scapegoat of anybody. In the first place, the enemy succeeded in getting possession of the strongest defensive position that could possibly be conceived of; in fact, a natural fortress held by a largely superior force in numbers, which we must concede was handled both with skill and energy. It was General Lee's intention no doubt, and it was so ordered, that there should be a simultaneous attack made all along the line, and if it could have been done I believe we would have won a great victory; but, owing to the difficulties of the round and some confusion of orders caused by the rapid concentration of the enemy, the result was a series of isolated conflicts which wasted the strength of the army without being able to utilize the advantages gained. And so, after the failure of Pickett's charge on the third day, General Lee withdrew his army and retired, which he did at his leisure and without being molested by the enemy.[4]

Private Henry Haywood Daniel
Third Arkansas Infantry
A Memorial, Henry Haywood Daniel, Confederate Soldier

H. H. Daniel lived in Smith County, Texas, for about twelve years and applied for his pension there. He was poor and never owned land, but his family of ten girls and two boys would hire out to neighbors to pick strawberries. They were in great demand according to my grandmother, because H. H. was the kind of man that insisted on the job done right. Claire Kirk.

Our Grandpaw Daniel was born on a plantation in Lowndes County, Alabama, July 3, 1840. He was the fourth child in a family of fourteen. At the age of 23, he enlisted in the 3rd Arkansas Infantry, Company I, at Camden Arkansas. The 3rd Arkansas Regiment, along with the 1st, 4th, and 5th Texas Regiments, made up the famous Hood's Brigade; the only Texas troops to serve under Lee in the Army of Northern Virginia.

6 June 1863, Hood's Brigade was in excellent condition and were ordered to cook three days' rations and prepare to move out early next morning into Pennsylvania towards Washington. They left at dawn in a heavy rain and dragged through mud until 10.00 that night. They slept under dripping trees on the wet ground, then marched back to their original campsite! Orders had been received during the night to return to the camp at Summerville until further orders. Finally on June 13th, new orders came and they moved from Culpepper Station to Cedar Run where they spent the night. Next day, under a burning sun, they headed up the Blue Ridge Mountains toward Ashby's Gap. The hot, sticky march, conducted by 'that unmerciful driver, our beloved General Hood, who simply strikes a trot and is satisfied that the Texas Brigade at least will camp with him at night fall,' was 25 miles to Gaines's Crossroads. The rapid pace cost 200 men who collapsed from sunstroke and sheer exhaustion—some died. Next day, they marched 20 miles to Markham Station, the next day a 14 mile march and then into the Shenandoah Valley, where they camped near Millwood. They finally crossed the Potomac at Williamsport, Maryland. The bridge was clogged with artillery, so the Arkansans and Texans stripped off their shoes, socks, pants and underwear, and with clothes, guns and ammunition held overhead, they started wading across. Just then a buggy-load of young Maryland ladies forded from the other side. There was no turning back! Colonel Van Manning, the commander of the 3rd Arkansas, remarked later '50,000 men without their trousers cannot be passed in review every day in the week!' Needless to say, the men moved across the river as quickly as possible and the young ladies did the same.

The Confederate army moved further into Yankee territory, confiscating food, clothes and whiskey as they went. After a long, hot march on an empty stomach, Lee allotted the troops a ration of whiskey. No one ever saw so many drunk men at one time! Van Manning dunked his men in a nearby icy stream until they were sober. Grandpaw never did like to take a cold bath after that! This episode set a record unbroken by anyone. Never had anyone been in five states in less than twenty-four hours—breakfast in the state of Virginia, lunch in the state of Maryland, supper in the state of Pennsylvania and sleeping in the state of intoxication!

By this time, the brigade was a queer lot to look at. Many of them had discarded their shoes in the mud and all were ragged and dirty, but full of good humor and confidence in themselves. They were in the Yankees' back door and getting closer all the time. As they marched through a small Northern town where all the ladies were out in the yards waving Union flags and making derogatory remarks at 'Hood's Ragged Jacks,' one particularly buxom lady had a red, white and blue banner across her chest. A voice from the ranks was heard to say in a definite southern drawl, 'Take care, Madam, for Hood's boys are great in storming breastworks when the Yankee colors is on them.' The lady beat a hasty retreat amid much guffaws.

Lee's army left Chambersburg on June 30, and after a slow march, moved into the valley of Willoughby Run behind Seminary Ridge on July 2nd. They cooked breakfast, then marched to position on Lee's right. Thus began the Battle of Gettysburg. Hood's Brigade formed their line of battle in a large clearing 200 yards behind a timbered area fronting on Emmitsburg Pike. The 3rd Arkansas on the left, the 1st, 4th, and 5th Texas in that order on the right. At 4.00 p.m., on July 2nd, a Confederate cannon sounded a single shot, and Hood's Brigade advanced at the double-quick with bayonets affixed and the Rebel Yell sounding along the entire line. As they approached the shallow valley of Plum Run in front of the Round Tops, they came under heavy fire from the Federals posted at Devil's Den. Men buckled, staggered and fell, but without faltering, Grandpaw and the rest of the brigade pressed on and flushed the sharpshooters. Robertson, in command of Hood's boys, started to shift his men to the right to support Law's hard-pressed forces, when a strong Federal force attacked the 3rd Arkansas on his left flank. The 1st Texas was ordered to their assistance, thus dividing the brigade about equally between Law and in the smoke of battle, he joined Robertson on the left. Therefore the 15th Georgia Regiment under Bennington was intermingled with the 3rd Arkansas and the 1st Texas. The casualties were terrible, especially among the officers. General Hood was dangerously wounded, General Robertson and Colonel Van Manning were also wounded. Regardless of the losses, 'the Texas Brigade, at Gettysburg, gave one of its great exhibitions of courageous fighting.'

The 1st Texas and the 3rd Arkansas fought desperately through and north of the Devil's Den, an unusual outcropping of granite boulders west of the Round Tops. During the first half-mile of their advance they were exposed to Federal long-range artillery barrage and sharpshooters' miniballs. Colonel Van Manning's 3rd Arkansas was locked in battle with the 6th New Jersey and the 40th New York. The Arkansans were suddenly assailed on their left and rear by a superior Federal force just as they were in the act of driving the two Union regiments from the field. They were ordered to fall back and establish a line of defense and await reinforcements. The 1st Texas was sent to their aid. Rejoined by their

Texas comrades, Grandpaw and the rest of the 3rd Arkansas engaged the Federals in bitter battle that lasted more than an hour. They finally drove the enemy through the boulder-strewn Devil's Den and back to a patch of timber north of Rocky Ridge. The fighting was so desperate that the men soon exhausted their original supply of ammunition and had to strip the cartridge boxes of the dead and wounded to keep firing. Officers in some cases threw down their swords, seized rifles, and fought in the ranks. General Robertson wrote later, 'For an hour and upward, these two regiments maintained one of the hottest contests against five or six times their number that I have ever witnessed.'

Reinforcements to both sides made the fighting heavy, but with little change in positions. At dusk, Robertson's regiments fell back to a shallow ravine below Little Round Top and reformed in line of battle. Here they were exposed to a terrific fire of artillery that killed and wounded many men, some losing their heads, and others so horribly mangled that their identity could scarcely be established. There was little sleep the night of the 2nd for the moans and cries of the wounded lying among the rocks and crevices made it nearly impossible. During the night, there was only spasmodic firing while both sides worked feverishly to construct barricades in anticipation of the next day. Then, before dawn, the 1st Texas and the 3rd Arkansas were moved to the right through Devil's Den, to join the 4th and 5th Texas. Law reported that, on July 2nd, one fourth of Hood's Brigade were casualties.

On July 3rd, Lee made his ill-fated attack on the center of Hancock's stout 2nd Army Corps. Longstreet's battle-weary forces were ordered to hold fast on the right. They saw little fighting that day on the 4th of July, withdrew to the Emmitsburg Pike from which they had started at dawn on the 2nd. The Battle of Gettysburg was over. The 3rd Arkansas had a total of 597 men killed, wounded, or missing.

The Texas Brigade moved south during the night of the 4th, slowed by heavy rain, high wind, and rutted roads. They finally camped on the 6th at Hagerstown. Grandpaw Daniel later told how the men would drive the hogs out of their wallows so they could curl up in their warm holes for a few hours' sleep on that terrible march back to Virginia after Gettysburg. The wounded suffered horribly in the hard wagon beds on the muddy rutted roads. Their moans could be heard all up and down the line of march.

When they reached the Potomac, it was at flood and they would have been in a bad position if General Meade had pressed after them. But the overcautious Meade waited, and the Confederates were safe until the river subsided and the bridge rebuilt. On the night of July 13th, Lee's battered Confederate army crossed safely into Virginia. As Hood's men crossed over, Lee, aside Traveler, watched as they passed—each soldier bared his head. No salute, no cheer, no word was spoken as they marched by. The great invasion was over and the Confederate army was badly damaged.[5]

Private John Allen Wilkerson
Third Arkansas Infantry

By evening our ranks were getting thin. It was fight all the time. Each side wanted the protection of those rocks. One in particular, it was very large, about 4 or 5 feet high. I saw smoke coming from behind that one and made a run for it, swerving to the right, with my gun ready. I cried, 'Hands up,' they dropped their guns and came out from behind the rock. There were six of them. One said, 'Young man, where is your troops?' I told them I was it, and showed them to the rear, and saw to it that they went. I went for that same rock, but went on the wrong side, right into the muzzle of the Yank's gun. He could easily put his gun in my face. He jabbed the gun out and fired, but it didn't touch me. Then he threw the gun up and begged me to spare his life. At that instant a comrade came on the other side of the rock and would have shot the Yank, had I not stopped him. As the sun started its descent, resting on the low crest of Seminary Ridge, Houck's Ridge and Devil's Den were occupied by boys from the South. Three guns of Smith's Battery were trophies in Southern hands, but the Confederates had to take a breather. The stress of battle and heat had taken a toll on Hood's troops. Empty canteens were no comfort to parched throats. Devil's Den offered a grisly haven from the deadly contest, and the men rested behind its fortress-like boulders. Away on the left, in a peach orchard, steady firing signified that McLaws was still heavily engaged, but only the distant furry of battle invaded the senses of Hood's men. When the sun was about an hour high in the evening we made another charge and drove the enemy back a short distance. Then we were ordered to fall back. The smoke was so thick, and the roar of the muskets so loud, we didn't hear all the command. I, with those who had not heard the order, went on forward and got too close. We thought our regiment was still back of us. The enemy were reinforced into two lines of battle, one directly behind the other. I dropped on my knees and fired at the two lines. When I raised up my comrades were gone and it seemed every Yank shot at me. Fortunately they shot too low. I was alive, but my left leg was shattered, below the knee. I fell, and they did not shoot at me anymore. They thought I was riddled with bullets. I crawled on my back and dragged my leg to a large rock nearby, on the side next to our men. I was then between two fires. W. S. Cockman found me. He said, 'John, if I live until it is over, I'll come and get you.'

About ten o'clock in the night he called for me, and at least fifty answered. I heard him tell the boys with him, 'Let me call again.' This time he yelled 'Seven Pines.' None answered but me. He was from my home town 'way down in Arkansas. They put me on a litter and carried me back to the rear of our lines, near a brick barn that our men were using for a hospital. I was left in that wheat field with about one hundred of my regiment, too badly wounded to be moved with my regiment, and the army.[6]

Arkansas at Gettysburg

Note: The following account of the part played by Arkansas troops in the Battle of Gettysburg was prepared by the Pennsylvania State Commission in connection with the forthcoming Gettysburg Battle Anniversary and Reunion Program, to be held at Gettysburg, Pa, in 1938 when the United Confederate Veterans and the Grand Army of the Republic will meet in a joint reunion on the field where they met in battle seventy-five years before.

Arkansas was represented in the Battle of Gettysburg by only one regiment, the 3rd. Under Colonel Van H. Manning this regiment formed a part of Robertson's Brigade, Hood's Division, Longstreet's Corps. Arkansas was a part of the Trans-Mississippi Department and was therefore subject to attack and invasion from three directions. The hard-pressed Confederate government could afford little aid, the state was forced to depend in a large measure upon its own resource. These proved quite adequate, and the appeal from Richmond for men to protect the capital was answered by the dispatch of the 3rd Arkansas Regiment. These men were noble examples of the soldierly qualities of Arkansas's sons. These were men as brave, but none braver; there were men as true to the cause they served, but none truer; there were men of valor in both uniforms both blue and gray, but none possessed more intrepid courage than the youthful veterans from Arkansas. Their state, their section, their nation will always be proud to honor the memory of these immortal sons.

The 3rd Arkansas did not reach Gettysburg until the morning of 2 July. Therefore it took no part in the first phase of the fighting, but it played a conspicuous part in the events of the second day. While Longstreet was getting his corps into position on the Confederate right, Sickles was moving the third corps of the Army of the Potomac from Cemetery Ridge westward to the Emmitsburg Road. This new position left his flank unprotected. Hood's Division, of which the lads from Arkansas formed a part, was directed to strike Sickles's exposed flank. When they moved to the attack the 3rd Arkansas found its way blocked by that formidable natural fortress, Devil's Den. Here nature has conspired to construct one of those weird spectacles which man has found impossible to intimidate. Giant granite boulders are heaped one upon another in massive profusion. On the east there is a sheer fall to Plum Run 40 feet below. This granite face shows one huge monolith heaped upon another and each is worn round and smooth by the gentle caresses of nature's kindly elements. On the west and north there is a gradual slope liberally sprinkled with granite boulders. On this natural fortress Smith's 4th New York Battery was planted.

Could this position be taken? The lads from Arkansas thought it could. With the objective in sight the advance was begun. From tree to tree, from boulder to boulder plunged the boys in gray. Shot and shell went screaming through the air or ploughed up the earth, and the rattle of musketry rounded out the weird staccato. The boys from Arkansas were intent upon their deadly business but they must have thought of the appropriateness of the name of this particular spot. They probably did not know that even the origin of the name had been lost in antiquity. Had they inquired of local people they might have learned that some, hesitating to pronounce his Satanic majesty's name in such connection, referred to this as the Big Rocks. However, they might have found someone who could have told them it was called Devil's Den by the ancients, because horse thieves had at one time made it their headquarters. Others would have related how, because of the unprecedented number of rattle snakes which formerly dwelt among these rocks, it had been christened Devil's Den. No matter how the name came to be applied, the 3rd Arkansas would have agreed that the locality was properly named. They were painfully aware of the fact that it was infested with engines of death and destruction, cannons and muskets. It might have been that these men thought what a tower of strength this position would be in their possession, how once they were safely ensconced the enemy would be made to believe the forked, tall and cloven-footed master had returned to his own. At any rate, the charging gray columns swept on in face of the leaden ball. They swarmed over the boulders and captured three of Smith's guns. This rendered Sickles's position untenable and threatened the whole Federal left.

Assisting in the capture of the Den and the New York battery was the tide of the achievement of the Arkansas troops at Gettysburg. On 3 July they occupied a position in this vicinity and kept up an intermitting skirmish with Federal forces along their left flank on Round Top. The purpose of this was to screen the movement along the center and later, when the attack was under way, to prevent Meade from reinforcing this center from this portion of the line. When the bombardment which preceded Pickett's ill-fated charge began, the boys from Arkansas had an excellent position from which to watch the most spectacular event of the entire war, the most tremendous artillery preparation ever undertaken previous to the World War. The 3rd Arkansas witnessed this forerunner of modern artillery usage, which was far more spectacular than an action by a thousand heavy pieces of the present type.[7]

Arkansas Soldiers Buried at Gettysburg

Dr J. W. C. O'Neal has furnished *The Gettysburg Compiler*, a revised list of the names of those Confederates buried on the battlefield of Gettysburg, whose graves can still be identified.[8] We publish for the information of their friends, the following list of those from Arkansas:

Sergeant J. W. Castlemann, 3d Ark.
J. A. Noble, 3d Ark.
C. C. Beeman, 3d Ark.
M. Reeves, 3d Ark.
S. A. Wallace, 3d Ark.

Memorial Will Honor Arkansans at Gettysburg

The state Gettysburg Memorial Commission picked a Georgia firm Monday to design and build a $50,000 memorial to honor Arkansas soldiers who took part in the Civil War battle.

The memorial will be on the battlefield.

Cobbs Memorial of Marietta, Ga, proposed a memorial 36 feet long, 9 feet high, and with a base 16 feet wide. The firm said the base would support a 2-foot thick slab, which will be etched figures and the tribute to the 3rd Arkansas Infantry Regiment.

A Little Rock firm also submitted a design.[9]

Arkansas Civil War Monument Dedicated

A $50,000 stone monument commemorating the men of the 3rd Arkansas Infantry Regiment was dedicated on the battlefield of Gettysburg Saturday.

The regiment led an assault on Little Round Top 2 July 1863, during the Civil War battle. The regiment acquitted itself [so] valiantly [that] it was granted the unusual privilege of keeping its colors when the Confederate Army surrendered.[10]

Arkansas Monument at Gettysburg. (*Patricia Rich*)

The Generals' Correspondence

General John Bell Hood
New Orleans, La, 28 June 1875
To General James Longstreet[1]

General—I have not responded earlier to your letter of April 5th, by reason of pressure of business, which rendered it difficult for me to give due to the attention to the subject in regard to which you have desired information.

You are correct in your assumption that I failed to make a report of the operations of my division around Suffolk, Va, and of its action in the battle of Gettysburg, in consequence of a wound which I received in this engagement. In justice to the brave troops under my command at this period, I should here mention another cause for this apparent neglect of duty on my part.

Before I had recovered from the severe wound received at Gettysburg, your corps (excepting Pickett's division) was ordered to join General Bragg, in the west, for battle against Rosencranz; my old troops—with whom I had served so long—were thus to be sent forth to another army—quasi, I may say, among strangers—to take part in a great struggle; and upon an appeal from a number of the brigade and regimental officers of my division, I consented to accompany them, although I had the use of but one arm.

This movement to the west soon resulted in the battle of Chickamauga, where I was again so seriously wounded as to cause the loss of a limb. These severe wounds in close succession, in addition to the all-absorbing duties and anxieties attending the last year of the war, prevented me

General John Bell Hood. (*Texas Heritage Museum*)

General Jerome B. Robertson. (*Texas Heritage Museum*)

from submitting subsequently, a report, as likewise one after the battle of Chickamauga, in which engagement—whilst you led the left wing—I had the honor of commanding your corps, together with the three divisions of the Army of Tennessee, respectively under A. P. Stewart, Bushrod Johnson and Hindman. Thus, the gallantry of these troops as well as the admirable conduct of my division at Gettysburg, I have left unrecorded. With this apology for seeming neglect, I will proceed to give a brief sketch from memory of the events forming the subject of your letter:

My recollection of the circumstances connected with the attempt, whilst we were lying in front of Suffolk, to reach General Lee in time to participate in the Battle of Chancellorsville is very clear. The order directing your corps to move to the support of General Lee was received about the time General Hooker crossed the Rappahannock.

Unfortunately, we had been compelled by the scarcity of forage to send off our wagons into North Carolina to gather a supply from that state. A short delay necessarily ensued, as couriers had to be dispatched for the requisite transportation before the troops could move. Every effort, however, was made to get to Lee at the earliest moment. If my memory betrays me not, you repaired in advance of your corps to Petersburg or Richmond, having issued orders for us to march with all possible speed to Lee on the Rappahannock. I was most anxious to get to the support of my old chief, and made strenuous efforts to do so; but, whilst on a forced march to accomplish this object, I received intelligence of our victory at Chancellorsville, and of Jackson's mortal wound. We, nevertheless, continued our march, and eventually went into bivouac upon the Rapidan, near Gordonsville.

After the Battle of Chancellorsville, preparations were made for an offensive campaign. Accordingly, my troops moved out of camp, crossed the Rapidan about the 5th of June 1863, and joined in the general move in the direction of the Potomac. We crossed the river about the middle of the same month, and marched into Pennsylvania. Hill's and Ewell's Corps were in advance, and were reported to be in the vicinity of Carlisle. Whilst lying in camp, not far distant from Chambersburg, information was received that Ewell and Hill were about to come in contact with the enemy near Gettysburg. My troops, together with McLaws's Division, were put in motion upon the most direct road to that point, which, after a hard march, we reached before or at sunrise on the 2nd of July. So imperative had been the orders to hasten forward with all possible speed, that on the march my troops were allowed to halt and rest only about two hours, during the night from the 1st to the 2nd of July.

I arrived with my staff in front of the heights of Gettysburg shortly after daybreak, as I have already stated, on the morning of the 2nd of July. My division soon commenced filing into an open field near me, where the troops were allowed to stack arms and rest until further orders. A short distance in advance of this point, and during the early part of the same morning, we were both engaged, in company with Generals Lee and A. P. Hill, in observing the position of the Federals. General Lee—with coat buttoned to the throat, sabre belt buckled around the waist, and field glasses pending at his side—walked up and down in the shade of large trees near us, halting now and then to observe the enemy. He seemed full of hope, yet at times, buried in deep thought.

Colonel Fremantle, of England, was ensconced in the forks of a tree not far off, with glass in constant use, examining the lofty position of the Federal army. General Lee was seemingly anxious you should attack that morning. He remarked to me: 'The enemy is here, and if we do not whip him, he will whip us.' You thought it better to await the arrival of Pickett's division—at that time still in the rear—in order to make the attack; and you said to me, subsequently, whilst we were seated together near the trunk of a tree: 'The General is a little nervous this morning; he wishes me to attack; I do not wish to do so without Pickett. I never like to go into battle with one boot off.'

Thus passed the forenoon of that eventful day, when, in the afternoon— about three o'clock—it was decided to no longer await Pickett's division, but to proceed to our extreme right, and attack up the Emmettsburg Road. McLaws moved off, and I followed with my division. In a short time I was ordered to quicken the march of my troops, and pass to the front of McLaws. This movement was accomplished by throwing out an advanced force to tear down fences and clear the way. The instructions I received were to place my division across the Emmettsburg Road, form line of battle, and attack. Before reaching this road, however, I had sent forward some of my picked Texas scouts to ascertain the position of the enemy's extreme left flank. They soon reported to me that it rested upon Round Top mountain; that the country was open and that I could march through an open woodland pasture around Round Top and assault the enemy in flank and rear; that their wagon trains were parked in rear of their line, and were badly exposed to our attack in that direction. As soon as I arrived upon the Emmettsburg Road I placed one or two batteries in position and opened fire. A reply from the enemy's guns soon developed his lines. His left rested on or near Round Top, with line bending back and again forward, forming, as it were, a concave line as approached by the Emmettsburg Road. A considerable body of troops was posted in front of their main line, between the Emmettsburg Road and Round Top Mountain.

This force was in line of battle upon an eminence near a peach orchard. I found that in making the attack according to orders, viz. up the Emmetsburg Road, I should have first to encounter and drive off this advanced line of battle; secondly, at the base and along the slope of the mountain, to confront immense boulders of stone, so massed together as to form narrow openings, which would break our ranks and cause the men to scatter whilst climbing up the rocky precipice. I found, moreover, that my division would be exposed to a heavy fire from the main line of the enemy, in position on the crest of the high range, of which Round Top was the extreme left, and, by reason of the concavity of the enemy's main line, that we would be subject to a destructive fire in flank and rear, as well as in front; and deemed it almost an impossibility to clamber along the boulders up this steep and rugged mountain, and, under this number of crossfires, put the enemy to flight. I knew that if the feat was accomplished it must be at a most fearful sacrifice of as brave and gallant soldiers as ever engaged in battle.

The reconnaissance by my Texas scouts and the development of the Federal lines were effected in a very short space of time; in truth, shorter than I have taken to recall and jot down these facts, although the scenes and events of that day are as clear to my mind as if the great battle had been fought yesterday. I was in possession of these important facts so shortly after reaching the Emmettsburg Road, that I considered it my duty to report to you at once my opinion, that it was unwise to attack up the Emmettsburg Road, as ordered, and to urge that you allow me to turn Round Top and attack the enemy in flank and rear. Accordingly, I dispatched a staff officer bearing to you my request to be allowed to make the proposed movement on account of the above stated reasons. Your reply was quickly received: 'General Lee's orders are to attack up the Emmettsburg Road.' I sent another officer to say that I feared nothing could be accomplished by such an attack, and renewed my request to turn Round Top. Again your answer was: 'General Lee's orders are to attack up the Emmettsburg Road.'

During this interim I had continued the use of the batteries upon the enemy, and had become more and more convinced that the Federal line extended to Round Top, and that I could not reasonably hope to accomplish much by the attack as ordered. In fact it seemed to me the enemy occupied a position by nature so strong—I may say impregnable—that, independent of their flank fire, they could easily repel our attack by merely throwing and rolling stones down the mountain side as we approached.

A third time I dispatched one of my staff to explain fully in regard to the situation, and to suggest that you better come and look for yourself. I selected in this instance, my adjutant general, Colonel Harry Sellers, whom you know to be not only an officer of great courage, but also of marked ability. Colonel Sellers returned with the same message: 'General Lee's orders are to attack up the Emmettsburg road.' Almost simultaneously, Colonel Fairfax, of your staff, rode up and repeated the same orders. After this urgent protest against entering into battle at Gettysburg according to instructions—which protest is the first and only one I ever made during my military career—I ordered my line to advance and make the assault.

As my troops were moving forward, you rode up in person: a brief conversation passed between us, during which I again expressed the fears above mentioned, and regret at not being allowed to attack in flank around Round Top. You answered to this effect: 'we must obey the orders of General Lee.' I then rode forward with my line under a heavy fire. In about twenty minutes after reaching the peach orchard I was severely wounded in the arm, and borne from the field. With this wound terminated my participation in this great battle. As I was borne off on a litter to my rear, I could but experience deep distress of mind and heart at the thought of the inevitable fate of my brave fellow soldiers, who formed one of the grandest divisions of that world-renowned army; and I shall ever believe that had I been permitted to turn Round Top mountain; we would not only have gained that position, but [would] have been able finally to route the enemy.

Trusting this sketch, however incomplete, may answer its purpose, I am, respectfully yours,

J. B. Hood
Witnesses H. B. Deas, R. J. Deas[2]

Major W. H. Sellers, Assistant Adjutant-General, Hood's Division
HEADQUARTERS TEXAS BRIGADE
Near Bunker Hill, Va, 17 July 1863

I have the honor to submit through you my report of the action of my brigade in the battle of Gettysburg, on July 2 and 3. I have been too much occupied with the duties imposed by the marches and maneuvers we have gone through to allow me to make this report at an earlier time.

The division arrived on the ground in front of the position of the enemy that we were to attack but a few minutes before we were ordered to advance. I therefore got but a glance at the field on which we had to operate before we entered upon it. I was ordered to keep my right well closed on Brigadier-General Law's left, and to my left rest on the Emmitsburg pike. I had advanced but a short distance when I discovered that my brigade would not fill the space between General Law's left and the pike named, and that I must leave the pike, or disconnect myself from General Law, on my right. Understanding before the action commenced that the attack on our part was to be general, and that the force of General McLaws was to advance simultaneously with us on my immediate left, and seeing at once that a mountain held by the enemy in heavy force with artillery to the right of General Law's center was the key to the enemy's left, I abandoned the pike, and closed on General Law's left. This caused some separation of my regiments, which was remedied promptly as the numerous stone and rail fences that intersected the field through which we were advancing would follow.

As we advanced through this field, for half a mile we were exposed to a heavy and destructive fire of canister, grape, and shell from six pieces of their artillery on the mountain alluded to, and the same number on a commanding hill but a short distance to the left of the mountain, and from the enemy's sharpshooters behind the numerous rocks, fences, and houses in the field.

As we approached the base of the mountain, General Law moved to the right, and I was moving obliquely to the right to close on him, when my whole line encountered the fire of the enemy's main line, posted behind rocks and a stone fence. The 4th and 5th Texas Regiments, under the direction of their gallant commanders (Colonels Powell and Key), while returning the fire and driving the enemy before them, continued to close on General Law, to their right. At the same time, the 1st Texas and 3rd Arkansas, under their gallant commanders (Lieutenant-Colonel [P. A.] Work and Colonel Manning), were hotly engaged with a greatly superior force, while at the same time a heavy forced appeared and opened fire on Colonel Manning's left, seriously threatening his left flank, to meet which he threw two or three companies with their front to his left flank, and protected his left.

On discovering this heavy force on my left flank, and seeing that no attack was being made by any of our forces on my left, I at once sent a courier to Major-General Hood, stating that I was hard pressed on my left; that General McLaws's forces were not engaging the enemy to my left (which enabled him to move fresh troops from the part of his line down on me), and that I must have re-enforcements.

Lieutenant-Colonel Work, with the 1st Texas Regiment, having pressed forward to the crest of the hill and driven the enemy from his battery, I ordered him to the left, to the relief and support of Colonel Manning, directing Major [F. S.] Bass with two companies to hold the hill, while Colonel Work with the rest of the regiment went to Colonel Manning's relief. With this assistance, Colonel Manning drove the enemy back, and entered the woods after him, when the enemy reoccupied the hill and his batteries in Colonel Work's front, from which Colonel Work again drove him.

For an hour and upward, these two regiments maintained one of the hottest contests, against five or six times their number that I have witnessed. The moving of Colonel Work to the left, to relieve Colonel Manning while the 4th and 5th Texas were closing to the right on General Law's brigade, separated these two regiments from the others. They were steadily moving to the right and front, driving the enemy before them, when they passed the woods or ravine to my right. After finding that I could not move the 1st and 3rd to the right to join them, I sent to recall them, ordering them to move to the left until the left of the 4th should rest on the right of the 1st; but my messenger found two of General Law's regiments on the left of my two (the 4th and 5th Texas), and did not find these regiments at all.

About this time my aide, Lieutenant Scott, reported my two regiments (the 4th and 5th Texas) in the center of General Law's brigade, and they could not be moved without greatly injuring his line. I sent a request to General Law to look to them.

At this point, my assistant adjutant and inspector general reported from the 4th and 5th that they were hotly engaged, and wanted re-enforcements. My courier, sent to General Hood, returned, and reported him wounded and carried from the field. I sent a messenger to Lieutenant-General Longstreet for re-enforcements, and at the same time sent to Generals [George T.] Anderson and Benning, urging them to hurry up to my support. They came up, joined us, and fought gallantly; but as fast as we would break one line of the enemy, another fresh one would present itself, the enemy re-enforcing his lines in our front from his reserves at the base of the mountain to our right and front, and from his lines to our left. Having no attack from us in the front, he threw his forces from there on us.

Before the arrival of Generals Anderson and Benning, Colonel J. C. G. Key, who gallantly led the 4th Texas Regiment in, up to the time of receiving a severe wound, passed me, being led to the rear. About the same time, I learned of the fall and dangerous wounding of Colonel R. M. Powell, of the 5th, who fell while gallantly leading his regiment in one of the impetuous charges of the 4th and 5th Texas on the strongly fortified mountain.

Just after the arrival of General Anderson on my left, I learned that the gallant Colonel Van H. Manning, of the 3rd Arkansas, had been wounded and carried from the field, and about the same time I received intelligence of the wounding and carr[ying] from the field of those two able and efficient officers, Lieutenant-Colonel K. Bryan, of the 5th, and B. F. Carter of the 4th, both whom were wounded while bravely discharging their duty. Captain [J. R.] Woodward, acting major of the 1st Texas, was wounded near me gallantly discharging his duty.

The 4th and 5th Texas, under the command of Majors [J. P.] Bane and [J. C.] Rogers, continued to hold the ground of their original line, leaving the space over which they had made their successive charges strewn with their wounded and dead comrades, many of whom could not be removed, and were left upon the field. The 1st Texas, under Lieutenant-Colonel Work, with a portion of Benning's Brigade, held the field and the batteries taken by the 1st Texas. Three of the guns were brought off the field and secured; the other three, from the nature of the ground and their proximity to the enemy, were left. The 3rd Arkansas, under the command of Lieutenant-Colonel [R. S.] Taylor, ably assisted by Major [J. W.] Reedy, after Colonel Manning was borne from the field, sustained well the high character it made in the earlier part of the action.

When night closed the conflict, late in the evening, I was struck above the knee, which deprived me the use of my leg, and prevented me from getting about the field. I retired some 200 yards to the rear, leaving the immediate command with Lieutenant-Colonel Work, the senior officer present, under whose supervision our wounded were brought out and guns secured, and our dead on that part of the field were buried the next day.

About two o'clock that night, the 1st Texas and 3rd Arkansas were moved by the right to the position occupied by the 4th and 5th, and formed on their left, where the brigade remained during the day of the 3rd, keeping up a continuous skirmishing with the enemy's sharpshooters, in which we had a number of our men severely wounded, I sent my assistant adjutant-general, Captain F. L. Price, at daybreak to examine the position of the brigade, and report to me as soon as he could, and, while in the discharge of that duty, he was either killed or fell into the hands of the enemy, as he has not been seen or heard of since.

About dark on the evening of the 3rd, the brigade, with the division, fell back to the hill, and formed in line, where it remained during the 4th.

Lieutenant [J. R.] Loughridge, commanding Company I, 4th Texas, who commanded the skirmishers in front of the 4th, and who was left when that regiment moved to the right, joined the 1st Texas, and did gallant service during that engagement.

In this, the hardest fought battle of the war in which I have been engaged, all, both officers and men, as far as my observation extended, fully sustained the high character they have heretofore made. Where all behaved so nobly, individual distinction cannot with propriety be made.

I cannot close this report without expressing my thanks to my personal staff for the able and satisfactory manner in which they discharged their duties. The wounding of so many commanding officers, among them the division commander, rendered their duties peculiarly arduous. They were discharged with zeal and promptness. Captain F. L. Price, my assistant adjutant-general, whose loss on the morning of the 3rd I have to deplore, was an active, efficient officer, and did his duty nobly. My aide-de-camp Lieutenant John G. Scott, my assistant adjutant and inspector general, Lieutenant John W. Kerr, and Lieutenant John Grace, volunteer aide, discharged their duties with a promptness and ability that merit special notice.

A list of the casualties in the several regiments, together with the reports from each of the regimental commanders, is herewith submitted.

J. B. ROBERTSON,
Brigadier-General, Commanding Brigade.[3]

Obituary of General John B. Hood

Not only throughout the South, but throughout the North and everywhere, where gallantry and true heroism is appreciated, the news of the death of General John B. Hood will be received with profound regret. Especially will this be the case in Texas, where so many reside who followed that noble chieftain in the saugulnary [*sic.*, 'sanguinary'] battles of Virginia, Maryland and elsewhere, during the conflict between the two sections, and where he was so well known on account of his active service on the Texas frontier previous to the war.

General Hood was born in Bath County, Kentucky, in 1831. He entered the Military Academy at West Point and graduated in 1853. He was assigned to duty in the 4th Infantry, then stationed in California, where he remained two years. He was transferred to the 2nd Cavalry in 1855, and served with that famous regiment which furnished the South some of its best generals and which was then stationed on the Texas frontier, until the commencement of the late civil war.

He resigned his commission in the US Army in April 1861, and hastened to Richmond where he tendered his services to the Confederate States of America. He served some time as major of cavalry on the Peninsular, and in September was placed in command of the gallant 4th Texas. Soon after, the famous Texas Regiment was formed, consisting of the 1st, 4th, and 5th Texas Regiments. His subsequent career as leader of Hood's Brigade was a most brilliant one. Gaines's Mill, Seven Pines, and Malvern Hill bore evidence to his military talent and to his bravery. After McClellan's retreat, General Hood was promoted to the command of a division in Longstreet's Corps and participated in the Second Battle of Bull Run, and in the sanguinary battles in Maryland on Lee's first invasion. At Gettysburg he was severely wounded in the arm, and at Chickamauga in the leg, which rendered amputation necessary. For gallantry in the last named engagement he was promoted to the rank of Lieutenant General. He then served under Joseph E. Johnston in Georgia and was assigned to the command of the Army of Tennessee, after the retreat to Atlanta, when General Joseph E. Johnston was relieved. He attacked and defeated General Schofield at Franklin, in November 1864, and after a series of strategic movements, attacked General Thomas in Nashville in December. After one of the fiercest battles of the war, he was forced to retreat. This virtually ended the campaign, and he took leave of his army at Tupelo, Mississippi, on the 23rd day of January 1865.

After the surrender General Hood located at New Orleans, where he married a daughter of A. Hennen, a distinguished member of the Louisiana legislature. For several years previous to his death he was representative of the Life Association of America in New Orleans.

His wife died a few days previous to his own death, which utterly crushed him. Two of his children are lying at the point of death, with the same disease which deprived them within a few days of their parents. It is the duty of the South to see that these children are not permitted to want.[4]

The Speeches

In the decades after the Civil War, soldiers of Hood's Texas Brigade formed the Hood's Texas Brigade Association and would meet annually at various locations around Texas. One of the most important reunions occurred on 26 and 27 October 1910 when a monument to Hood's Texas Brigade was dedicated on the Capital Grounds in Austin, Texas. The two-day event attracted thousands of the remaining veterans, who heard speeches given about the exploits of the brigade during the Civil War. Many of the speeches given by the veterans and dignitaries included the actions of the brigade at Gettysburg and at other battles. The following excerpts were pronounced by some of the brigade's heroic soldiers to fight at Gettysburg.

Dr John O. Scott
Hood's Texas Brigade at Gettysburg

Of all the battles fought on this continent none compares with Gettysburg.

Take it all in all, the historian must conclude that it was the grandest, greatest and most important battle in history.

Greatest, for during the three days' contest—1, 2, and 3 July 1863—there were displayed more acts of daring, persistent, dauntless bravery, than in any battle yet chronicled, and most important, for the retreat of General Lee was the death knell of the Confederacy, forever settling the permanency of a free, united government of compact States, and abolishing slavery from this land.

For the failure at the Battle of Gettysburg some writers unjustly criticize General Lee for permitting the corps of his army to be so far from each other when the battle commenced. Very many without just cause reproach General Ewell for not advancing on the evening of the first day's battle and taking possession of Cemetery Heights.

Not a few, without reflection, censure General J. E. B. Stuart, the great cavalry chief, for not being with General Lee in time of battle. Why he was not there no one has ever known. The secret died with General Lee.

Others have unkindly abused General Longstreet, partly through prejudice and partly through ignorance, for not making the charge on the morning of the second day's battle, instead of waiting until four o'clock in the afternoon, when the enemy were reinforced and were in convenient instance to concentrate troops on the Round Tops.

If anyone is culpable posterity must decide that question, for after this generation has passed off the state of action this great pivotal battle of the war will be read and discussed as of Saratoga, Waterloo, Pharsalia and other memorable contests.

The daring, reckless bravery of the Cossacks placed the name of Peter the Great among heroes of Christendom.

The Old Guard that bore the eagles of Napoleon from Marengo to Waterloo, shed a halo of glory on the name of their adored leader which yet charms the people, enthuses the historian to write and gives the orator subject matter for his audience.

For heroic acts collectively and individually there has been no collection of armed men, under any commander, that has surpassed Hood's Brigade of Texans.

Colonel Philip Alexander Work, in his narrative of this battle, has truly written that the success of the Texan regiments was not due to the training of Hood or any other commander, but that they were composed of the very pick and flower of an intelligent, educated, adventurous and high-spirited people. Infused with the spirit of chivalry, the Texans on every battlefield displayed the sublime, fearless, exalted courage of the heroes of the Alamo and San Jacinto, adoring their Lone Star flag and guarding its unsullied record as a dutiful son [would] the name of an honored father. We believe that if General Hood had not been wounded at the commencement of the charge 2 July 1863, he would have led the Texans in rear of the Round Tops and gained a glorious victory. For Colonel Robert Michael Powell writes that 'my regiment was on the extreme right 400 yards from the left wing of the brigade, and in the very commencement of the battle, before the firing of the great signal gun, General Hood rode up to me and pointed to Great Round Top as the direction for me to take with my regiment, whose flag should be the leader for the brigade. Before us stood in serried, rugged defiance Great Round Top, with Little Round Top leaning against it.'

Colonel P. A. Work has given a little history of the glorious achievements of the heroic Texans in this battle, which as yet no historian has recorded, and has rendered the Texans that need of praise which the patriotic people of this grand State will rejoice to hear of, remember and treasure forever.

Colonel Work writes:

I sent from my regiment Charles Kingsley and William H. Barbee to reconnoiter Little Round Top to ascertain and report the probable force and number of the guns of the Federals in possession of it, there being no other thought than that the enemy has taken possession of the vantage ground and the key of the whole field.' The scouts reported in my hearing and presence that they had ascended Little Round Top and there was not a man or gun on it; that from the summit they saw a ridge all the way 2½ miles long to Gettysburg, and behind this ridge a line of Federal infantry, and battery after battery of artillery, whereupon General Hood said to one of his staff, Major W. H. Sellers: 'Go as fast as your horse can carry you and explain all this to General Longstreet, and ask him to permit me to move by the right flank, so as to be able to envelop that knob,' pointing to Little Round Top, 600 or 800 yards in the distance, a little southeast of where the Texans were in line of battle. In a few moments Major Sellers returned with the message from General Longstreet: 'You will execute the orders you have already received.' Thereupon General Hood remarked: 'Very well; when we get under fire I will have a digression.'

Charles Vidor, A. Wakelee, Wm Schadt, W. A. Bedell and Wm Von Hutton of the Galveston Company, 1st Texas were witnesses to this scene on the eve of battle, saw the scouts return and heard their report. A few moments later, about four o'clock, the great signal gun was heard, when General Hood, rising in his stirrups, being about 20 feet in advance of the First Texas said: 'Forward, my Texans, and win this battle or die in the effort!' His thrilling words, like an electric shock, passed along the Texas regiments arrayed in line of battle impatiently waiting the shrill notes of the bugle for advance, their beloved general, Robertson, in command. Presently I saw a spherical case shot explode 20 feet over General Hood's head, saw him sway to and fro in his saddle and then start to fall from his horse, when he was caught by one of his aides. Seeing a battery 600 or 800 yards on the crest of Little Round Top, I directed my command to it, as it was always my rule when under fire in battle not to halt until I took the battery in front of me.

The distance from the Spring Branch (Plum Run), at the base, to the summit of Little Round Top is 75 to 100 yards, and is a mass of granite stone piled on each other, and must have been very difficult to climb, for

Mr James Williams of Coleman County writes that his company came to a large rock which they could not get over, when Mr H. H. Hendricks, a very tall man, placed his back to the stone and assisted his comrades to climb over him. When all were up they in turn assisted him over.

Captain W. E. Barry of Navasota, whose brother John Barry, was severely wounded in this battle, afterward killed at Chickamauga, in a litter to us described the charge up Little Round Top, narrates that while ascending he came across a deep crevice in the rocks and looking down he saw in the bottom a German soldier, so besmeared with white clay as to be scarcely recognizable. The German was so frightened that he begged piteously for mercy. He was so terrified from the deafening yells and threatening shouts of the advancing Texans that he chose the alternative of jumping in the deep hole and going to the devil rather than face the coming Texans. Privates Knox, J. and B. Milam, Woodhouse, E. Newsome, Thompson, Parker, Davis, Wren and others of that heroic band saw George A. Branard of Houston go in front of all. Finding the highest and largest rock on the crest of Little Round Top there he planted the adored standard of the Texans, adorned with the Lone Star, shining far off to friend and foe with the effulgence of its glory.

Pretty soon it attracted the attention of the enemy, who, firing a shell at the signal, broke the flagstaff and hurled the hero unconscious down the slope of the mountain. He was tenderly cared for by his brave color guard, Alex J. Watts and Ira Parker. The latter died of wounds received here. The flag was immediately replaced and the advancing column of the Texans, by their steady aim killed and drove away to the other side of the ridge, some 600 or 800 yards distant, the infantry supporting the battery.

Colonel Work relates: 'After the First Texas captured the battery the Third Arkansas on my left, was being hard pressed.' In this critical juncture I ordered Major Bass to face about with one-half the First Texas and the flank the enemy, which maneuver he bravely and skillfully executed, thereby preventing the Third Arkansas from being routed and enabling it to get into line on the crest of the mountain under shelter of the rocks with the First Texas.

Willis James Watts of Palestine, in a history of the battle writes that in assisting the Third Arkansas, which recoiled as far back as the stone fence, Lieutenant Ben Campbell and C. W. Butler were killed, and Captain Woodard, a physician from Palestine, who was afterward killed at Front Royal, was severely wounded.

J. E. Stinson and W. J. Watts were among the first to reach the captured battery, and rejoicing in the heroism of the Texans, Stinson, mounting a captured gun exultantly 'shook the fragment of his blade and shouted victory.

Captain George T. Todd of Jefferson and E. P. Derick, after fighting gallantly to almost the summit of Little Round Top, sheltered themselves behind a large boulder. While firing on the enemy a bullet from the foe struck E. P. Derick, scattering his brains in the face of Captain Todd. Andrew Dennis and W. A. Duvall were killed with hands on the captured guns. Immortal heroes!

T. L. McCarty of Corsicana, who was in that famous charge—which is an imperishable honor to him and his family—says that Sergeant William Porter was mortally wounded by a shell and his comrades buried him with the honors of war on the side of the mountain; that Jack Lewis, who was killed at Chickamauga, and Rich Curtis, took hold of the trail of one of the captured guns and turned it around with the muzzle pointing toward the enemy. For want of ammunition the gun could not be fired.

Privates C. L. Freeman and Beavers were witnesses, among others, of the heroism of Alf M. George who was among the first to reach the captured cannon.

Alf M. George of Albany, Texas informs us that he followed the retreating foe some distance on the top of the mountain, where he and his comrade, C. L. Freeman, were severely wounded.

J. E. Hickman of Bibb, Texas relates that when the 1st Texas Regiment ascended nearly to the top of the mountain the regiment halted. It was a 'hot situation, almost like the bad place.' Here Colonel Work asked Lieutenant John T. Smith if with seventy men or more he could take the hill. The lieutenant replied: 'I will try.' At the same time shouting to his comrades 'Come on, boys!' leading them to death and glory.

The top of this mountain where this battery was captured by the 1st Texas is a level plateau 60 to 75 yards from east to west; and from this place to the opposite side of the ridge, northeast, where the enemy was firing at them, was a distance of 600 to 800 yards, and from where the battery was captured to the end of the ridge a distance of 75 yards.

During the night Captain Sam A. Wilson requested of Colonel Work permission to bring off the captured cannon. He, Colonel Richard J. Harding, Jeff Brady and others crawling to the cannon, picked out of the path over which the guns were to be drawn, all stones and large pebbles, not speaking above a whisper, wrapped the wheels with blankets and brought the guns off so carefully that the noise was not heard 100 yards away. Colonel Harding was one, with Major W. H. Martin and other Texans, who at the Battle of the Wilderness prevented General Lee from leading the charge in person. The guns were delivered to Major Riley, quartermaster of the division.

Col. Work writes:

> After nightfall the Federals were as mute as mice, not sounding a bugle or gun. They were making a retreat or getting ready for one, but General Lee having no cavalry, had no means of ascertaining it, and after the firing ceased the Confederates were busy caring for the wounded.

The night was dark, still on the field of carnage, after the horrid strife, the stars were shining through the smoke of battle silent witnesses, dimly lighting the death scene. There weltering in their life blood cold and pale in the embrace of death, on the slope and the top of the mountain, lay the gray clad warrior from the banks of the Trinity, side by side with the blue trousered veteran from the heights of the Hudson.

At two o'clock in the morning of 3 July 1863, General Law ordered Colonel Work to withdraw the command from the top of the mountain.

Colonel Work left Lieutenant J. J. Quarles with his company as picket guard in Devil's Den, a dismal mausoleum of glory crowned Texas heroes. This weird rocky glen, destitute of vegetation, appeared as the habitation of witches, hobgoblins, ghosts and devils to the Texans passing through it in the night to join the 4th and 5th Texas, whom they found at the western base of Round Top, one-quarter of a mile distant.

During the afternoon of 3 July, Colonel Work ordered Major Bass with the 1st Texas to intercept some Federal cavalry that were making their way to the rear. In the encounter General Farnsworth was wounded by Armand Taylor of the 1st Texas Cavalry. After being wounded, General Farnsworth killed himself with his own pistol. The cavalry was put to flight and the baggage train of General Lee's Army was saved by the bravery of the 1st Texas under Major Bass.

Having narrated how the brave Texans under the heroic Work charged through the open field and fearlessly ascended the rugged heights of Little Round Top, the mountain in front of them spouting destructive fire from batteries on its summit like the dreadful volcano, we rejoice and are proud to relate how the 4th Texas, under the intrepid Colonel B. F. Carter, that eventful charge, diverging to the right from the 1st Texas, climbed the monster boulders and waded through the bloody chasms of Devil's Den, every inch of ground being stained with the best blood of Texas' noblest sons, and their joining the 5th Texas, hand in hand, shoulder to shoulder made the most daring, reckless and bravest assaults ever yet chronicled in prose or verse, driving the enemy to the crest of the mountain, killing two generals, many subordinate officers and privates.

William H. Martin, an honored son of Texas, who was a captain in the 4th Texas, in answer to a letter writes:

Most of the thrilling scenes of this battle have passed from my memory. When General Longstreet ordered the charge he galloped his horse in our front, leading the Fourth Texas.

Hon. John M. Pinckney of Homestead, in answer to our request for his experience at Gettysburg says:

I was a mere boy when I fought that battle under the colors of the Fourth Texas. I remembered the regiment charged over a plain through Devil's Den to a mountain covered with large rocks 400 or 500 yards away. Here we charged and recharged, every one striving to get to the summit.

The heroic Ed Francis, with measured step, like Mars himself, fearlessly upholding the Lone Star banner, 'by angels hands to valor given,' tattered and torn by balls and shell and sealed with the crimson blood of the brave Colonel Warwick, inscribed the name of Texas in imperishable characters on the escutcheon of fame.

Mr Val C. Giles of Austin thinks Colonel Carter was wounded after passing Plum Run, the ravine at the foot of mountain, where the fighting was very severe. He remembered seeing him before he crossed the ravine and recollects a courier riding up to Major Rogers who, having a shrill voice said to the courier: 'Present my compliments to General Law and ask him if he expects me to hold the world in check with the Fifth Texas.'

Dr J. C. Loggins of Ennis, Texas, was captured in this battle about one-half way up Great Round Top. He was taken further up the mountain side, where he saw Colonel Powell a wounded prisoner, the Federals supposing him to be General Longstreet. He says it was a severe ordeal charging through the Devil's Den, that rocky tabernacle of unsepulchered heroes, and that Colonel J. C. G. Keys was wounded in that disastrous place, where the precious blood of Texas sons stained every boulder.

Having spoken of the journey of the 1st Texas over chasm and boulder and the precipice to the formidable summit of Little Round Top, of the 4th Texas' trying ordeal through that calamitous Devil's Den, where death held high carnival, where huge destruction shook the earth beneath with its giant strides and with flaming sword felled with pitiless force the heroes from the Texan land, we will describe those memorable charges of the 5th Texas at the slaughter pen in the gorge of the mountain. We will use Colonel Powell's language:

After crossing the pike we came to a small meadow, where we were greeted with a volley of grapeshot, which did but little damage. Then, hurrying on the to the foot of the Great Round Top, thence to the gorge of the two mountains, we met the Fourteenth United States regulars, whom we soon demolished. We then moved up the side of the mountain to a level plain, which reached across the slaughter pen, where I could see the enemy hurrying up, getting into line. Wishing to secure a position on the opposite side of the gorge I appealed to Law's brigade to support my right and give me protection in the flank. The Fifth Texas boldly rushed to the struggle, but Law's brigade made no effort to protect my flank, and for the first time in its history the Fifth Texas recoiled in the slaughter pen and yielded the field. Here the stubborn and aggressive Lieutenant-Colonel King Bryan was wounded and the gallant Rogers permanently disabled. The valiant Cleveland, whose voice was like a thunder in the roar of battle, called out: 'Fifty dollars to the first man who crosses the work at Round Top!' Sergeant Ross sprang forward when Cleveland spoke: 'Come back to your place Sergeant Ross; color file not included!' I have always thought the Fourth Texas had the brunt of battle at the Devil's Den and the Fifth Texas the tough end at the slaughter pen.

After being wounded and captured I was carried further up the mountain and laid beside Lieutenant White of the 2nd Minnesota, who was severely wounded with two bayonet wounds. [1] During our stay together on that ever memorable night of suffering, grief and misery, Lieutenant White, who was the bitterest foe I ever met, said to me: 'If the charge had been made two hours sooner it would have been a complete victory for the Southerners.' He informed me that a Texas soldier made three efforts to get his colors, and in the last encounter he killed him. The flagstaff was lost, but the lieutenant still held in his clinched hand where he lay wounded the treasured flag of the 2nd Minnesota. He praised the Texans and said they were the best marksmen in the army. Every bullet from the Texans did its execution. When five pieces from the artillery were rushed to the front all the horses were killed, and out of the regiment of 247 men of the 2nd Minnesota 200 were wounded and slain. On the mountain side, facing this death carnival, while the bright stars shining in the firmament were weeping bitter tears over this ghastly sight and the winds were moaning for this agonizing scene, the two warriors of the blue and gray lay side by side, so horribly mutilated that their attendants supposed they must die. Colonel Powell and Lieutenant White spent most of that lonely and dismal night together on that gloomy mountain slope, consoling each other in their painful sufferings; beneath them the bloody chasm, the slaughter pen, the crimson trench of destruction, this valley of death, where the grass has ceased to grow and the flowers refuse to bloom, there the sunburnt veteran from the verdure clad steppes of the Brazos and the pale faced boy from the frozen lakes of Minnesota make one common funeral pile.

Judge J. W. Stevens of Hillsboro, who was captured when Colonel Powell's flank was unprotected, says that the enemy came up the gorge in his rear, and while he was in the act of firing a lieutenant seized his musket, ordering him to quit shooting and surrender.

Col. Campbell Wood of San Saba County, who was adjutant of the 5th Texas in this battle, gives some history of the battle. He says that after passing through Devil's Den and crossing the creek at the foot of Great Round Top the 5th Texas struck a bluff that they could not climb. Behind this bluff under cover of a stone fence the infantry of the enemy were stationed. Here the Texans met with a severe repulse and the mortality was very great.

Colonel Wood thinks Colonel Carter was mortally wounded at this bluff. Colonel Wood writes that he saw Colonel C. M. Winkler several times in command of the 4th Texas. Once he called his attention to the crimson stain of blood on his pants. The colonel was so enthused in his deeds of glory as to be unaware that he was wounded in the fleshy part of the thigh.

After a terrible ordeal, the 5th Texas reformed and fell back twice, making three charges in all in the slaughter pen. The last two charges were made without any order from a commander, the soldiers all, or someone, saying, 'Let us charge them again.'

Colonel Wood relates that in this last charge on the side of the mountain he was wounded in the foot; that Judge J. M. Slither, W. B. Campbell, and J. M. Green assisted him to mount General Law's wounded mare, which he rode down the mountain side to Dr W. P. Powell's field hospital, where the mare fell. From thence he was conveyed by William A. George to the division hospital, where his foot was attended by Dr Robert Breckinridge, the division surgeon.

Captain W. T. Hill of Maynard, who was severely wounded in this last charge, says he saw Major Jeff Rogers waving his sword over his head, bravely leading the men to the battle, and Boss Campbell being exposed to enemy fire refused to take shelter behind a rock when ordered by his commanding officer.

General Law, in his article in the *Century*, speaks of the gallantry of Sergeant Barbee, who climbed one of the huge boulders in Devil's Den and recklessly fought until he fell severely wounded.

L. A. Daffan, being a private in the 4th Texas, climbed and re-climbed those immense rocks in Devil's Den, followed the flag of the 4th Texas on the side of Little Round Top, through the slaughter pen and saw it wave on the crest of Great Round Top, where the gallantry of Texas festooned the mountain with garlands of unfading glory.

In his last charge on Great Round Top, R. H. Skinner, now living in Corsicana, was shot through the lungs, and Lieutenant Joseph Love mortally wounded.

W. D. Pritchard of Crockett, Texas, who is justly proud of his record as a member of Hood's Brigade, writes that he was sick when this great battle was fought, but his neighbors, Colonel A. A. Aldrick and A. D. Oliphant, claim the distinction of having been engaged in that battle. Captain Joe Polley, who his comrades say, was like the rest of Hood's Brigade, who were to Lee as the 10th Legion to Caesar, tells us that Jack Southerland fought bravely through all that battle with the Texans, where their valor shed a halo of glory around the name of Texas which will shine when the works of art that deck that battlefield have faded.

When the future historian writes the history of this battle; when the mother at the fireside relates to her children how her ancestors fought under the stars and bars at Gettysburg; when the poet, enthused with the fire of inspiration, writes his stanzas for future generations; when the orator of the second day of July, every year for centuries, arouses his audiences with frenzied enthusiasm of what transpired at that battle they each must tell of our heroic Texans. How the plume-crested warrior Work, fearless of death with the 1st Texas, stormed the cannon crowned heights of Little Round Top, directly in front of him, capturing and retaining the only battery taken by the Confederates during the battle.

Posterity must be told how the 4th Texas under the brave and lamented Colonel B. F. Carter, charged and recharged over hill and large boulders, through chasms, cleft rock and thorny bushes in Devil's Den, where the death dealing bullet of a determined and patriotic foe on their own soil resisted every foot of ground; how the 4th Texas unheeding the demon death in the shape of a bullet, shell and grape, went to the base of Little Round Top, where Colonel Carter fell, driving the enemy before them like chaff before the whirlwind, killing Generals Zook, Vincent and Weed, Colonel Cross and Captain Hazlett, then going up the gorge of the mountain and assisting the 5th Texas in the three most desperate charges in all history.

The orator, the poet, the historian, must tell how Colonel Powell, obeying General Hood's instructions saw the banner of the 5th Texas, borne by the gallant Fitzgerald and stained with the life blood of the fearless Upton, go direct to Great Round Top, penetrate the gorge, drive the enemy from the side of the mountain and fight through the slaughter pen up the side of Great Round Top, where the blood of our brave Texans flowed in rivulets down the mountain side; where every Texan was a hero; where their gallantry erected an indestructible cenotaph to their memory; where the rising sun ever smiles in ecstasy over their renowned deeds; where the pale moon is in her midnight wanderings sheds a halo of glory over the hallowed spot; where the night wind mourns their sad requiem among the rocks where they fought; where their glorious actions have made a page in history imperishable as the granite beneath their crumbling bones, as lasting as the coming and going of the rainbow, or the roaring billows of their sea girt home.[2]

Dr John O. Scott
Battle Flags of Hood's Texas Brigade

To attempt to narrate all the heroic acts, which gave the Texans immortal fame, is a task endless as counting the glittering stars that stud the diadem of night, arduous as climbing the dizzy heights of the snow-clad alps.

To tell in worthy language of the patriotic and noble women who gave the flags to the Texans, the brave acts, daring and reckless exploits, noble deeds and dying words of those who fell defending them, is a task beyond the capacity of mortal man. We, in our humble nature will try, that some of the names of the deathless dead, and their patriotic acts may be known to the present and coming people.

In the year 1861, two young ladies and their mother made the long and arduous journey from their home in Marshal, Tex., to join their father in Virginia, who was the commander of the 1st Texas Regiment. The memory of the mother, Mrs Wigfall, and the young ladies, Misses Louise and Fannie Wigfall, is as dear to the Texans, as their father was admired by them for his eloquence and loved for his many virtues.

The first flag that graced the ranks of the 1st Texas Regiment was the handiwork of Mrs Wigfall. Her daughter, Mrs Louise Wigfall Wright, informs us that the large white star on that flag was the special work and pride of her mother. This beautiful silken sheet, striped with the blue, the white, and the red, was presented to the regiment at the fairgrounds, Richmond, Va., in 1861, when the dread toesin of war sounded from Red River to the Rio Grande, when the clarion notes of the bugle called to arms the 'rose and fair expectancy' of the state, the first offering of the Texan land.

On this memorable occasion, Jefferson Davis made the presentation speech in which it was related that he said, 'We have seen the Texans in battle and know that one Texan is equal to ten ordinary men.'

This flaming signal of battle, renowned in dreadful war and reverenced in serene peace, was accepted from the distinguished president of the Confederacy by Louis T. Wigfall, colonel of the 1st Texas, in behalf of the regiment, with the ever-to-be remembered words, 'I will lead them where the battle's wreck lies the thickest and death's brief pang is quickest.'

For conspicuous gallantry at Eltham's Landing, George Branard was appointed color bearer. At Gaines's Mill, Branard was with his regiment when it stormed the heights of Powhite Creek. The regiment was compelled to reach the battery on the summit of the fort.

Branard dexterously threw his flag over the abatis, and then crawled under and through the works, a shout that almost split the welkin greeted the color bearer, as he with a few others was seen standing on the summit of the works with the silken banner decked with the lone white star floating over them. This precious offering from queenly hands, was bravely borne by its color bearer, Branard, at Seven Pines, Malvern Hill, Freemans Ford, Through Fare Gap, Second Manassas, and Boonsborough Gap.

During the journey to Sharpsburg, Branard was bare-footed. His feet becoming sore, he was ordered to the hospital by Major Dale, when the Lone Star Flag was committed to the care of another.

At Sharpsburg much heroism was displayed by the Texan Brigade, 'whose achievements,' say Hood, 'have never been surpassed in the history of nations.' Jackson complimented them 'for their almost matchless display of daring and desperate valor.' Lee has written that 'the Texans fought grandly and bravely and the contest in the corn field and lane was the hottest ever witnessed on any battlefield.'

In that ever-to-be remembered corn field, being overwhelmed by numbers, the 1st Texas to their great sorrow lost their flag. When the 'fallen banner' was discovered by the enemy, eight dead and six wounded Texans were found around and over it. One of them was immortalized in death with this beloved standard of the Texans wrapped around his lifeless body as his winding-sheet.

Someday the people of this grand Lone Star empire state in gratitude for their heroism will erect a monument to their memory. Let the granite from the laughing waters of the Llano be its pedestal and the marble glistening with the spray of the Colorado be its shaft. May dew-eyed pity engrave on its crowning stone, 'Here lie embalmed in everlasting glory the bodies of eight Texans who met death with the Lone Star flag in their hands.'

With reverence and holy love for the memory of the heroes, we commit to the youth of Texas the sacred names of those who fell crowned with glory under the shadow of that Lone Star flag, which is now in Washington City—Major Matt Dale, Lt James C. S. Thompson, Sgt. A. A. Congleton, Sgt. Stephen Carpenter, Sgt. J. C. Hollingsworth, Wm. Hollingsworth, Jacob Frank, William Zimmer, killed; John Hanson, William Leach, Peter Gillis, Chas. Kingsley, Joseph Ashbrook, Austin Jones, wounded.

On the tattered silk can yet be deciphered the words, Malvern Hill, Ganies' Mill, Seven Pines, and Etham's Landing. Blood stains are still visible. The bullet-holes and shell rents show that it went through the hurricane of battle 'where thick and heavy was the work of death.'

After the battle, far in advance of any one, the dead body of Lt R. H. Gaston was found by the foe. In acknowledgement of his heroism, he was accorded an honorable burial by them with a head mark over his grave extolling his conspicuous gallantry; 'Tears and love for the gray.'

In the cornfields lie the crumbling bones of Texas' beloved heroes, Captain Cotton, Lieutenants Hoffman, Perry, Runnels, Waterhouse, Sandford, Drake, A. H. Baker, color bearer of the 5th, and many others whose names, like shining stars on the milky baldrie of the skies, glitter with perennial glory; whose heroic deeds the cherubim and the seraphim chant to rhythmic lays in angelic choirs; whose renowned exploits are carved on a monumental shaft made of the ruby, the emerald, and the sapphire.

After the battle of Sharpsburg another silk flag was presented to the 1st Texas regiment. It was a Lone Star flag like the one lost at Sharpsburg. We are informed by one of the color guard, Capt. Dave Bronaugh, that it was given to the regiment by Mrs Davis, Wigfall and Mckeen and was craped in mourning for the heroic dead of the brigade who fell at Sharpsburg.

Would that we were gifted with genius to speak in language adequate to the heroism of the Texans at Gettysburg who followed the flaunting folds of that gay banner, studded with a large white star of the morning. It was the star of Texas. It was the star of glory. It was the star of victory.

A little before the commencement of the battle, Gen. Hood, the idol of the Texans, with the beloved Robertson by his side, rode in front of the 1st Texas Regiment. After making them a short speech, he arose majestically in his stirrups to the full height of his manhood, like Mars himself, and in a loud stentorian voice, which is still ringing in the ears of his invincible soldiery, gave the order, 'Fix bayonets, my brave Texans; forward and take those heights.'

Col. P. A. Work, commanding the 1st Texas, as heroic as Napoleon at the bridge of Lodi, pointing to Little Round Top in the distance, bristling with a huge ordinance of war, gave the order to his brave comrades: 'Follow the Lone Star flag to the top of the mountain.' On right on, death's danger braving, through showers of shell, canister and grape, that Texas flag, that Lone Star banner in the hands of George Branard, without waver or halt, steadily advanced to the mountain top, supported by the Texans, who encircled among the nations of the earth with a halo of immortal fame—the name of Texas.

After one-third of the Texans had been killed or wounded, the enemy driven and their battery captured, George A. Branard, the brave and daring color-bearer of the 1st Texas Regiment, hoisted on the topmost summit the streaming banner of the victorious Texans. He held the post of glory and honor, like Jasper at Moultrie, until he fell almost dead from a shell wound on the head. As he lay by his flag his color guard, James

Willis Watts, James Williams, Elias Newsome, and David Bronaugh, were by his side to preserve the unblemished honor of the sacred colors and hoist them afresh, high up in the bright firmament above the mountain top, that friend and foe from a distance could see the lone star standard of our Texans shining with the effulgence of heavenly glory.

The 4th Texas flag was a gift to the regiment by Miss Louise Wigfall, now Mrs Wright of Baltimore, president of the Daughters of the Confederacy for Maryland. This historic piece of faded silk, mutilated by ball and shell in dreadful battle, years ago came into the possession of a brave soldier, gifted scholar and honorable gentleman, Val C. Giles of Austin, who with watchful care has preserved it to the present hour.

Gen. Hood, who was at that time colonel of the regiment, received the adored colors from the hands of Miss Louise Wigfall. Upon the spearhead of this precious treasure was printed in gilded letters, 'Fear not, for I am with thee.'

Chaplain Davis writes that when he saw the flag on review the last time, 8 October 1862, after the Battle of Sharpsburg, nine ensigns had fallen under it on the field of battle. It had the scars of sixty-five balls and some shell marks.

This historic silken standard of the Texans was borne in triumph through the battles of Eltham's Landing, Seven Pines, Gaines's Farm, Freeman's Ford, Second Manassas, Boonsbrough Gap and Sharpsburg. On the 8th of October, 1862, this tattered, and mute witness of the heroism of the Texans was committed to the care of Captain Stephen H. Darden by the commander of the regiment Col. Ben H. Carter, to be taken to Austin, Tex., to be delivered to Gov. Frank Lubbock. In a letter to the governor Col. Carter writes the following words, which are a lasting memorial to the exalted character of that heroic Texan:

> More than 500 of our command have fallen beneath its folds; an emblem of gallant and dauntless courage in the storm of battle, let it be preserved sacredly that the remnant of our little band may in future days gaze upon its blood-stained colors, recall to mind the suffering they endured in their country's cause, and their children be incited to renewed vigilance in the preservation of those liberties for which we contended.

There are many dead heroes connected with the history of that silken pennon of the 4th Texas that make it sublime—subject for the post, the sculptor, the painter, and full of interest to those who love the recital of noble acts and the chivalric deeds of patriots, in the defense of the honor liberty of their country.

Lt Col. Bradfute Warwick, Col. Ben F. Carter, Edward M. Francis, the color bearer, and other brave officers and many privates, 'the untitled heroes of the war,' for individual acts of heroism deserve more than a passing mention from the pen of the historian.

We are informed by the soldiers of the regiment that at Gaines's Mill, or farm, Gen. Hood led the 4th Texas after the brave Col. John Marshall fell at the head of his regiment, crowned with glory.

We are informed that Ed. Francis was at his side with the flag of 'the red field and the blue starry cross' which he, like Wolfe at Quebec, waved in glorious ecstasy on the battlements of the fort when victory crowned the supreme heroism of the Texans.

We are informed that some other regiment, as they fell back, repulsed under the destructive fire of the enemy's batteries, lost their battle flag. In the desperate charge of the Texans, Col. Warwick being among the foremost, picked up the lost bunting of the stars and bars and hoisted it in gleeful triumph on the captured guns of the retreating foe. Amidst the deafening shouts the conquering legions, in the joyful moment of success, with the flag in his grasp, bleeding from a death hound, like Dessiax in the supreme hour of victory at Marengo, he nobly fell to earth shrouded in glory's pall. At the Battle of Second Manassas, after Ed. Francis was wounded, Col. William H. Sellers of Hood's staff, one of Texas' beloved heroes, with the Louise Wigfall flag of the 4th Texas in his hands, the words emblazoned on it, 'Fear not, for I am with thee,' shining like glittering diamonds on the diadem of eternity, side by side with Col. Carter, Townsend, Martin, Winkler, Hunter, Darden, Barziza, Bassett, Bilingsly and other brave Texans, hoisted that victorious banner over a United States battery, like the Spartan band at Thermopylae, none were left to tell the tale of the heroism of their comrades.

The lieutenant commanding, bleeding from many wounds, fired the last shot. The Texans, admiring his heroic action, withheld their fire until he attempted again to crawl up to a cannon to make one more desperate effort in the work of death.

Col. Carter sent the body of the brave federal artillery officer with sword, watch and pocket book inside the federal lines under a flag of truce—'Love and tears for the blue.' For this act of courtesy to a brave and fallen foe Col. Carter was soothed in his dying hours by the dead officer's brother after he was captured at Gettysburg.

This battle, planned by Lee under the strategic eye of Stonewall Jackson, was a grand victory for the Confederacy. Hood obeyed Longstreet's order like Marshall Ney at Friedland. When all seemed lost he was there in time with his Texans to rush headlong like a thunderbolt and break the enemy's center. It was a dear bought victory to the Texans, for it scattered the weeds of mourning all over the state for the loss of its first born. Clustered around the blood-stained body of the heroic Upton, 'where the bravest love to die,' rest crowned with the palm of victory, in the arms of death, on this 'fame's eternal camping ground,' the brave Thomas, Fawcett, Herndon, Johnson, Dean, Martin and hundreds of others, whose names, wreathed around in glory, all Texans hold sacred.

Here the gally attired zouave from the heights of the Hudson and the blue-trousered veteran of New England, lay cold in the embrace of death beside the gray-clad Texan from the verdure-clad fields of the Brazos or the flowery steppes of the Colorado.

On this field of fame, renowned in song and story for all time to come, beneath the laurel ever rejoicing to deck the victor's brow, the blushing wild rose with the morning's dew glistening on its fragrant petals, blooming over their almost hidden graves, whispers to the passer-by, 'Forget me not, forget me not.' When this, tattered ball-rant silken memorial of the glorious deeds of the Texan girl was sent home, Colonel Carter had written that 'our general,' meaning Hood, 'gave us another flag.'

Later on at Gettysburg this new ensign of liberty waved over brave men performing deeds of valor unparalleled in the history of the world. Edward M. Francis, with martial step advancing 'on, on, no fear, no halt,' carried that blue-crossed bunting of the 4th Texas—that new device of chivalry, lit with its dazzling stars from glory's land-in the dreadful storm of battle through sheets of fire and rain of shot and shell in Devil's Den, to the iron mantled heights of Great Round Top, where the laurel-wreathed name of Texas is carved in imperishable letters on the granite rock of the mountain; where the glory of our dead heroes is painted in unfading grandeur on the escutcheon of fame; where the morning stars with heavenly music chant their last reveille and the winds of the evening sing their requiem; where the skies above are grandly and gorgeously decked with panoramic scenes of deeds of unparalleled heroism of those who fought under the stars and bars, the idol emblem of the Southland.

Here in this furious tornado of battle, where death held high carnival and huge destruction with giant strides shook the earth beneath, and all creation trembled for the work of the demon war, in sight of the star-crossed emblem of liberty, glory, patriotism, and honor, which Hood, his famous general, had given him, Colonel Ben F. Carter at the head of his column 'on to death and glory dashing,' like the torn and mangled Marshal Lannes at Lobau was hurdled in 'the crimson trench of death, no more to rise in arms or shine in war again.'

Ed Francis, with his blue and crimson star-glittering standard, which had been the guide of renowned warriors to victory in the awful shock of battle, was reserved by the hand of providence for a fate not less glorious. On Sunday, 20 September, at Chickamauga, when our Texans were victorious and driving the enemy at Snodgrass Hill, Edward M. Francis ran ahead of the regiment out of sight among the trees. On that 'field of death and slaughter,' followed by his faithful guard, he proudly unfurled his radiant colors by the rail breastworks, crying in a loud voice so as to be heard by friend and foe, 'Rally, Texans, Rally.' His last words were 'Here I die.' Amid perils, dread, appalling, encircled with a halo of dazzling glory he sunk to the ground, enshrouded with the bloodstained banner of the 'brave Texans,' as Lee called them.

After Francis was killed two other ensigns, William Daugherty and John Barry, shining with glory like the ethereal seraphim on the walls of paradise, were stricken down by his side while grasping 'the star-flowery banner' of the Texans, streaming with dazzling blaze of glory. A fourth ensign, Fred Makeig, from the bleeding bodies of the dying heroes, raised the weeping colors, rejoicing in glorious triumph, until the Texans, like a hurricane blast, 'came dashing on to on to victory or death.'

The flag of the 5th Texas has so many acts of brave men connected with them that we with great diffidence in this address speak of them. We feel the need of utterance sufficient to describe all the acts of gallantry, the daring reckless bravery, the supreme courage, exhibited under these silken banners which the fair ones of Texas gave to our heroes.

The first standard that floated over these Texans, every one of them whom was a gentleman, scholar and natural born soldier was presented to the regiment by Miss Fannie Wigfall, now Mrs Taylor of Maryland. Col. Archer made the speech of acceptance, denominating it as the fled of 'the red field and blue starry cross,' which poetic description of the flag we love so well, the fallen banner of the Southland, with his name shrouded in chivalry, glory and honor, will ring across the centuries, sung with rhythmic lays, read in romance and spoken in outbursts of thrilling eloquence.

This blazing device of freedom in the hands of its custodian, George Onderdonk, waved in triumph over the heights of Gaines's Farm until, all gashed and scarred with bloody wounds, he transferred the blessed banner to another of the brave Texans, as they were styled by Lee and his entire army. This silken standard, lit with glittering stars on the azure blue, was the Texans' guiding star to grand achievements at Eltham's Landing and the Seven Pines. The whereabouts of this emblem of love, chivalry and liberty so dear to the Texans, after many months of search, we are unable to tell. Perhaps it may be a chained captive in some prison vault, or pet idol by some comrade, or trophy of its captor, and like the long lost ship it may return to its moorings after the storm has passed, or, like the wandering child of doting parents, it may someday come back to the caressing arms of its mother, the State of Texas.

There is another flag of the 5th Texas draped in mourning, for the brave Upton, Color bearer Onderdonk and eight other heroes who perished under its crimson folds. It is a Lone Star flag, one that was reviewed by Longstreet and Hood after the Sharpsburg fight, 8 October 1862.

Chaplain Davis, in the history of the brigade has written:

> From the manly step of its ensign, Fitzgerald, one could see he was proud of his colors, pierced with ninety-eight balls, three canister shot and a piece of shell, passing through fire and blood and craped with the glorious memory of nine ensigns.

This flag was made under the direction of the officers of the regiment, all of whom with the privates wished to go to battle under a Lone Star flag, which was contrary to the order of Generals Longstreet and Hood.

Adjutant Campbell Wood and Captain John Smith Cleveland by a little diplomacy succeeded in having the flag carried by the regiment in the Second Battle of Manassas, where it won so much distinction.

At this battle the Texans came up to Jackson's relief at double quick. The famous Fifth New York Zouaves were opposing the 5th Texas. While thy in battle array were in front of the fearless Zouaves making ready for the onset, Captain John Smith Cleveland grandly standing out in front of the regiment, like the towering Ajax, pointing to the beautiful Lone Star flag waving majestically over the Texans, said, 'Cling to it boys, as you would to your sweethearts.'

At one time when the fate of the battle was wavering, the color bearer, Onderdonk, being wounded and eight other color guards shot down with the flag in their hands, the gallant Upton, reckless of his life, seized the flag with his left hand, and with his drawn saber in his right exclaimed in a loud voice, 'Come on, boys, follow me.' With Bryan, Farmer, Roberdeau, McBride, Hill, Baber, Cleveland, Turner and many others by his side, he led the regiment to glory and victory. When the 5th New York Zouaves were about to be demolished, 243 killed on the spot, and victory was certain, the brave Upton, the hero of this battle, with this flag in his hand, pierced with a shot over his right eye, fell lifeless from his horse in the arms of his brave Adjutant, Campbell Wood.

Hunt Terrell, J. S. Miller, Leroy Mitchell were among the color guard who fell. When one of the color guard, J. K. P. Harris, a boy fifteen years old, was wounded, his expiring words were, 'I am shot through but I shall carry this flag until I die.' Another ball from the enemy made his name and dying words 'go sounding down the ages' imperishable on the scroll of fame. 8 October 1862, Col. J. B. Robertson sent this same Lone Star flag home to F. R. Lubbock, Governor of Texas, with a letter from which we quote the following words from that great and good man:

In sending this flag to your Excellency, in addition to the evidence it bears, I will be excused for adding my testimony to the gallantry, bravery and chivalrous bearing of the regiment over which this flag has floated in the sanguinary Battle of Virginia.

In the name and in behalf of the 5th regiment I send this flag to you to be deposited in the archives of the State with the hope that as the sight of it amidst the battle's furious storm has cheered and nerved us to bear it on to victory, so a view of it may nerve those who come after us to sustain with the same unfaltering devotion to liberty it symbolizes.

Thou Lone Star flag, the pride and glory of the Texans, emblem of liberty to the oppressed, an asylum to the exile and comfort to the homeless; bright star planted on the azure blue beside the white and the red symbols of purity and love, in smiling peace, in bloody war, be ever first thou star.

Thou Lone Star flag, thou wert the sacred device of Houston, Travis, Fannin, Crockett, Sidney, Sherman, Johnston, Hood and a host of others in horrid battle and glorious death. Blessed flag of the 5th Texas, we leave thee now to the keeping of thy patriotic custodian, William H. George whom Hood has declared to be the rightful owner.

A gifted and lovely lady of Houston, Mrs Maud J. Young, presented the 5th Texans a beautiful silk flag. At that great and grand Battle of Gettysburg it had the honor to be designated by General Hood in his order to Colonel Powell as the flag to lead the Texans to the Round Tops, which loomed up in the distance in magnificent grandeur, 'standing in serried rugged defiance, great round top with little round top leaning against it.'

In this battle the gallant Fitzgerald was the hero who bore that silken banner, dear to all Texans, which should be sacredly preserved as it was the guiding star that lit the pathway of the 5th Texas to the slaughter pen between the mountains, where every Texans was a hero, where the gallantry of the Texans encircled the mountains with festoons of unfading renown, where Colonel Powell at the lead with the Texans, like Jeff Davis at Buena Vista, made those three desperate charges where the bones of one-third of the brave Texans lie embalmed in glory. Where the mountain dells still echo the words of the private soldier from the bleeding ranks of the Texans, 'Let us charge them again.' At Chickamauga this same Mrs Young flag smiling with delight over the renowned deeds of the Texans was seen flaunting in the breeze like a thing of triumphant joy, when Hood with his Texans like Napoleon with the old guard at Austerlitz, broke the center, and the shouts of the Texans rent the welkin with huzzas of victory.

With bleeding wounds, the dauntless color bearer, William Hobson Clark, hoisted the ball-rent silk on the ramparts of the fleeing foe. At the terrible and destructive Battle of the Wilderness where the pale flag of death and despair waved from every pine tree, this blazing torch of liberty, this fiery beacon to the field of immortal fame, this loved banner of the Texans, saluted the skies and decorated their inner vaults with triumphant glory.

After an all night's march, as the rising sun crimsoned the eastern skies with rosy hues, with flying banners and the soul-stirring music of the 'Bonny Blue Flag,' the Texans under General Gregg, all jubilant and ready for battle, were met by General Lee with the words, 'My brave Texans, I know you can and will drive these people back; I can always depend on you in tight places; follow me, I will lead you.'

Then it was that Martin, Harding, Watts, Mahle, Randall and others surrounding him, declared that the flags of the Texans knew not defeat; that they had never been hurled to the dust except to rise again; that if the enemy were not defeated like the 188 of the Alamo, there would be none of them left to tell the story of death; that war is our business, fighting our pastime, death or victory our battle-cry, the crown of laurel the gift to the victor, our guerdon, our glory; that if he would go back they would drive the enemy. 'General Lee to the rear,' was the shout of the entire troop of Texans. Clark, the color bearer of the 5th Texas, was seriously wounded and many ensigns were wafted to glory with the radiant colors of the 5th Texas.

The color bearer of the 4th Texas, Lane Wilson, and Ensign Brown and Durfee met glory and death with garlands of victory and eternal renown under the blue cross of St. Andrew's glittering with radiant stars. The Texans did what they promised; fighting through fire and blood, they halted the exultant victors and drove them into their works, thus saving Lee's Army from defeat. When Lee saw the blood-stained banners of the brave Texans, 'decked in sad triumph for one-half of their number lying prostrate among the pines,' then it was that Capt. W. E. Barry lying wounded from many wounds, near a battery, heard Lee say: 'It is all sunshine now; the brave Texans have repulsed the enemy and cut them in two.'[3]

Hood's Brigade
A Grand Gathering of Confederate Veterans, The Annual Reunion of Hood's Brigade

Honorable J. D. Sayers, Congressman, also made an address, which contained an ably drawn outline of the history of the brigade during the war and the battles in which it took part, dwelling particularly on the Battle of Gaines's Mills, where the Texans were the first to break McClellan's lines. He drew a vivid picture of the charge of the brigade on Seminary Ridge, at the great Battle of Gettysburg, and closed by saying the command, though its cause was lost, had won a title of imperishable renown.

Mr Martin, during his speech, held up to gaze of the vast audience a red cap which, he said, had been captured at the Battle of Manassas.[4] But the hearts of the veterans beat high, and the multitude who listened under the shades of the trees held their breath and looked on in amazement as the tall speaker bent down a moment, then raising himself to full height held out in his hand and displayed the gray coat of a Confederate general. It was stained with time, but the insignia, the well-known insignia was there. It was the coat worn by General Hood at the Battle of Gettysburg. At this moment a yell, the famous old rebel yell, clear and keen as of yore, went up while tears stood in the eyes of many of the brave men who were with Hood in the fearful charge at Seminary Ridge.

Colonel William Preston Johnston
Speech of Col. Johnston

At the late banquet, given by the Texas boys at Washington and Lee University, to which we alluded to in our last: The Confederate Dead. Col. Wm. Preston Johnston responded: But I am warned by the presence here of many invited guests that this is no place for personal reminiscence or state pride, that we are assembled as brethren of a sacred cause, and although no state can answer more nobly than Texas at the roll call of the Confederate dead, yet it is from no narrow standpoint we must look, as we lift the veil that shrouds our holiest and tenderest griefs.

Permit me to add some verses called forth by the threat to plough up the graves of Confederates buried at Gettysburg. Since I wrote these lines, the kind ladies of Richmond have been removing the bodies of our soldiers from Gettysburg to Hollywood. They have been diligent in all good works, for they have loved much:

> *They call to the Southrons from the North,*
> *'Come, take your dead away,*
> *Or we'll plough up the sod*
> *And break the clod*
> *That covers the rebel clay.'*
> *The loyal hands that carried the flag,*
> *The men who wore the blue,*
> *On whatever of earth*
> *They had their birth,*
> *They continued good and true.*
> *They raise for their own the sodded graves,*
> *And range them row by row;*
> *And the billowy grounds*
> *Lift up in mounds—*
> *The furrows of death and woe.*

And hireling gangs contract for the job,
Paid from the public purse;
And they pillage the grave
Of rebel or slave,
With laughter and ribald curse;
They toss the bones of the gallant dead
With mattock, pick, and spade;
And the coffins they fill
With what they will.
What matters it? They are paid!
Our dead died too for the dear-loved land,
Whose soil had given them birth,
And wherever they fell
It served them well—
A handful of mother earth.
No pious hands have lifted the dust
Of men who nobly died,
But they sleep with a sleep
As sweet and deep
As if urned in marble pride.
A voice by the ear of faith is heard,
'My people keep your trust,
And behold with your eyes,
Beyond the skies
That your heroes are not dust.'
Their home is with those who fought for truth,
For God, for fatherland;
With the blessed they dwell,
And not where swell
These battle-scarred mounds of sand.
They live on the lips of Seraphim
And on the tongues of man;
In the unheeded grave
Or 'neath the wave
Their glory will bloom again.
Then, tender mother! Weep not your boy,
Though no stone record his name;
In brave hearts he will dwell
When minstrels tell
His story of deathless fame.

(Col. Johnston was interrupted by frequent applause).

At the conclusion of Col. Johnston's speech Mr Fisher said, 'Rise and drink to the memory of the illustrious father of the noble son, who has paid so just a tribute to the memory of "Our Confederate Dead."'

Lexington, Va. Gazette[5]

Mrs C. M. Winker

At Gettysburg, General Hood was ordered to attack up the Emmettsburg road, the enemy being entrenched upon Round Top Mountain. Sending out his scouts, he ascertained what a fearful loss of life would be the price, as it was up a steep declivity, over huge boulders of rock, with the Federal cannon sweeping their ranks. Three times he remonstrated, and urged to be allowed instead to turn Round Top Mountain by a flank movement, as his division occupied the extreme left, but the request was refused. He led his men under the heavy fire, and in about twenty minutes was severely wounded in the arm and borne from the field. The assault was unsuccessful, as, although the 1st Texas managed to gain temporary possession of the Federal lines and captured three guns, yet the others were unable to scale the rocky declivity, driven back by grape and canister, and the slight advantage was lost, the troops in advance being compelled to retire.

General Hood always contended if he had been allowed by General Longstreet to use his own judgment, that part of the field would not have been lost. General Hood was now under medical treatment for his wound, which did not, fortunately, necessitate the amputation of his arm.

While still in Richmond under the surgeon's care, Longstreet's Corps passed through the city, on their way to join General Bragg in the west, and although but partially recovered, he determined to follow, with his arm still in a sling. Reaching Ringgold, Georgia, he was ordered to proceed to Reid's Bridge, on the Chickamauga, and assume command of the column advancing against the Federals. There he met his men for the first time since Gettysburg, who gave him a touching welcome.[6]

The Other Texans at Gettysburg

Many soldiers, both Union and Confederate fought at Gettysburg and settled in Texas after the Civil War. Soldiers from Barksdale's Mississippi Brigade described charging through the Peach Orchard during the late afternoon of the second day of battle. Other soldiers fought at various locations during the battle. From the first day of battle to Pickett's Charge these Texans never forgot the three days of the battle.

William A. Abernathy
17th Mississippi Infantry
Drew Our Rations

About noon on the first day of July we drew rations. It was flour and some pretty good beef. We had, somehow or other, got hold of some lard, and for the only time after it became War, we had shortened bread.

I was the cook that day. The dough was made up on a rubber cloth tent and I had another skillet and the lid was hot when 'Long Roll' beat and that meant to march. Skillet, and lid was red hot nearly, but it was no time to dally. It meant a rapid march to the battlefield. I never saw that skillet anymore, but the boys do say that the 18th Mississippi, the thieving Mississippi, 18th Mississippi, got it. You know it was commonly true that they could steal anything in the commissary line from a red hot skillet to cold soup with tallow on it, and when we missed anything all we had to do was to go over to the thieving 18th and get somebody's there. I have tried to get Judge Gerald of Waco, who was a Major of the 18th to return that skillet or its equivalent, but as far as I could get him to commit himself was

'Forward to the Foe!' General William Barksdale leading the Mississippi Brigade at Gettysburg, 2 July 1863. (*Mark Maritato*)

Private William Abernathy. (*John Hoopes*)

something in the nature of a champagne bottle. You know the Judge was a gallant soldier, and I guess I will have to leave it at that.

Just about the time we got our blankets rolled up, haversacks, canteens and cartridge boxes all on and in line, Edward Johnson's Division of Jackson's Old Corps came piling into the road from some place they ought not to have been, and we lay there waiting for them to pass, and when the wagon train, piloted by a dunderhead major who had less sense and more obstinacy than any army mule in Longstreet's corps, filed in ahead of us and delayed us for hours, while we lay there and said soft things about the rations we did not get a chance to coop up, and were delayed from going to the battlefield. When finally the old idiot did get his wagon train out of the way we were set for Gettysburg, 22 miles away. Late at night we passed the battlefield on which the two other Mississippi Brigades had fought and greeted old friends as with rapid steps we hurried by.

A Tribute

About two o'clock we laid down for a short rest. Before day we were up and hurrying without halt until we got within about two hundred yards of General Lee's headquarters, and now, confound you, I will tell you how I know it was Lee's headquarters. You like to have put me in the guardhouse for slipping off up there. The regiment lay there something like two hours when Colonel Johnson of General Lee's staff rode up to direct us where to take position in battle. We followed him on a half trot and half walk until we started to cross a high hill. We were then the leading division of Longstreet's Corps, and we were in front. The head of the column came in sight of the Yankee line and shot from a battery told us they could see. There was an immediate halt, and true to my instincts, I bolted into a Yankee's barn, and got me some flour. We did not stop long before McLaws, commanding the division, and Colonel Johnson came back. McLaws was saying things I would not like to teach my grandson, Dan Thompson, to repeat. The object of the move being to place the Confederate lines on the left flank of Meade's Army.

It was manifest that we would have to turn and go back and follow a ravine which ran parallel with the Federal line, but General Hood, who had been following us in him impetuous way, had lapped over and the two Divisions were considerably mixed, and so McLaw's Division was halted and Hood's Division took the lead. That is how Hood's Division came to be placed in front of Little Round Top and directed to make the attack through Devil's Den. You and I, my dear sir would have faced that problem had the staff officers from General Lee's headquarters had properly advised the location of the ground. But after all, Hood's Division did not go sufficiently far until after the battle opened, but that retrograde of the head of the column placed us in the rear of the two divisions and opposite the peach orchard when the attack was made, and now dear sir, I want to take you to task. You are the historian of Texas. You were along, you played a full man's part in that great battle. You knew we were in front, and you knew that Colonel Johnson of Lee's staff, gave us the order to move, and guided us to the position we were to take in the battle. You knew the terrible march we had made the night before. You knew that we got up before day and hurried until we got to Lee's headquarters, and yet, I have never seen one single word from you in vindication of the greatest leader in the field of battle the Confederates had.

Longstreet deserved better at the hands of a historian of Texas and this is written in spirit of caption. I have seen you on many a battlefield and I never saw you falter. Aye, I heard your call for volunteers from your own regiment of infantry to help man the guns of Moody's artillery. I saw Dundy Gunn and his brother of Company A, Robertson and Mimms of our own company, and others spring from the ground and help to serve the artillery (it was part of Ewell's Corps and its wagon train that delayed us hours on the march. It was Ewell's Corps and Early's Division that failed to occupy Cemetery Heights on the evening of the first, and it was Fitzhugh Lee's Cavalry and Stuart who failed to give Lee warning of the approach of the Federals, and yet, they are the ones who mainly hounded Longstreet for not attacking earlier on the morning of the second. Mindful of these things, I can only wonder that a gallant soldier as you were, you have said nothing in praise of your commander).

Gettysburg Incidents

And now of the incidents of the struggle at Gettysburg. The Confederates had driven Meade's advance back nearly 4 miles and Meade had taken position on Cemetery Heights throwing a part of his command forward so as to include the peach orchard, and running back through the Wheat Field and beyond Little Round Top. His army faced west and this was his left wing. His right extended along the range of hills over Culp's Hill, and back again somewhat in the nature of a bent fishhook, his right wing and his left wing were closer together than other parts of his army something in the order of a bent semicircle. Hood's Division was intended to overlap the southern part of his line at Little Round Top and to swing around like a gate, and the line of battle as he drove them in was to advance. We were lying behind Moody's Battery, just under a little hill, when General

Longstreet and McLaws rode up and gave our Brigadier his instructions, that when Hood's Division had driven them until his line was at an angle or 45 degrees then we were to advance. It was expected that the Confederates' line of battle would be composed of two lines. Wofford's Georgia Brigade was to support the Mississippi Brigade and Sims (Cobbs) Brigade was to support Kershaw South Carolina Brigade. Unfortunately, Hood's Brigade did not go sufficiently far to the right and in place of enveloping the Federal lines on Little Round Top, the Yanks were beyond them and Hood had to move to the right, and that left a space between Hood and Kershaw, and when Kershaw moved so as to keep in touch with Hood, Wofford's Georgia in the front line, and that left us without any support whatever. Hood's Division first advanced, driving the enemy steadily back towards and on Little Round Top to Devil's Den, and climbed up the sides of the mountain. Kershaw's, Sims' and Wofford's brigades all went into and through the Peach Orchard driving the Yankees from Emmitsburg turnpike, and then Meade began to take all the troops from the right wing and hurl them upon the two divisions of Longstreet's Corps.

As these brigades advanced they were compelled to face the advancing Yankees coming from almost every direction. One who goes upon the battlefield will see a line of monuments erected by some grateful northern state to commemorate the valor of its troops. And here the line faced west. Scarcely turning from his tracks he will see another line of monuments erected by another Northern state to commemorate the valor of its troops, and here the line faces another direction, and so again, he will see another line further on facing in another direction. And thus it is that on that field of the Federal line without unexampled activity and earnestness, line after line had been brought from the right wing of Meade's Army to break the attack of the southern warriors. When the attack finally stopped and Ewell first advanced, he found the enemies' great works empty. Ah! But if Ewell had only held Meade's right wing that stern old soldier Longstreet would have swept every vestige of the Federals and beyond the Baltimore turnpike.

Our Part in It

We, too, had our part in this fearful struggle. When the time came we went forward and first encountered a New Jersey Brigade. Two of the regiments were the 26th and 27th New Jersey. The grateful state of New Jersey has erected a line of monuments here to commemorate the valor of her troops. We drove them back through the Peach Orchard, and on to and among a line of Indiana troops. The grateful state of Indiana has erected a line of monuments running through the Peach Orchard to commemorate the valor of her troops. We drove those back and on to the New York Excelsior Brigade, and here, another desperate struggle resulted. Here was a battery of artillery, and around this battery a terrific struggle ensued. Twice we took it, and then on a final charge we ran up over it. The writer of this article, like the fool that he was, sprang on one of the guns and was shot off of it, but we held the battery, and then came another effort to retake it, but without avail.

And then came the order 'Forward with bayonets' and over the Wheat Fields, beyond the Trostle house and u the sloping sides of Cemetery Heights, nearly a mile, away, the old Mississippi Brigade crowded three dense lines, New Jersey, Indiana, and New York troops, upon a line of Wisconsin troops, who had been brought from Culp's Hill far away on the right of the Federal line, and there the Confederate advance was stopped. Barksdale, chivalric soldier as he was, was killed just as he gave the order to halt, but the Brigade held the field. Federal bullets had however played sad havoc. Frank Ross, manager of the circus, was killed in the thickest of the fight with New Jersey, close to the Emmitsburg turnpike. Billie McRaven, a polished, cultivated gentleman, was struck in the breast and died in the thickest fray with the Indianans. Scott Lynch got hit about the same time. Charlie Connelly was shot through the body just as the Indiana troops broke and fled. Cul Cummings was hit just as we started. All these were shot close to the writer of this article.

Our Killed and Wounded

With wild yells we went on to the New York Excelsior holding the battery. One of the boys sprang on a gun and was shot off of it. The New Yorkers, too, gave way, and Fizer on his little blaze face bay horse rode along the lines calling the troops to halt and form. The three brigades, New Yorkers, Indianans, and New Jerseys had rallied and were coming in solid mass to retake the gun. Jim Ramseur was shot through the mouth and through the left hand, and there he stood unable to utter a word or make a sound, waving his old battered hat with broken hand, and his sword in the other. Brown, a native of England, but a Southerner every inch of him, fell. Billie Gast, another native of England, stepped up to a little bush, knelt, and placing his gun between the branches of a bush, took deliberate aim, and fired kneeling. Just as he did so, a bullet struck him square in the forehead and with a gasp he settled back head on his knees. The writer here got his third bullet. Jim Crump sprang over him, calling for a 'forward charge with bayonet' and the line went forward leaving a ghastly row around and about the Federal guns. Arch Lee had run up with the flag of the old 17th.

On it had been embroidered the names of the battles in which it had fought. Manassas, Leesburg, Yorktown, Williamsburg, Seven Pines, Gaines Mill, Savage Station, Frazier's Farm, Malvern Hill, Sharpsburg, Fredericksburg, and then the cry for another forward movement. The writer, with the other Confederates, wounded, was carried back to the hospital, and the first man to find him was his old colored servant, Simon. Ah! But Black faces filled with sympathy and love such as his are sometimes welcome. It has been more than forty-six years since Simon came, but in all these years I can still see and bring back vividly the picture of that devoted Negro. Time effaces many things from our memory; care, sorrow, and trouble making us forget, but nothing but the coming of the Master shall take the Negro from my recollection.

Many Confederate Wounded Left

Many of the Confederates were left behind when Lee retreated two days after. Those who were disabled were carried to New York in time to be swapped for able-bodied Yankees. They carried us through Philadelphia, the city of brotherly love. Philadelphia had been the pride of the Southern people; the Southern dandy and the Southern belle did not think they were well dressed unless they were clad from the markets of that city of brotherly love. Southern merchants had dealt liberally with the shopkeepers of that city. It was this city of all the American continent, the pride and boast of all the Southern people, and with all the homes of Frank Leslie's periodical.[1]

W. M. Abernathy
17th Mississippi Infantry
Gratitude of Ex-Slave, Old North Carolina Negro Made Happy, X-MAS Gift from Texas

Faithful and devoted even amid horrors of the fiercest battles of the Civil War. The following letter has been received by Hon. W. M. Abernathy of this city, from his old black servant, which breathes a spirit of loyalty and humility that forever enshrines the memory of the old time darkey in the heart of his former master. Old Simon served Mr Abernathy devotedly throughout the war, carrying him wounded from the battlefield of Gettysburg and surrendering with him at Appomattox. Though separated for forty years and hundreds of miles apart, the white master of the long ago has not forgotten the faithfulness and devotion of the slave.

Private William
Abernathy after the war.
(*John Hoopes*)

Every Christmas a substantial remembrance is sent him and the following
letter acknowledges receipt of the last one:

Arden, NC, Jan 10, 1905
Mr W. M. Abernathy, McKinney, Tex.
My dear old and fond Master:
I received your Xmas remembrance as usual and I want to tell you that
it seemed to get next to me this time in truth, and indeed I could not help
from shedding tears. I had to say out loud 'God bless that dear friend
of mine whom thou has preserved.' Dear Mr William I am well, can't
complain. Of course I am old and feeble, but thank God, for some cause,
some purpose he has given me health and strength to work and make a
living, somehow, some say the Lord will provide.

Oh you wrote me a beautiful letter, the very thought is beautiful. You
commenced your letter by saying, 'Last night I went to church and my
preacher talked of home, and you ended by saying, 'not many years will

come ere and all of us are gone.' And sometimes I wonder in my soul, will I meet you in that bright shining world, where God is to give us light, where we will rest. For I am so tired sometimes I feel like how happy I would be to change worlds. May it be your highest aim to strive, to honor his great name. Please remember me to all your family.

I am as ever till death, your old and loyal servant,
Simon Abernathy[2]

C. C. Cummings and W. M. (Billy) Abernathy
17th Mississippi Infantry
War Times Are Recalled[3]

The Dallas News of a few days ago since contained an interesting article from C. C. Cummings, of Fort Worth, Historian Texas Division U.C.V., containing the fierce charge of Hood's Texas Brigade at the Battle of Sharpsburg (Antietam) and Barksdale's Mississippi Brigade at Gettysburg. In closing his article and noting the passing away of Col. Manning and Col. Fizer who took such a prominent part of the battle he says:

> The only witness I can summon to sustain these reminiscences is Judge W. M. (Billy) Abernathy of McKinney, Texas, my whilom messmate, who was there shot off the enemy's batteries as we took it, and there I left my right hand to rest with the braves who still sleep there in this 'fatal flooded field.'

In regard to this article, which contained the reference to him, Mr Abernathy was seen by this reporter of this paper today and after being questioned concerning it, he said:

It is very pleasant to be remembered by a comrade like Cul Cummings, who never missed a fight or shirked a duty. We broke a New Jersey Brigade first, then a brigade of Western troops and then attacked New York Excelsior supporting the guns. I've been over the ground and seen their monuments. Those guns were the storm center of a fearful struggle of our own company. Billie Gart, killed while kneeling with his gun pointed. Frank Ross, a young man of great promise, Billie McRaven, one of God's noblemen. Brown and Richardson killed in the struggle. Cul Cummings shows a stump of an arm. Scott Lynch, a broken leg, which never healed. W. J. Phillips, a mangled arm. Jim Ramseur one half his hand torn off, a shot through his mouth, and his tongue lacerated, waving his old black hat with his two fingers and his sword in his right hand, not able to utter a word, but every action FORWARD. The two Osler boys, the two Blackburn's, and Charlie Cameron of Company F, all right there and down.

Arch Lee ran up with the colors and in falling they were taken by Estes who died a few months ago maimed and scarred beyond recognition, when Lem Morris grasped them.

It was on that field that my Negro, Simon, by his devotion, earned a 'gratitude,' which years cannot dim nor time efface.

It is a matter of pride and also a mournful pleasure that I feel able to say that though far from being the strongest brigade in Lee's Army, Barksdale's Brigade in that battle lost more men killed and wounded than any other brigade in Lee's Army, Hood's and Pickett's Brigades not excepted. This much is due to my old comrades.

This is taken from reports, but does not include those captured.[4]

C. C. Cummings
17th Mississippi Infantry

Judge C. C. Cummings enlisted as a private in Company B, 17th Mississippi Regiment (Col. Featherston), in his native town, Holly Springs, Miss., in April 1861. This regiment was ordered to Virginia and his command was in many fierce battles, among them First Manassas, Leesburg (or Ball's Bluff), Savage Station, Malvern Hill, storming of Maryland Heights, Harper's Ferry, Sharpsburg (or Antietam), Fredericksburg, and Chancellorsville. Judge Cummings was in all these, and escaped unhurt except in the peach orchard at Gettysburg, 2 July 1863, where he lost his right hand. He was sergeant major of the regiment. He started in the retreat in an ambulance with his then Col. W. D. Holder who was also wounded. Col. Holder is well known through the VETERAN as Commander of the Mississippi Division, U.C.V.

Judge Cummings was captured at Cashtown. He was imprisoned at Chester, the oldest town in Pennsylvania, a few miles run from Philadelphia. Compared to Fort Delaware, Chester was a fairyland. Sympathizers were admitted, and ladies from far and near visited them as heroes instead of 'Rebels.' The regular prisons were then overcrowded. This was a temporary hospital, and romance caused the treatment of prisoners to be sentimental. Pierce Butler, a Georgian of South Carolina lineage (akin to Senator Butler), married the then celebrated actress Fanny Kemble. She had caused him to free his slaves and move to Philadelphia. When the war began she took the Union side, and wrote a book about the 'Old Flag,' while he and his daughter Fannie, an only child, sided with the south. There was disunion in the family in consequence. Fannie, the daughter, was fair-haired and charming, and an heir to rice fields and much gold. A number of young surgeons served in this hospital, and Miss Fannie and her father had *carte blanche* to pass to and from our prison, and made things very pleasant. After all, Miss Fannie married a titled Englishman.

Judge Cummings was at the Florence Wesleyan University, Florence, Alabama from 1856 to 1860, as a schoolmate of J. B. Polley of 'Charming Nellie' fame, and Hayward Brahan, whom he mentions often as among Hood's 'orphan boys' in Virginia. He recalls vividly the last time he met the Texans. It was the day before the peach orchard charge at Gettysburg. He went over to see the 'wild and wooly orphan boys,' so far from home and ragged. He wore a new sergeant major's uniform of bright Confederate gray, just received from home. They took him for 'fresh fish,' and exclaimed: 'Lordy, he's mine!' 'I sah him fust!' 'Look at the chicken fixens on his arm!' 'See them air locks!' 'Ef I was a louse, I would swim the Mississippi River to crawl in his head!' 'Let me kiss him for his mother!' 'Put him in his little bed!' They evidently mistook him for a 'tenderfoot,' and no explanation that he had been in from the first would be received. He failed to see his friend Joe Polley, and never has till this day, but he is glad to see the last reunion of Confederate veterans in Texas has made him Major General of the State Division, U. C. V.

Judge Cummings was elected two terms as judge of his county and Commander of Lee Camp at Fort Worth two terms. He has also been Commander of the Fort Worth Picket of United American Veterans, organized at Eagle Pass, on the Rio Grande, in 1892, its object being to unite the blue and the gray into a brotherhood of American soldiery.[5]

C. C. Cummings
17th Mississippi Infantry
My Prison Days Spent at Chester on the Delaware River
(Written for the *Fort Worth Gazette* by C. C. Cummings, 17th Miss. Regiment)

They were short—only about six weeks—and they were short because truth won over suggested error, as you will see. I pass over as a horrid dream the retreat with Lee's miserable all day the 4th of July 1863 on the pike from Gettysburg, the lay off at Cashtown only 8 miles from the battlefield from loss of blood; the two weeks misery and suffering at the old barn hard by the pike in the village with thirty officers, the day I gave up life as lost and look on the last time I thought, on the full blown meadows and the silvery dream and the blue sky and the towering mountain at whose foot like village nestled, the hard-tanned faces of the Pennsylvania Dutchman that stood over me in its tawny beard and said, 'you steal my horse, hogs, corn and now you die and I be'a glad,' and the soft voice of his frau pleading 'now Hans pity the poor roost,' and then she gave me apple butter, which with the foots of abuse caused new life in me to live again. We pass through Gettysburg about the 18th of August the ambulance of the corps of blue left to gather us in. On the Baltimore, up the Chesapeake, through some locks and dams of a canal, in canal boats out into the broad majestic Delaware River. Are happy in passing the frowning Fort Delaware in the middle of this stream, which looked grim and black and monstrous, as it was with its unfeeling commandant. We land at Chester, 15 miles from Philadelphia. The object town in the good state of Pennsylvania. As the bow bears the shore I climb out of the hole and catch onto the first ambulance and mount by the side of the drive in blue with a talking mouth, a match to my own. I see you are an officer and you will fare better than the privates in the wards. They are in the wards to the left out there about a mile. The officers are in the high school building on the right. They get to see the ladies and get pies and things and sweet words of cheer and such. Heap of ladies every day. Rebels big show here, never had any before. A ward of our blue boys out there is deserted, they say, for you Rebs. Not an officer ward said drawing a long breath out of that well. You look like a full grown Brigadier General with all them buttons and chicken fixins on your arm.

We are at the Chester Hotel. As I dismount, I paused as did Caesar on the brink of the Rubicon, and after a short debate between truth and error, such as Paul writes about, truth won, and into the wards I turned with 2,000 officers of my kith and kind. Three wards in a division, sixty men to each ward, each man on a single iron bulkhead, dressed in cotton drawers and a long short branded 'Chester hospital' covered by a single snow-white sheet. This was our uniform, and I had to ask as I passed on down to my ward, No 3, 2nd Division; 'Boys are you all rebels in here?' 'Yes, all rebels,' they sang out cheerily. Flags were there, more flags than I ever saw before in one place. Big flags, little flags and the 'old flag,' waved from chandeliers and hung pendant so that as you passed under them or be slashed in the face by them as was John Wilkes Booth in his great tragedy. Bible motives were there as profuse as the flags. Such as 'Whom He loveth, He chastieth,' and I knew I was sorely chastised. And another I remember, 'Trust in the Lord and He will bring it to pass,' so that in six weeks we as humble privates were exchanged, while the poor officers were sent to Johnston's Island, many of them to perish that winter from starvation and deprivation. So, truth was my best friend. As a sample of the pure democracy of our prison life, without regard to race, color, or previous condition, I will tell a story of the Texan and the Yank. They went out one night on a lark, the Yank was one of the guards. The Texan one of Hood's men that fell at Round Top in the 'Devils' Den' among the rocks there. They came back late, pretty well tanked up with bug juice. One of the faithful flags slapped the Texan in the face because he failed to bow to it. The Texan reached up and tore it down. The Yank bounced him and they waltzed each other out in the court between the wards and had a nip and tuck in the moon's pale light. The wiry cow puncher was more than a meal for the blue boy. He bit off, 'more'n he could chaw' and so was content to turn the tiger loose, seeing that the tiger was on top. One of the happiest incidents was the kindly ministrations of Prince Butler and his beautiful daughter, Fannie. He was a Georgian and a relative of the South Carolina family, now represented in the United States Senate by one of the name. He had married the then celebrated Fannie Kemble, and this fair Fannie was the only product of that union. Not content with having him free his slaves and move north before the war, the wife would change his politics also. But there he drew the line and she drew a divorce and wrote a book about the old flag and the union. Fannie, the fair and debonair, sided with her father and they ministered unto us in prison with lavish hands. The Federal doctors, young and old, were not insensible in the witchery of the little beauty backed by here golden booty, and ran over each other to do her obedience. But she was for none of them. A year or more after the war I read in the labors of her renunciation of the Monroe Doctrine and embracing foreign intervention in the shape of titled lord, who steamed over, doing America, and there down in her father's rice fields in old Carolina, he walked right into the parlor of this pretty little rice bird with her golden plumage of something more than wavy hair, and the twain were made one flesh, and flew away to merry England, where I hope they have reared a full nest of rice birds, and as gay as happy as Fannie, fair and debonair with golden hair. It was with many regrets at parting from the good folks at Chester that one October day we left in the good steamer *New York*. Captain Chisholm (peace to his ashes, he gave his cabin passage.) Out in the broad ocean away out of sight of land. We passed Fortress Monroe, afterwards as the prison place of Jefferson Davis; and Hampton Roads where in the Cumberland went down to everlasting renown under the withering breath of the Monitor, and land at City Point, below Richmond, with the lines of Scott's 'Lay of the Last Minstrel' sweeping the tendrils of our hearts:

Breathes there a man with soul so dead
Who never himself hath said,
This is my own, my native land,
Whose heart hath ne'er within him burned
As home his footsteps hath turned
From wandering on a foreign strand?
If such there breathe, go mark him well.
For him no minstrel raptures swell.
High tho his office, proud his name,
Boundless his wealth as which can claim.
Despite those, titles, power and self.
The wretch, concentered all in self.
Living, shall forfeit high renown.
And nobly dying, shall go down,
To the vile dust, from whence he sprung,
Unwept, unhonored and unsung.[6]

J. T. Cone
13th Mississippi Infantry
Barksdale's Last Order

Kosse, Texas, 6 January. One by one the old Confederates disappear and soon we'll all be hushed in death, and then our children can say: 'I've heard father speak of such and such a fight and what a hard time he had in prison, etc.'

It was my luck to be in Lee's Army and the last battle I was in made the deepest impression that was the Battle of Gettysburg. Our command got into it the worst—Texas Brigade on the right, the Mississippi Brigade next and the Alabama next. These brigades had a hard time that evening, July 2nd. I belonged to the 13th Regiment and it was our duty to dislodge the blue coats from a large barn. As we went into the fight, Nute Nash turned to us and said, 'You know who is in the habit of running. Keep them in line.'

I'll say here it was just all I could do to keep myself in line and let them be. Poor Nute! That was the last word I ever heard him utter. He was killed. Clem Buck, Craig Davis, Hock Brister, and others from our company fell that evening and many were wounded. John Durham was our color bearer. He lost an arm and had to leave the colors on the field. Jack Boyd bravely picked them up and carried them to the front. Last, but by no means least, our Brigadier General William Barksdale fell. Much good blood was spilt that evening, but none braver than General Barksdale (he was in the first year of the war as our Colonel). I suppose I was the last man who ever heard General Barksdale give orders. His last word was 'forward.' I looked around to see where our line was, and we had none. The blue coats came with a solid line. Barksdale was killed. Poor me. I just had to obey orders and forward—to Fort Delaware to stay until June 1865.[7,8]

W. T. Bell
51st Georgia Infantry
Oakwood, Texas

After the Battle of Chancellorsville we took up the line of march and went into Pennsylvania and encamped at Chambersburg. On July 2nd we left on a forced march and after three days we drew three days of rations. Some got their rations cooked, others did not. I was fortunate enough to get a little bread. When we went into the engagement I was taken prisoner and delivered to Kilpatrick's command that evening (the 3rd) and on the night of the 4th we were marched all night and boarded a train for Baltimore, where we received the first food we had since the 2nd.[9]

J. D. Boring
3rd Georgia Reserve
Merkel, Texas

I was in all the battles in which my regiment participated. There were three brothers of us. R. M. and T. W. were with Gen. Lee in Virginia, and I wanted to be there too. The others were in Company K, 4th Georgia. There were in the first company from Americus. R. M. was killed at Gettysburg in Pickett's Charge. He fell with the colors of the 4th Georgia. He was not a color bearer, but picked them up when the color bearer fell. I think he was the seventh man that met the same fate that day.[10]

Newton Jasper Brooks
14th Alabama Infantry
Breckenridge, Texas

While on our way to Gettysburg food became scarce, and we had to forage for a living. A man by the name of Jack Ross and I were out in search of food. Calling at a man's house and seeing some nice chickens, we proposed to buy some from him, but he refused to sell. After being without food for some time, our appetites were keen for chicken, but we could not prevail on him to sell us any, so I told my companion to go around the chickens and drive them towards me. I made one quick lunge with the ramrod of my gun and that one stroke killed four. Of course the owner made many threats, but we stubbornly refused to pay. By this time our business lay rolling. And what a time we had that night feasting on chicken![11]

R. W. Ferrell
1st Mississippi Cavalry
Cleburne, Texas

In memorial to my brother S. D. Ferrell, I write this: He lived in Texas at the beginning of the war. Enlisted in Company G, 4th Texas Infantry (Hood's old regiment), was attached to Gen. Hood's Brigade, and served in the Army of Northern Virginia. Was wounded at Gaines's Mill and killed in the Battle of Gettysburg, Pa., 3 July 1863, and his body was buried by the enemy. After the war, my father had the body brought back to Mississippi, and reinterred by the side of our mother near Holly Springs, Miss. From our family went out six brothers, namely, B. H., H. H., J. H., S. D., R. W., and W. S. Ferrell, of whom only one was killed. All are now dead except the last two mentioned, R. W. and W. S.[12]

G. B. Ford
16th Mississippi Infantry
Bangs, Texas

After Chancellorsville, Lee rested at Fredericksburg and made preparations to invade the North. So in June we began to march to Pennsylvania. Nothing of any moment on the way and we reached the battlefield of Gettysburg on July 1st. The battle lasted most of three days and is now history. Our division covered the retreat all the way back to the Potomac as we had been held in reserve at Gettysburg. Rations were a little short, coming back. I had a Negro boy with me as cook and I told him to get out in the country and get us something to eat. He found a place where some ladies asked him to stay with them and be free and work for them. He agreed to this provided they would give him enough to keep him in hiding till we were gone. About sundown he came in with a load of goodies. I asked him where he got all that. 'Boss, I outgeneraled dem Yankee women back dar.'
    After Gettysburg Gen. Lee fell back by way of Shenandoah Valley to a place on the Rapidan River near Orange Court House.[13]

M. M. Hines
23rd North Carolina Infantry
Iatan, Texas

At Gettysburg out of twenty-seven men, the loss was twelve killed. The wounded were all captured except Comrade Finger and myself and he started out with one wound and got four more flesh wounds before he got away. In other battles our losses were not so much. The company was small and favored by chances of war.[14]

John W. Jones
14th South Carolina Infantry
Mambrino, Texas

I walked from Gettysburg to Staunton, Va., with my shoes about worn out when I started. Was in the Battles of Seven Days around Richmond, Fredericksburg, Chancellorsville, Gettysburg, Wilderness, and Spotsylvania Court House. James W. Jones, the only brother in the Company with me, was in all the principal battles with me and was killed at Gettysburg in July 1863. I was wounded 27 June 1864, at Gaines's Mill, and also wounded in the thigh at Gettysburg, and in the foot at Richmond.[15]

E. J. Lake
Bonham's Brigade, Company E., ANV
Lindale, Texas

About the 21st of June we crossed the Potomac on our way to Gettysburg, and this battle was fought on the first three days of July 1863, where on the second I was wounded. I fell into the hands of the enemy and was a prisoner at Devil's Island. I was disabled in this last battle for the balance of the war. I will give a little incident of a messmate of mine.

At the Battle of Gettysburg, Thomas Sligh, an orderly to the Colonel, was told to hold horses in the rear until called for. Sligh begged to be permitted to go into the battle. During the battle when several flag bearers were killed or wounded, Sligh ran and raised it, when he, too, was soon killed.[16]

J. F. Lewis
23rd North Carolina Infantry
Austin, Texas

The Battle of Gettysburg was the worst battle I was in. The entire field was covered with dead and dying men. When I first went into the army, it made my heart ache to see my comrades falling on every side, but I, like the rest, got used to it.[17]

Henry C. Lindsey
47th Alabama Infantry
Waco, Texas

At the Battle of Gettysburg it was thought the Lieutenant-Colonel was killed, and I was elected by the regiment as Colonel, but it afterwards developed that Bulger was only wounded and a prisoner. He afterward came back to be retired as a Colonel. This process being arranged when the war closed and thereupon my election as Colonel fell through.[18]

H. B. Love
4th Alabama Infantry
Paris, Texas

I was with Gen. Lee in Virginia, and soon after went to Gettysburg, Pa. They had very fine barns in that part of the country, so one day I went out of camp with the intention of burning some of these big barns; but I had to get mad first. I could not set fire to them in cold blood, so I decided I would go and talk to the owner and tell him how mean the Yankees were, and how they had burned my grandfather's place. They agreed with me that they were very bad and had done wrong, and that they were sorry etc., so I killed a chicken and returned to camp. In the Battle of Gettysburg my command was on the extreme right of the line of battle, at Round Top.[19]

M. Dwight McNeely
42nd Mississippi Infantry
Fort Worth, Texas

Was wounded by fragment of shell striking me on the nose, while carrying the regimental flag at Gettysburg. At that battle four men were killed under the colors. For my conduct on the field of that battle I was made first lieutenant and ensign of the regiment. Was captured on the retreat from Gettysburg and taken to Mercersburg, Pa., and paroled; made my way back to Richmond and was furloughed home for sixty days, or until exchanged and reported back to my regiment, not knowing whether or not I had been exchanged.[20]

Henry A. Morehead
11th Mississippi Infantry
McGregor, Texas

Once more we waded across the Potomac, took a long march through Pennsylvania and on to Gettysburg, where we fought the three days' battle, which I think were the hardest battles of the war. At least I saw more dead men on both sides than any other battlefield of the whole struggle. Our train of 400 wagons fell into the hands of the enemy. They were loaded with supplies of all kinds, together with our ammunition, the loss which caused us to fall back to our own side of the Potomac. We drew no rations, but learned how to forage.[21]

George W. O'Neal
31st Georgia Infantry
Wolfe City, Texas

At this stage of the game, our officers and soldiers had such unbounded confidence in Gen. Lee that it seemed nothing was impossible. If Gen. Lee decided to do it, it would be done, so we again crossed the Potomac River into the enemy's country with I suppose two objects in view: first, to get the enemy to withdraw their army from our once fertile valley of Virginia, but now laid waste by the two armies. We had, therefore, need of borrowing supplies from our neighbors across the Potomac. Then I suppose Gen. Lee had concluded to defend Richmond by threatening Washington. Our orders were very strict not to molest private property or non-combatants.

As we were approaching the city of York, Pa., the mayor and many of the business men met us outside the city limits and requested us not to destroy their city and property. They returned satisfied, as Gen. Gordon assured them that we were not there for the purpose of destroying private property or molesting non-combatants. And we passed through the town without breaking ranks and on to the little town of Wrightsville, on the Susquehanna River, where we encountered a small force of the enemy, but as we gave them a few shots they made a hasty retreat across the river and set fire to the bridge, so that when we arrived we went to work to extinguish the fire and call for buckets to carry water, but there were no buckets to be had and the fire continued, catching the lumber yard, and getting near a fine residence. Gen. Gordon explained to them that if we had plenty of buckets we might be able to extinguish the fire, so they then brought plenty of buckets and tubs and by heroic work we saved the residence and stopped the fire. The lady who owned the house, late that night, sought Gen. Gordon and, when she was directed to his quarters, told him that she had come to invite him and as many of his men as could get into her dining room for breakfast the next morning. She wanted to do something to show her appreciation for saving her residence from the fire. The next morning we turned our backs on the village and retraced our tracks to Gettysburg, and we when arrived the two armies had met and the big Battle of Gettysburg had just begun. We were thrown out to the left of our army and were soon in combat. Our attack was so sudden or unexpected that the enemy was not well formed when we struck them, but after a short and stubborn resistance they began to retreat and we drove them through the city and on to the heights beyond, when night put an end to the first day's light. At this particular time we found all the commissioned officers of my company were wounded or gone off the battlefield, and several comrades were wounded. As I was the highest non-commissioned officer on the field it fell to me to take command of the company for the next three days, and I was captain in the army for three days, some of my old friends call me captain yet.

The next two days the big battle was on with varying success for one side and then the other. At the end of the third day we fell back about 1½ miles for a new and better position and waited for them to come out into the open field and renew the attack, but they did not come, and as we could not stay there we had to fall back to our base of supplies.

After this we fell back into Maryland and formed our battle line again and waited for an attack, but they again refused. While we were stopping in Maryland for a few days, I thought I would go out into the country and secure some butter, bread and milk, if possible. So I approached an old fashioned residence and halted at the entrance. A lady made her appearance and as I was explaining to her my mission a gentleman made his appearance and asked me what I wanted and what I was doing there. I explained to him the object of my visit and also told him that I was not trying to steal anything; neither was I begging, but I wanted something to eat and had the money to pay for it. He said that he was well supplied with Confederate money. I then told him that I would pay him with greenback. He then wanted to know how much greenback money I had. I told him that I had $20.00, and he became very much interested in my affairs and wanted to make a trade with me and told me that he would give me $40.00 Confederate money for my $20.00 in greenback, and the bread and butter and milk in the bargain. I told him that trade suited me exactly. He loaded me up with the butter, light bread and milk and gave me the $40.00 and I gave him the $20.00 and went on my way rejoicing. We came back into Virginia and it felt like we had gotten home.[22]

W. L. Owens
12th Mississippi Infantry
Blooming Grove, Texas

Was at Gettysburg, had a hard time, and oh, what a bad fight—saw so many good men lose their lives. I will tell of one sad incident of this battle. We were all lying down and I was laying with my head behind a post when a young man came running down the line and lay down by my side. I turned to see if I knew him, but did not. I asked him to what command he belonged, he replied, to 'G.' He remarked, 'This is a hot place.' I said, 'You bet' (almost afraid to speak). Just at that moment a ball struck him between the eyes and he said, 'I am a dead man.' Those days have been long passed, but will never be forgotten.

In the afternoon we could hear the enemy say, 'Shoot low, they are lying down.' We left that night to cross back over the river-marched all night in the rain. I lay down in the rain and went fast asleep and was glad to get the rest.[23]

Walters Pendergrass
6th South Carolina Infantry
McKinney, Texas

The second big battle I was in was at Gettysburg, Pa., three days. On the second day I thought my time had come. Gen. Hampton charged a Yankee battery and we went to the mouth of the guns and took them. I never knew how I escaped being killed.[24]

James Jackson Manning Smith
31st Georgia Infantry
Dallas, Texas

I was barefooted and feet bleeding from marching over stone roads. I am proud to tell this. Our brigade held the rear in Lee's retreat from Gettysburg. We fought a battle at Wrightsville on the Susquehanna River east of York, Pa., which was the farthest east of any of Lee's troops.[25]

Alf H. H. Tolar
18th North Carolina Infantry
Houston, Texas

Had a serious wound in the groin at Gettysburg and was relieved from further service. At the reorganization of the regiment in 1862, I was elected to second lieutenant and after the Battle of Gettysburg was promoted to captain for meritorious conduct.[26]

David H. Williams
13th Mississippi Infantry
McGregor, Texas

We got to Gettysburg on the 2nd of July 1863, and went into battle on the 3rd. We charged the first line at the barn on the left of the peach orchard and carried the place with very small loss. We then passed on to the second line and charged a battery where we had a heavy loss and I was shot down in 20 feet of the cannon, and was reported dead and lay there till midnight, but the boys captured the battery and turned the Federal's own guns on them.[27]

Ed C. Wilson
3rd Louisiana Infantry
Childress, Texas

Went out as a captain, but was transferred to duty as a scout and then acted as a spy, carrying dispatches to Lee on his march to Gettysburg.

I was wounded twelve times in the third day's fight at Gettysburg. I was with Pickett's Division that day. Received two saber cuts on back of the head, had end of thumb shot off, wounded in knee and several small wounds. I was in the Battles of Gettysburg and Bull Run. At Gettysburg we drove the enemy 40 feet and had a hard hand-to-hand fight. I lost my father and four brothers that day. After the battle, I was told to report to Kirby Smith in Louisiana, which I did, and stayed with him till the close of the war.[28]

W. L. Young
17th Mississippi Infantry
Dallas, Texas

At Gettysburg, I was in Longstreet's Corps, with Pickett's Division, resting on our right. We were the center of Lee's Army. I think this was the 2nd day of July, the day of the great battle. We were ordered in line about 2:00 p.m. We moved on the enemy, the 17th and 13th in front, with the 18th and the 21st Mississippi Regiments supporting us. As I was first sergeant I knew how many guns we had and know that we went into battle with 416 men and came out with sixty-seven men unhurt. My regiment took thirteen pieces of cannon and held them, but we could have walked on dead men for quite a distance. We had three color bearers killed that day and I had one man killed on each side of me in less time than it takes to write this. I can never forget that day. On the next day our entire artillery was brought to bear and they fought a duel for three hours; and strange to say, that while we supported the artillery that day, we did not lose a man. The earth fairly shook, but there was so much smoke that there was much wild shooting. I have been in many hard fought battles but this was the most heart-rending of any that I ever witnessed.[29]

A. J. Baker's Mission

A Washington special to the *Fort Worth Gazette* of January 23rd, says: A. J. Baker of Tom Green County, who is here on professional business, has also an interesting mission in view. He says that there is some mistake in marking the charge made by the Jon Davis Brigade at Gettysburg in which he served together with many Texans.

He accounts for this by the wounding and death of General Pettigrew, in command of the division at Falling Waters, which prevented a report of the Gettysburg charge. Baker says their charge was more vigorous and disastrous than the Pickett charge, as the Davis Brigade lost 897 men, as against 575 lost by Pickett. He expects to go from here to Gettysburg to take steps to have the position of the brigade and its gallant work corrected.[30]

RG CARTER

Got Back the Watch he Lost at Gettysburg

A strange experience recently befell George Dietz, formerly a resident of Chester, but at the present time in the jewelry business away off in

Honolulu. Mr Dietz has just recovered a watch which he lost thirty years ago while fighting at Gettysburg. He was fighting for the north on that bloody battlefield when he dropped it. The watch was recently brought into the jewelers shop by Harry Ellis of the Kansas Volunteers. The soldier, who was bound for Manila, wanted to sell the watch. On being asked where he got it, he said his father, who had found it on the battlefield of Gettysburg, had given it to him. The jeweler opened it, and found his name scratched on it. He lost no time in making a trade with the soldier.[31]

The Reunion
By Sadi Kirgan

A cloud of dust—and a baby's cry,
A bugle's notes on the strangled air;
Red balloons, and the children's shouts,
And a new flag waving there.
A blood-barred flag with the stars that shine,
Smiling there on the bank of blue.
Passing, the lads go laughing by,
Gay in their khaki—two and two.
In a shaded space the old men sit,
Remnants of those who wore the gray;
Only a few—lone old heads,
Sensing the thrill of a lived out day.
Almost—we've forgotten—safe and secure,
Fingers cling to the yellow gleams,
Grass and poppies hiding the scars,
Gettysburg, only a dream
And the old men sit in the shaded space,
Remembering the gray—remembering the blue
Passing, the lads go by,
Gay in their khaki—two and two.[32]

A. P. Clark
10th Alabama Infantry
In Memory of A. P. Clark

Mr A. P. Clark, formerly of Palacios, died at 2:20 p.m. Wednesday, 26 December 1928, at the home of his son, Joe W. Clark, in Melrose, New Mexico, at the age of eighty-eight years, eleven months and eight days.

He was born in Georgia, but when a small child his parents moved to Jacksonville, Calhoun County, Alabama, where he grew to young manhood. He was educated in the schools of his county.

When the war was waged between the States he cast his fortune with the Southland, and at the age of nineteen he was mustered into the state service in February 1861. He went with the state troops to Mobile, and took possession of Ft. Morgan on Mobile Bay, remaining there until the Confederate government was organized. The state troops were then discharged, and he returned home where he found the country actively preparing for war. Ft. Sumter had been captured and the war dogs turned loose. He at once listed in Company D, 10th Alabama Regiment C. S. A., under Captain F. Woodruff and Colonel John H. Farney. The regiment was at once ordered to Richmond and from that time on Private Clark was in every engagement of the Army of Northern Virginia up to the Battle of Gettysburg.

Private Clark was in General R. H. Anderson's Division, General C. M. Wilcox' Brigade, whose position was on the right of Pickett's division to the attack on Cemetery Ridge, 2 July 1863. In this bloody charge up 'Little Round Top' Private Clark was captured—he being among the boys who did not know the extent of the repulse, remained too long after the retreat of the Confederates, and could not escape as the enemy's line had been formed in the rear.

He, with other prisoners, were taken to Baltimore, thence to the northern prison at Ft. Delaware, New Jersey. Here he and his friend, C. C. Cook, of the 51st Alabama planned to escape. The prisoners were granted the privilege of bathing in the bay within marked limits. If any prisoner passed these limits he was at once fired upon by the guards, and many who made the venture were killed and left for the fish.

After about three weeks of earnest daily practice of at swimming they made the attempt on the night of 12 August 1863. They passed through a closet, which extended out over the water with a sentinel at each end. But they were not seen and entered the water and swam away with the lights of Delaware City as their objective point. But the tide was against them and drifted them out into the channel.

After hours of hard swimming in the direction the tide was drifting them, they saw a light on the shore, and they swam for the newly discovered light. In a short time they reached the shore. The place proved to be New Castle, Delaware.

The fast-approaching dawn warned them that something must be done, and that quickly. Bare-footed and bare-headed and insufficiently clad, they agreed to enter the first house and steal some clothing. They had only walked a short distance when they came to a good looking house with the doors standing wide open. Cook passed and waited a short distance from the house, with the understanding if Clark was captured, he would make his escape. With light steps his bare feet approached the gallery. He stopped to listen. All was quiet. He cautiously ascends the steps and stops again. He goes to the door and listens. All is quiet except for the heavy breathing of the sleepers. He enters the room and feels cautiously around for men's wearing apparel, and finds a pair of pants and a coat on the wall. With these trophies he quietly leaves the sleepers to enjoy their morning nap. After joining his companion one put on the coat and the other the pants; then one was dressed in a coat and a pair of drawers, the other in a shirt and a pair of pants. By this time the light of the new day was spreading over the earth and they hurried out of the city into the woods.

Although they were far from home, in an enemy's country, yet these unpleasant feelings were subdued by the prospects of a speedy return to Dixie.

They travelled by the stars at night for the south and hid in secluded places in the day. They raided orchards and spring houses for sustenance, and when almost back to friends and Dixie they were re-captured and sent back to the prison at Ft. Delaware and locked in a dungeon as punishment for leaving the Fort without permission. Cook died in prison; but after a few months Private Clark was transferred to Point Lookout, Maryland, where he remained until the next winter, when he was exchanged at Savannah, Georgia, and furloughed for twenty days. Over half of his time having expired before he could reach home. At its expiration he reported to Brigadier General Ben Hill and was assigned to the quartermaster's department. He laid down his arms when Lee surrendered at Appomattox, and he returned to his home in Alabama to find the country devastated and under military rule.

His home was a wreck and one brother dead. But he was not a man to give up. He knew he just live on, hope on and help rebuild the country he loved so well. This was not time for lagging.

He took the oath of allegiance to the U. S. government and began to do his part to rebuild his home, his country, and his state.

Mr Clark came to Texas in 1873, and settled in Jacksonville, where he went into the grocery business.[33]

James Hamaker
50th Virginia Infantry

In the last 230-plus years, many brave Americans have died of wounds they received on the battlefield. They are our heroes, and their names should be remembered.

Aledo veteran James Phillips Hamaker had a story, which must be unique. Even though it ended three-quarters of a century ago, it bears retelling. When he died in 1938, articles about his unusual demise appeared in both the *Fort Worth Press* and the *Dallas Morning News*. Few country folks in those days made it into the big city papers. James Hamaker was born in 1843 in Montgomery County, Virginia. His father, Michael Hamaker, was a beloved country doctor. When the War Between the States began, James Hamaker and two of his brothers enlisted in the Confederate Army. James enlisted in June 1861 and eventually became a sergeant in the 50th Virginia Infantry. His regiment was sent to Tennessee, where he took part in the Battle of Fort Donelson in 1862. One of the turning points in his life came during the Battle of Gettysburg, Pennsylvania in July 1863, when he was wounded twice and taken prisoner by the Union Army. He remained a prisoner for the next twenty-five months. James took an oath of allegiance to the Federal government and was released to go home at Fort Delaware, Delaware, on 20 June 1865, more than two months after General Lee's surrender. After he returned home, James worked for several years as a music teacher. About 1885 he married his wife, Bettie, and they had four children.

About 1894 James brought his family to Aledo in eastern Parker County, where they spent the rest of their lives. By the time the census taker visited their home in 1900, three of the children had died. Only one, their son Frank, remained. Frank died childless in 1909 and was buried at Aledo. For most of the years after he came to Texas, James worked as a stockman. As the years passed and most of his comrades in the Confederate Army answered the last roll call, James spent time thinking about the years he'd spent in the service. Bettie Hamaker died in 1937, leaving James completely alone. When James heard there was to be a final, seventy-fifth reunion at Gettysburg, Pennsylvania, in 1938 he determined to go. He hoped to find the tree where he'd been wounded. He got his train ticket, and the trip began. Not long before the train arrived in Gettysburg, James fell from his berth in one of the cars and broke his shoulder. The people of Gettysburg were ready and welcoming when the old veterans began arriving, and plenty of medical help was standing by. James got plenty of attention during his painful stay at the reunion. Through an incredible coincidence the hospital to which they took him to treat his broken shoulder sat on the same spot where he was taken to treat his gunshot wounds in 1863. Helpful friends took him all over the battlefield as he tried to find the old tree. They never found it. Then as now, a fall and broken bone is always serious, especially for a ninety-four-year-old man. After spending two weeks in the Walter Reed Army Hospital, James returned home to Aledo, but his Gettysburg wound—his third one, suffered seventy-five years after the guns were silenced there—would be the one that ended his life. He was helped in his last years by a housekeeper, Mrs Charles Trigg. She said on his last day, 6 September 1938, he had been sitting on the porch. He got up, walked to the bathroom, and returned to his chair. A short time later she found him dead. The next day, James was buried beside his wife in Aledo Cemetery. He has a headstone, which simply has his initials, J. P., and his surname, misspelled 'Hamacker.' With no living family members to mourn him, one wonders who got him the stone. The Veterans Administration furnishes new headstones for Confederate veterans who lie in unmarked graves. When local historians applied for a stone for him, they were told his grave was considered marked, even though it contained very little information, and some of that incorrect.[34]

John Hunter
2nd New York Fire Zouaves

Captain John Hunter, who resides at 686 Washington Avenue, Dallas, Texas, was born in New York City, 4 June 1831. The subject of our sketch received his education in the private schools of New Jersey. He learned the trade of blacksmith, and followed that trade nine years. When the war came on Mr Hunter was among the first to offer his services to protect the Union. 16 July 1861, he enlisted in Company C, 2nd New York Fire Zouaves. He entered the service as a private, and after the Battle of Antietam, was made captain, his promotion being made for bravery in action at that battle. The first engagement in which he participated was that of Williamsburg, Maryland, and there he was wounded in the thigh the effects of which he still suffers. He was in all the battles of the Army of the Potomac up to, and including Gettysburg. There, on 2 July 1863, at 4:00 p.m., he lost his arm by a shell from the enemy's gun, and was at once taken prisoner from the field. He spent the night in General Lee's headquarters, and it was three days and nights before he received anything to eat. What he suffered at that time can be better imagined than described. He was fourteen days a prisoner at Williamsport, Pennsylvania, and his arm received no medical attention until 18 July, when it was amputated near the shoulder by Dr Fitch, of the Union Army, at Hagerstown, Maryland. He was paroled on the 16th, and as there was no hospital at Williamsport, went with four others to Hagerstown to be treated. Twelve days later he went to Frederick City, Maryland, remained in the general hospital there till 10 October, and was then discharged and returned home.[35]

L. P. Jennings
9th Virginia Infantry

L. P. Jennings, who died here 18 May, was born 23 November 1841. He united with the Baptist church when quite a young man. He fought four years in the Civil War and was wounded five times. He was first married to Miss Isabell M. White, 10 August 1865. To that union eleven children were born. Two died in infancy and one daughter at the age of twenty-four years. The first wife died 12 April 1883.

Mr Jennings was a member of the 9th Virginia Regiment. He enlisted in 1861 in Company B, 19th Virginia Hunting Brigade, Pickett's Division, Longstreet's Corps. His company was organized at Buffalo Springs, Amherst County, in the spring of 1861, with Richard Taliferro as captain. From there he went to Charlottsville and on to the Battle of Bull Run, which was the first he participated in. This was his first fight of the Civil War. Next was the Battle of Williamsburg, May 1862, then Seven Pines. The next fight he was in was the Seven Days fight around Richmond on 27 July. He was at Gaines Mill and in that battle was wounded in the left hip. After he was wounded he was sent home, where he remained for some time. As soon as he sufficiently recovered he next went back into the war and his next battle was Fredericksburg, 13 December 1862. He was also in the Battle of Chancellorsville, and the next battle he participated in was the battle that everyone remembers, the bloody fight of three days at Gettysburg. In this battle, Mr Jennings was shot in the right breast. He does not remember how long he lay wounded in the field, but a long time. He was taken in the hospital, where he remained about ten days, and having been taken prisoner, was carried from there to Baltimore, where he stayed three months. Mr Jennings came near dying from the wound, the bullet having been cut out of his back.

When he recovered so he could travel he was paroled and sent to Richmond. Mr Jennings should never have gone back as a prisoner of war, but he was and it was eleven months before he was exchanged. He joined his command at Gordonsville, and his next fight was the Wilderness. He was there when Grant tried to blow up the Confederates at Petersburg, but instead of getting the Confederates got his own soldiers. He was in the Battle of Five Forks and was wounded in the left foot and was sent home just a few days when Lee surrendered.[36]

Dr Callhoon Sams
Assistant Surgeon, Army of Northern Virginia

Callhoon Sams, the subject of this memoir, attended the Furman University at Greenville, South Carolina. At the age of twenty years he began the study of medicine, entering, in the fall of 1858, the Charleston Medical College, where he graduated in the class of 1860. After practicing his profession for a short time he joined the Confederate Army; was appointed Assistant Surgeon in the Army of Northern Virginia; in 1862 was transferred to the hospitals of Virginia, and just prior to Lee's march into Pennsylvania was returned to field service, also promoted as surgeon of his regiment. They were attached to General Hampton's Cavalry, and took part in the Battle of Gettysburg. Dr Sams was fortunate not to be wounded, a shell from the enemy's gun burst near where he stood and many near him were killed or wounded.[37]

Samuel F. Tenney
3rd Georgia Infantry
For the *Crockett Courier*

A few old Confederate veterans are left in Crockett who participated in this most terrible of the battles of the Civil War. This writer is one, who as a private in the 3rd Georgia Regiment, Wright's Brigade, joined in the charge, July 2nd, on the strongly fortified position of the Federals. A recent article in the Christian Herald of New York is of so much interest that I give extracts from it.

For three terrible days the conflict raged on the meadows and hill-slopes, the advantage lying first on one side and then on the other until at last came Pickett's magnificent charge ending in defeat. A month hence the Blue and the Gray will meet again on the famous battlefield this time to cement the ties, which half a century ago they fought to sever.

In accepting the invitation to take part in the Gettysburg commemorative jubilee, General Walker of the Confederate Veterans declared to his former companions-in-arms: 'Your commander feels that the time has come when, by invitation of our one-time foes, we can unite with them in celebrating that permanent peace which we pray may forever bless this our great and glorious country.' General Trimble of the G. A. R. sent greetings to the former Confederate leader saying:

> Let us assemble there and inaugurate a great peace movement under which shall be entombed forever any lingering prejudices and bitterness, to symbolize to all our people and to the generations yet to be that even out of the dead dust and ashes of war under the sunlight of our Christian civilization the fragrant flowers of peace and amity may grow and bloom.

In this same article is a quotation from General Pickett's letter after the battle:

> At about a quarter hour to three o'clock, when his written order to make the charge was handed to me, and dear old Peter (Longstreet) after reading it in sorrow and fear reluctantly bowed his head in assent,

I obeyed, leading my three brigades straight on the enemy's front. They moved across that field of death as a battalion marches forward in line of battle upon drill, each commander in front of his command leading and cheering on his men. Two lines of the enemy's infantry were driven back: two lines of guns were taken, and no support came. Pendleton, without Alexander's knowledge, had sent four of the guns which he had loaned him to some other part of the field, and the other three guns could not be found. The two brigades which were to have followed me had, poor fellows, been seriously engaged in the fight of the two previous days.

It is deplorable that so many lives were sacrificed, but it may not be in vain, if the peace of our country is permanently assured, and if the men of both sections have learned to respect the honest convictions of their opponents.[38]

Samuel F. Tenney
3rd Georgia Infantry
For the *Crockett Courier*

Through the kindness of my church in affording me a vacation, and supplying means for my expenses aided by the Daughters of the Confederacy and other Confederate friends, I had the privilege of attending the reunion at Gettysburg. Through the weather was intensely warm, and the crowd great, yet the reunion had been so well planned by the U. S. Government and the Pennsylvania authorities that it was an immense success. Good order was preserved and wise precautions were taken to protect life. Mounted soldiers were stationed at the street corners and crossings, to see that no one should be run over by automobiles or other vehicles. A brother minister remarked as to the happy reunion of the North and the South, that the blue and gray had faded into the khaki—the khaki being the uniform of the U.S. soldiers, that is, their undress or everyday uniform, while the blue uniform is still being used for dress parade occasions. The mounted soldiers ride beautifully, erect and graceful, and seemed to be very attentive to their duty in endeavoring to protect life and keep and keep order.

There was very little dust in the camp, or on the streets of the city, in some places the streets had been oiled. By the way, I noticed that the streets in Fort Smith, Ark., had been oiled, and even the county roads around the city. I was told that they were oiled once every two or three months. The soldiers' camp was well supplied, with pure drinking water, cooled with ice, in drinking fountains, while there were also hydrants to supply other water. The tents were roomy, apparently made of khaki colored canvas.

The cots were new and good and the new blankets issued to the veterans were needed, as the nights were cool.

It was a beautiful sight to look over the battle-ground, and see it occupied with a city of tents, with regular streets and avenues—the northern veterans in the tents of the side of the battle-ground that they held in the battle, and the southern veterans on their side. At night the camp was lighted with thousands of electric lights, and was a beautiful sight. The food supply was good and abundant, and all the accommodations for the old soldiers infinitely superior to what they had fifty years ago, when they were engaged in deadly strife on the same ground. The veterans from Georgia were placed in certain rows of tents and those from Virginia in other rows, and so on for each state. The quartermaster's tents were kept supplied by great loads delivered by a kind of army wagon-automobile. The hospital tents with physicians, nurses and ambulances were conveniently located. The old veterans were treated with the utmost respect and kind attention by the young U.S. soldiers.

The general effect of the management was to make the veteran feel proud that he belonged to a happy, united, prosperous and strong nation, one well equipped with an army of noble young soldiers such as commands the respect of the world for our country. The bearing of the blue and the gray veterans toward each other was courteous, kind and cordial, all rejoicing that the war is a thing of the past and that we are now firmly united as a nation—the blue veterans often speaking in complimentary terms of General Lee and our other generals, and the bravery of our Confederates. The writer and his Georgia comrade were awakened early the first morning by a brass band marching around playing 'Dixie,' and 'My Maryland,' awakening recollections of our times that filled us with laughter and tears. The line of battle of the Confederates was longer than that of the Federals, the Federals having the inside of the semi-circle. Both lines are marked with stone tablets, with inscriptions showing what brigades, divisions and batteries fought at certain places in the line. The writer tramped until he was tired along the Confederate line, following a macadamized road called Confederate Avenue. And then the next day walked along the Federal line, the latter being adorned in many places with splendid monuments of certain generals, or certain troops.

I don't remember seeing any monument along the Southern line except for one erected by Virginia. I learn that it is to be completed with an equestrian statue of Lee, on the battle line opposite to the place where the equestrian statue of Meade stands. Of course much was said about the charge of Pickett's Division, and the place where it occurred was pointed out, and viewed with interest. I learned the following incident, which seems to be well authenticated. When George Pickett was a young man he wanted to be a soldier, and go to West Point for a military education. He found great obstacles in the way, but through the kindness of Mr Lincoln he was appointed to be a cadet. When Richmond fell, and Mr Lincoln visited that city, he sought out Mrs Pickett, and asked where George was. He was told that George was in the army with General Lee. Mr Lincoln then inquired about George's baby, and with great interest in fondling the little one. I learned that Mrs Pickett lived in Washington many years, and has had employment in a government office. Mr Lincoln evidently had more kindness in him then the South at one time thought.

The Cemetery Hill where the hottest of the fight was and from which Confederates were driven back, is such a beautiful spot, occupied as the National Cemetery (alongside of the old cemetery used by the citizens) adorned with monuments, green lawns, and graceful shade-trees. It is one of earth's loveliest resting places for the dead. In the midst of it is one particular beauty spot where the unknown dead (some of them Confederates) are buried in circular rows, each graved marked with a small marble headstone. At a little distance it seemed like a garden of beautiful purple flowers; but when I approached, I found that each grave was decorated with a little U.S. flag and a little blue Pennsylvania flag crossed over each headstone. The effect of these circular rows thus decorated was very pleasing, and I guessed that some good women had planned this arrangement.

On the whole God has highly favored the people of Gettysburg and its vicinity with a magnificent farming country. Even if one of the world's most famous battlegrounds did not attract visitors, the magnificent scenery ought to make it a very attractive place for tourists to visit. There is a steel tower about 100 feet high on each of the opposing lines of battle. From the top of one of these, as I took in the extensive and resplendent view, I thought of its having been the place of such a bloody conflict, the words of a familiar hymn came into mind. 'Where every prospect pleases, And only man is vile.'

If large bodies of men must fight in a scientific military way, then by nature Gettysburg is fitted to be the suitable battleground. As I saw the big loads hauled, on the U.S. automobile wagon, and the dozen or more passengers carried in a five-seated automobile omnibus, the suggestion came to me why not such automobile machines do for a time as a substitute for a railroad between such places as Crockett and Ratcliff—the big automobile wagon carrying the trunks and baggage, and the automobile omnibus taking the passengers.

In the financial point of view the Gettysburg reunion must have cause a heavy deposit of dollars in the Gettysburg banks, flowing in from the many lemonade stands and lunch stands, the hired automobiles, carriages, and the hotels and boarding houses.[39]

L. B. Stephenson
Army of Northern Virginia, An Ex-Confederate Soldier

The Herald editor has had the pleasure lately of meeting Capitan L. B. Stephenson of St. Louis, who is now visiting his daughter, Mrs J. D. Anderson of this city. The captain is a most welcome visitor to the sanctum sanctorum of The Herald, as he is a most entertaining conversationalist, and an excellent gentleman. He is a thorough Southron, being from the 'Old Dominion.' He was a Confederate soldier, having fought from the first to the last for the dear Lost Cause. At Manassas, the first great struggle of that fateful war, the captain fought with such heroes as Stonewall Jackson, Joseph E. Johnston, and Beauregard. He also had the honor of charging the stony heights at Gettysburg, in the gallant Pickett's command. It was here that he became a captain, having gone into that most gigantic struggle as a first lieutenant. Thirteen captains went down in the fearful charge made by Pickett's Division, among them the leader of Mr Stephenson's Company, and the latter at once assumed the command, leading his men on in one of the most daring charges made during the entire war. And again, at Appomattox Court House, the captain was present and laid down his sword, at the command of the noble Lee. The details of his life during those four eventful years are full of great interest.

After the war, Capt. Stephenson went to Illinois where he engaged in the legal profession. He was elected to the office of district attorney, and afterwards became a member of the Illinois senate, being the only ex-Confederate who ever sat in that body. He removed with his family to St. Louis about six years ago, and now makes his home there.

He is greatly enjoying his visit in Brownsville, although he finds the South not quite so 'sunny' as he expected from reports of the climate. However, he has the satisfaction of knowing that the mercury has not reached the 'below zero,' reported from St. Louis in the recent blizzard.[40]

Blue-Gray Reunion

After several years of disunion, a final reunion of Union and Confederate soldiers has been agreed upon, to be held at Gettysburg, Pa., in 1938, on the seventy-fifth anniversary of the decisive battle fought there 1, 2, and 3 July 1863.

The United Confederate Veterans unanimously agreed at their recent reunion in Amarillo, Texas, to accept the invitation of the governor of Pennsylvania to join with the Grand Army of the Republic in the 1938 reunion, but only on condition that they be allowed to carry the Confederate flag unfurled alongside the Stars and Stripes.

Some members of the G. A. R. insisted that the Confederate flag be furled during the ceremonies, but finally waived the point. There was a joint resolution at Gettysburg on the fiftieth anniversary of the battle in 1913, but on that occasion the Confederate flag was carried furled.

While the forthcoming joint reunion in 1938 will have high significance as a gesture of good will between former foes, it is doubtful whether say considerable number of veterans will be able to participate.

This year only about 500 veterans attended the G. A. R. encampment in Grand Rapids, the youngest being eighty-five years old. The ranks of the Confederates have likewise dwindled; few of either army will be under ninety by 1938, and it is inevitable that many of those who survive will be physically unable to attend.

But the spirit of the joint reunion will be the spirit of a unified country, and as much should prove an inspiration to every American.[41]
After the Battle of Gettysburg, when the battled Confederates, worn, weary, and heart sore, were re-crossing the Potomac, at dusk, many were groaning, some were cursing, while the majority felt too unhappy to express themselves boisterously. Finally they went into camp, cooked their frugal meal and settled down to a grim quarrel with fortune or lapsed into sullen silence. All at once swelling melodiously through the summer air came a noble, resonant tenor voice singing, 'Give me a Cot in the Valley I Love.' The soldiers listened with rapture, and the dear vision of home turned the bitterness in their hearts to sweetness and peace. All blasphemy, anger and unutterable anguish ceased. By the power of song Heaven descended upon the raging hells in their bosoms and when the ballad lulled into an echo, dying plaintively away, it was as if angel had passed and touched valiant men in gray with the healing of his wings.[42]

A Battle-Scarred Coat

A souvenir of the lost cause is in possession of Col. Will Lambert, commander of Dick Dowling Camp No. 197, of Houston. It is a captain's Confederate uniform coat of regulation gray and was worn by Capt. Bushrod W. Bell, commanding a company of the 5th Alabama Regiment, from 1862 to the close of the war. The coat has six bullet holes, two of the Yankee compliments cutting the cuticle of the wearer. It has the regulation captain's bars on the collar and chevrons on the sleeves, the latter being spoken of as regulations 'chicken guts' by the old solders during the war. Five of the bullet holes were received at Gettysburg and one at Sharpsburg.

Captain Bell has recently moved to Houston and is now a member of the Dick Dowling Camp. As there is some doubt as to whether he will be present during the reunion, Col. Lambert brought the souvenir of the war, which is the center of attraction wherever exhibited.[43]

West Texas Confederate Veterans Return to Gettysburg to Join Soldiers They Fought

West Texas veterans of the Confederacy yesterday began their 'march' on Gettysburg, where they eagerly anticipate the first and last reunion of the Blue and Gray. Pecos' J. W. Prewitt, ninety-nine, one of the first residents of Pecos County, Charles Robertson of Abilene, W. H. Browning, ninety-five, of Pecos, all set for the reunion, John Lewis Clark, ninety-four of Rotan, and his escort Raymond Eakin, a grandson.

There was a 4th West Texas veteran on the train when it reached Abilene, Cicero C. Martin of McCaulley, accompanied by his grandson, L. E. Rector. A fifth, H. T. McPheeters of Winters and his escort, Judge A. O. Strother, boarded the afternoon east bound train.

All of the veterans are travelling in air-conditioned Pullman comfort, their expenses and that of their escorts paid by the national government. Passing through Abilene enroute to the reunion, a special car for the veterans stopped briefly yesterday morning

From Cisco two other veterans left yesterday, David Blackshear Perdue, ninety-one, and Wild Wood Foster, ninety-four. Accompanying them as attendant was Fred Stelley, a son-in-law of Mr Perdue.

Mr Perdue served as a courier in the 27th Georgia Infantry and the 31st Georgia Cavalry from November 1861 to April 1865. He was slightly wounded once.

Wild Wood Foster enlisted in Capt. N. W. Dammers Company, Darnell's Brigade in 1861, later was imprisoned at Camp Douglas, exchanged and rejoined his command and fought under both General J. E Johnson and General John B. Hood against General Sherman's Army and the march through Georgia.[44]

The Soldier's Dream
Inscribed to the Daughters of the Confederacy

The Battle of Gettysburg was lost,
My soldiers In Gray, my soldiers in Gray
Were falling back before the host
And left the bloody field for their sway!

There lay by the hill a wounded boy;
He was a Texan, a Texan so brave!
No peer he had for his mother's joy,
And now his goal was the early grave!

He lay there with thirst in agony
Of his home he thought, of his dear old home,
Of the cosy walks by the Trinity!
Now all his hopes were buried and gone!

And while he wander'd in gloomy dream
And heard the cannons, the cannons roar,
His burning eyes were lit by a beam,
His pallid face a smile now bore!

Around his neck with most tender care,
An arm so white, an arm so soft,
From his true love, from his love so fair,
Is holding his manly form aloft!

And mild as Spring awakens the reed,
His lips were touched by a magic wand!
With a kiss so pure, with a kiss so sweet!
As only seraphs it can spend!

The Union soldiers were pushing on,
My soldiers in Gray, my soldiers in Gray!
The battle was lost, the heaven was won,
And through the darkness is piercing a ray![45]

Endnotes

Introduction

1. Simpson, *Hood's Texas Brigade: Lee's Grenadier Guard* (1970), p. 41.
2. Simpson, *Hood's Texas Brigade: A Compendium* (1977), p. 1.
3. Simpson, *Hood's Texas Brigade: A Compendium* (1977), p. 252.
4. Simpson, *Hood's Texas Brigade: Lee's Grenadier Guard* (1970), p. 88.
5. Simpson, *Hood's Texas Brigade: Lee's Grenadier Guard* (1970), p. 88.
6. Simpson, *Hood's Texas Brigade: Lee's Grenadier Guard* (1970), p. 214.
7. Simpson, *Hood's Texas Brigade: Lee's Grenadier Guard* (1970), p. 325.
8. Simpson, *Hood's Texas Brigade: Lee's Grenadier Guard* (1970), pp. 386-387.
9. Simpson, *Hood's Texas Brigade: Lee's Grenadier Guard* (1970), pp. 466, 468.
10. Flagel and Allers, *The History Buff's Guide to Gettysburg* (2006), p. 133.
11. Flagel and Allers, *The History Buff's Guide to Gettysburg* (2006), p. 131.
12. Flagel and Allers, *The History Buff's Guide to Gettysburg* (2006), p. 131.
13. Petruzzi and Stanley, *The New Gettysburg Campaign Handbook 9 July – 14 July 1863, Facts Photos, And Artwork For Readers Of All Ages* (2011), p. 66.
14. Flagel and Allers, *The History Buff's Guide to Gettysburg* (2006), p. 134.
15. Petruzzi and Stanley, *The New Gettysburg Campaign Handbook*, p. 107.

Chapter 1

1. Simpson, *Hood's Texas Brigade: Lee's Grenadier Guard* (1970), p. 1.
2. Simpson, *Hood's Texas Brigade: Lee's Grenadier Guard* (1970), p. 532.

3. *The War of the Rebellion: A Compilation of the Official Records of the Union and Confederate Armies*, Series I, Volume 27, 128 vols. (1880-1901), p. 409.

4. Todd, *First Texas Regiment* (1963), pp. 14-17. George T. Todd wrote about his wartime experiences in a series of articles for the Jefferson, (Texas), *Jimplecute Newspaper* in several instalments—2 April, 16 April, 30 April, 14 May, and 11 June 1909. The articles were later published in 1963 as *First Texas Regiment* by Texian Press, with notes and introduction by the late historian of Hood's Texas Brigade, Colonel Harold B. Simpson (USAF). On 3 July, 1863, General Judson Kilpatrick ordered General Elon J. Farnsworth to make what became a hopeless charge into the rear of Confederate General John Bell Hood's Division, resulting in Farnsworth's death. 'Farnsworth's Charge,' as it has come to be known, was made primarily by the 1st Vermont Cavalry under the command of Lt Colonel Addison W. Preston. The Vermont regiment suffered sixty-five casualties during the futile assault.

5. Todd, 'Recollections of Gettysburg' in *Confederate Veteran Magazine* (1900), p. 240.

6. *Cherokee County History*, Cherokee County Historical Commission, pp. 160-161.

7. Polley, *Hood's Texas Brigade: Its Marches, Its Battles, Its Achievements* (1910), pp. 167-172.

8. *The Eagle* (28 June 1926).

9. *The Eagle* (5 July 1926).

10. *The Houston Daily Post* (19 November 1899).

11. *Galveston Daily News* (20 November 1903).

12. *Galveston Daily News* (4 April 1904).

13. *Galveston Daily News* (7 May 1905).

14. Chilton, *Unveiling and Dedication of Monument to Hood's Texas Brigade on the Capital Grounds at Austin, Texas, Thursday, October Twenty-Seven, Nineteen Hundred and Ten, and Minutes of the Thirty-Ninth Annual Reunion of Hood's Texas Brigade Association Held in Senate Chamber at Austin, Texas, October Twenty-Six and Twenty-Seven, Nineteen Hundred and Ten, Together with a Short Monument and Brigade Association History and Confederate Scrap Book* (1911), p. 192.

15. *San Antonio Express* (18 March 1900).

16. Yeary, *Reminiscences of the Boys in Gray* (1912), pp. 104-105.

17. *Galveston Daily News* (11 July 1906).

18. *Jasper Newsboy* (Jasper, TX), 17 May 1911.

19. *The Orange Daily Tribune* (3 June 1903).

20. White, *Confederate Veteran*, Vol. 30 (May 1922), pp. 185, 187.
21. *Galveston Weekly News* (21 October 1863).

Chapter 2

1. Simpson, *Hood's Texas Brigade: Lee's Grenadier Guard* (1970), p. 114.
2. Hunt, Fourth Texas Infantry: Handbook of Texas Online.
3. Hunt, Fourth Texas Infantry: Handbook of Texas Online.
4. Simpson, *Hood's Texas Brigade: A Compendium* (1977), pp. 96, 103, 111, 117, 124, 130, 137, 146, 154, 160.
5. Henley, 'Lt Colonel Benjamin F. Carter', *UDC Magazine*, (December 2010), pp. 16-18.
6. *The War of the Rebellion: A Compilation of the Official Records of the Union and Confederate Armies*, Series 1, Volume 27, 128 vols. (1880-1901).
7. Shuffler, *Decimus et Ultimus Barziza, The Adventures of a Prisoner of War, 1863-1864*, (1964), pp. 43-46, 53-54.
   Editor's Note: Decimus et Ultimus Barziza (1838-1872), kept a diary of his experiences as a Captain in the Fourth Texas Infantry from 1863 to 1864. After being captured during the Battle of Gettysburg, Captain Barziza was a POW at Johnson's Island. A year later, as Barziza was being shipped to another prison, he escaped by diving through a window of a moving train. Making his was across Pennsylvania to New York, he took a train for Canada. There he became one of the first beneficiaries of an underground system which eventually returned him to North Carolina. Too sick from his early wounds and hardships of his escape from captivity, he spent the next few months writing his memoirs.
8. *The Tri-Weekly Telegraph* (12 December 1864).
9. Yeary, *Reminiscences of the Boys in Gray* (1912), pp. 9-10.
10. Chilton, *Unveiling and Dedication of Monument to Hood's Texas Brigade*, pp. 169-170. This is an excerpt of a letter sent by J. H. Cosgrove to J. B. Polley that was read at the dedication ceremony of the Hood's Texas Brigade monument in Austin, Texas, on 26 October 1910.
11. Lasswell, *Rags and Hope: The Memoirs of Val C. Giles, Four Years With Hood's Texas Brigade, Fourth Texas Infantry* (1961) pp. 176-187.
12. *Galveston Daily News* (11 May 1902). The Twenty-Second New York Infantry was not present at Gettysburg.

13. Polk, J. M., *Memories of the Lost Cause and Ten Years in South America* (1905) pp. 13-18.
14. Polk, *The North and South American Review*, (1912), pp. 26-27.
15. Polley, *A Soldier's Letters to Charming Nellie* (1908), pp. 130-139. J. B. Polley, a soldier of the Fourth Texas Infantry Regiment, wrote a series of letters to a fictitious woman named Nellie about his experiences during the war. Published as a book in 1908, *A Soldier's Letters to Charming Nellie* became a valuable resource of information about the life of a soldier in Hood's Texas Brigade. Interestingly, Polley was not present at the battle of Gettysburg. Polley was an unusually gifted writer with a talent for satire and humor unmatched by most Civil War diarists. While the collection met with an enthusiastic audience upon its publication, it has not been without controversy. Scholars have debated the authenticity of some of the letters; many appeared in the Confederate veteran magazine long after the end of the war, and questions remain about whether they were all written during the Civil War or if some were composed at the turn of the century or later.
16. *Corsicana Daily Sun* (21 October 1913).
17. *The Bryan Daily Eagle and Pilot* (28 June 1916).
18. West, *Texan In Search of a Fight—Being the Diary and Letters of a Private Soldier in Hood's Texas Brigade* (1901), pp. 79-103.
19. Chilton, *Unveiling and Dedication of Monument to Hood's Texas Brigade*, pp. 275-277.

Chapter 3

1. Simpson, *Hood's Texas Brigade: A Compendium* (1977), p. 167.
2. Simpson, *Hood's Texas Brigade: Lee's Grenadier Guard* (1970), p. 78.
3. Simpson, *Hood's Texas Brigade: Lee's Grenadier Guard* (1970), pp. 151-152.
4. Simpson, *Hood's Texas Brigade: Lee's Grenadier Guard* (1970), p. 154.
5. Colonel Powell wrote his recollections about the Battle of Gettysburg in an article entitled 'With Hood at Gettysburg', which appeared in the *Philadelphia Weekly Times* on 13 December 1884. Colonel Powell never wrote anything else about his Civil War experiences in Hood's Texas Brigade. In 1990, the late Civil War author and historian Gregory A. Coco edited the article that became the book *Recollections of a Texas Colonel at Gettysburg*. After Colonel Powell was wounded and captured on 2 July 1863, he spent several weeks at the Lutheran Theological Seminary's main building at Gettysburg.

He was later sent to the Federal prison camp at Johnson's Island, Ohio, until January 1865. Transferred to Fort Monroe, Virginia, he was paroled on 6 February 1865, two months before the war ended. Colonel Powell took command of Hood's Texas Brigade until the war's end. Colonel Powell later returned to Texas, where he lived for eighteen years before moving to St. Louis, Missouri, where he died on 15 January 1916. (Coco, *Recollections of a Texas Colonel at Gettysburg*, Thomas Publications (1990), pp. 9-16, 36)

6. *The War of the Rebellion: A Compilation of the Official Records of the Union And Confederate Armies*, Series 1, Volume 27 (1880-1901), p. 128.

7. *Ibid.*

8. *Galveston Daily News*, (30 March 1902).

9. Simpson, *Hood's Texas Brigade in Poetry and Song* (1968), p. 88. This poem by Sergeant Brantly was written for the 27–28 June 1906 reunion of Hood's Texas Brigade Association held in Somerville, Texas. Sergeant Brantly reminisces about his role at Gettysburg on a visit twenty years after the battle. He was captured by the Federals at Gettysburg on 2 July 1863 and confined at Ft Delaware prison until being paroled on 7 June 1865.

10. He was elected Captain in the Hood's Texas Brigade Association.

11. *The Bryan Daily Eagle and Pilot* (4 August 1911).

12. *The Houston Tri-Weekly Telegraph* (13 February 1865).

13. Stevens, *Reminiscences of The Civil War* (1902), pp. 111-119. Corporal Stevens' reference to 'General Stewart' is actually a reference to General James Ewell Brown (JEB) Stuart.

14. Yeary, *Reminiscences of the Boys in Gray, 1861-1865* (1912), p. 13.

15. *The Age* (1 December 1979). *The Age* was originally established in Houston, Texas, on 15 May 1871 by D. L. McGary, and moved to Wallisville, Texas on 16 May 1897. It was discontinued in 1908, and reestablished on 1 December 1979 as a newspaper highlighting historical news articles of past Texas history.

16. *Tri-Weekly Telegraph* (4 November 1863).

17. *Tri-Weekly Telegraph* (25 December 1865).

18. Fletcher, *Rebel Private Front and Rear, Experiences and Observations From the Early Fifties and Through The Civil War, The Greer Print* (1908), pp. 73-88.

19. Yeary, *Reminiscences of the Boys in Gray* (1912), pp. 471-472.

20. *Confederate Veteran*, Vol. 24 (February 1916), p. 69.

21. Cushing, ed., *Houston Tri-Weekly Telegraph* (8 March 1865). The Bayou City Guards was re-designated as Company A, Fifth Texas Infantry.

22. Yeary, *Reminiscences of the Boys in Gray* (1912), pp. 580-582.
23. Texas State Historical Association, *The Junior Historian*, Volume 25, Number 2 (November 1964), pp. 27-28.
24. Parker, *Touched By Fire: Letters From Company D, 5th Texas Infantry Hood's Brigade Army of Northern Virginia 1862-1865* (2000), pp. 64-67.
25. *The Southern Bivouac*, September 1884–May 1885, Vol. III (1992-1993), pp. 76-78. The Private from the Fifth Texas Infantry (who wished to remain anonymous) is referring to Big Round Top as Sugar Loaf Mountain.
26. *Waco-News Tribune*, (29 June 1925).
27. *The Eagle*, (23 October 1925).

Chapter 4

1. Simpson, *Hood's Texas Brigade: A Compendium* (1977), p. 252.
2. Van Hawkins, *Duty Bound: The Hyatt Brothers and Confederates of the Third Arkansas Infantry Regiment, Army of Northern Virginia, C.S.A.*, (2011), p. 15.
3. O. R., 27, pt. 1, pp. 407-408.
4. *Confederate Veteran*, Vol. 23 (December 1915), pp. 551-552.
5. Springfield, East Texas Genealogical Society, *East Texas Family Records*, Vol. 2, No. 2 (Summer 1978), pp. 1-4. Claire Kirk, the granddaughter of Henry Haywood Daniel, wrote about her grandfather's service in the 3rd Arkansas Infantry Regiment as a tribute to him. Obvious memories of talks with her grandfather gave her insight to his experiences during the Gettysburg campaign. She also referred to the following documents and books for the history of the 3rd Arkansas Infantry Regiment in her tribute to Henry Haywood Daniel: Civil War Muster Rolls, Company I, 3rd Arkansas Infantry, Henry H. Daniel, Washington, D.C.; Civil War Pension Application, Henry H. Daniel; Texas State Archives; Simpson, *Hood's Texas Brigade: Lee's Grenadier Guard* (1970); and Collier, *They'll Do To Tie To! 3rd Arkansas Infantry Regiment, CSA* (1959).
6. Joselyn, 'For Ninety Nine years and the War, the Story of the 3rd Arkansas at Gettysburg', *Gettysburg Magazine*, (1996), Issue 14, pp. 52-63.
7. *The Courier News*, (10 March 1937).
8. *Little Rock Daily Gazette*, (9 July 1866).
9. *Northwest Arkansas Times* (28 September 1965).
10. *Northwest Arkansas Times* (20 June 1966).

Chapter 5

1. Hood, *Advance and Retreat: Personal Experiences in the United States and Confederate States Armies*, (1880), pp. 55-59.
2. This report about the Battle of Gettysburg was only written in an informal letter to General James Longstreet following the war. After the war, General Longstreet wrote to General Hood for his recollections of the Suffolk and Gettysburg campaigns. General Longstreet noted that General Hood, who was seriously wounded on 2 July at the base of Big Round Top, had not turned in an official report for either campaign.
3. 'Report of Brig. General J. B. Robertson, C. S. Army, commanding brigade, 3 June-1 August, 1863'—*The Gettysburg Campaign*, O.R.—Series 1—Volume XXVII/2 [#44].
4. *Denison Daily News*, (2 September 1879).

Chapter 6

1. Dr Scott mistakenly referred to the First Minnesota Infantry as the Second Minnesota Infantry.
2. Chilton, *Unveiling and Dedication of Monument to Hood's Texas Brigade on the Capital Grounds at Austin, Texas Thursday, October Twenty-Seven Nineteen Hundred and Ten*, and *Hood's Texas Brigade Association Held in Senate Chamber at Austin, Texas October Twenty-Six and Twenty-Seven Nineteen Hundred and Ten Together with a Short Monument and Brigade Association History and Confederate Scrapbook* (1911), pp. 338-343.
3. Chilton, *Unveiling and Dedication of Monument to Hood's Texas Brigade*, pp. 348-354.
4. *Fort Worth Daily Gazette*. (28 June 1887). Congressman William Harrison 'Howdy' Martin (1822-1898) fought in the Fourth Texas Infantry, Hood's Brigade. Nobody is sure how he got the nickname of 'Howdy,' but one wartime legend has it that he saw General Robert E. Lee, stood up in his stirrups and yelled, 'Howdy!'
5. *Dallas Herald* (10 February 1872). After the Civil War, General Robert E. Lee became president of Washington and Lee University, located in Lexington, Virginia. Originally called Washington University, the university changed its name to Washington and Lee University after General Lee's death in 1870. Colonel William Preston Johnston (1831–1899) was the son and biographer of General Albert Sidney Johnston. During the war, he served as aide-de-camp to

Confederate President Jefferson Davis. After the war (at the invitation of General Robert E. Lee), he became a professor at Washington and Lee University in Lexington, Virginia. In 1880, he became president of Louisiana State University, but resigned four years later to become the first president of Tulane University in 1884.

6. Winkler, *The Life and Character of Gen. John B. Hood. Written at request of and read before Hood's Texas Brigade Association*, 27 June 1885 (1887), pp. 22-23. On 27 June 1885, Mrs C. M. (Angelina) Winkler delivered a speech at the Hood's Texas Brigade Association about the life of General John Bell Hood. The actions of General Hood during the Battle of Gettysburg are described in this excerpt from the speech. Mrs Winkler was the wife of Clinton McKamy (C. M.) Winkler (1821-1882), who formed the 'Navarro Rifles,' later Company I of the 4th Texas Infantry Regiment. Captain Winkler was wounded at the Battle of Gettysburg and later promoted to Major and then Lieutenant Colonel. After the Civil War, Lieutenant Colonel Winkler became a prominent lawyer and judge in Corsicana, Texas. The county of Winkler, Texas is named after him.

7. Hoopes, *The Confederate Memoir of William M. Abernathy* (March 2003), pp. 21-23. William M. (W. M.) Abernathy wrote his experiences as a Confederate soldier at the request of his friend and fellow veteran, C. C. Cummings. His account describes his service throughout the war, from April 1861 to April 1865. His great-great grandson John W. Hoopes submitted his entire memoir to Confederate Veteran Magazine in March 2003.

Chapter 7

1. *Democrat* (19 January 1905).
2. Both C. C. Cummings and W. M. Abernathy are referring to General William Barksdale's charge with his Mississippi Brigade during the late afternoon of 2 July 1863. This charge was famous for the ferocity of Barksdale's Brigade breaking through Union lines and capturing many prisoners, until fatigue and many casualties inflicted on the soldiers of Mississippi caused the charge to falter and retreat. General Barksdale was shot off his horse and died a few hours later in Union hands.
3. *Weekly Democrat-Gazette*, (26 September 1907).
4. *Confederate Veteran Magazine*, (September 1898).
5. *Fort Worth Daily Gazette*, (25 November 1894).
6. Prisoner of War Camp.

7. *Houston Daily Post*, (14 January 1900).
8. Yeary, *Reminiscences of the Boys in Gray* (1912), p. 52.
9. *Ibid.*, p. 67.
10. *Ibid.*, p. 83.
11. *Ibid.*, p. 222.
12. *Ibid.*, p. 232.
13. *Ibid.*, p. 336.
14. *Ibid.*, p. 390.
15. *Ibid.*, p. 415.
16. *Ibid.*, p. 435.
17. *Ibid.*, p. 439.
18. *Ibid.*, p. 450.
19. *Ibid.*, p. 505.
20. *Ibid.*, p. 538.
21. *Ibid.*, p. 578.
22. *Ibid.*, p. 584.
23. *Ibid.*, p. 598.
24. *Ibid.*, p. 696.
25. *Ibid.*, p. 752.
26. *Ibid.*, p. 798.
27. *Ibid.*, p. 806.
28. *Ibid.*, p. 834.
29. *The Waco Evening News*, (24 January 1894).
30. *Henderson Times*, (16 November 1899).
31. *Mexia Weekly Herald*, (7 August 1925).
32. *Palacios Beacon*, (10 January 1929).
33. *Cleburne Evening News*, (19 September 2013).
34. *Memorial and Biographical History of Dallas County, Texas: Containing a history of this important section of the great state of Texas, from the earliest period of its occupancy to the present time, and biographical of its pioneers, and also of prominent citizens of today*, (1892).
35. *Tulia Herald* (4 July 1919).
36. *History of Texas* (1892).
37. *Crockett Courier* (26 June 1913).
38. *Crockett Courier* (17 July 1913).
39. *The Brownsville Herald* (11 February 1895).
40. *The Alto Herald* (17 October 1935).
41. *The Standard* (15 May 1885).
42. *Waco Evening News* (5 April 1894).
43. *Abilene Reporter-News* (28 June 1938).
44. Rumpel, *Texas Souvenir: A collection of poems devoted to the scenery and historical events of Texas*, (1903), p. 9.

Bibliography

Anon., 'Pickett's and Hood's Charges At Gettysburg,' In *The Southern Bivouac,* September 1884–May 1885, Vol. III, Wilmington, DE: The Broadfoot Publishing Co., 1992-1993.

Carroll, H. B. (ed.), 'John Roberts, Austin, TX', *The Junior Historian,* Vol. 25. No. 2, 1964.

Carter, R. G., 'Inquiries and Answers', In *Confederate Veteran,* Vol. 14, 1906.

Chilton, F. B. *Unveiling and Dedication of Monument to Hood's Texas Brigade on the Capital Grounds at Austin, Texas, Thursday October Twenty-Seven, Nineteen Hundred and Ten, and Minutes of the Thirty-Ninth Annual Reunion of Hood's Texas Brigade Association Held in Senate Chamber at Austin, Texas October Twenty-Six and Twenty-Seven, Nineteen Hundred and Ten. Together with a Short Monument and Brigade Association History and Confederate Scrap Book,* Houston, TX: self-published, 1911.

Coco, G. A. (ed.), *Recollections of a Texas Colonel at Gettysburg,* Gettysburg, PA: Thomas Publications, 1990.

Flagel, T. R., and Allers Jr, K., *The History Buff's Guide to Gettysburg*, Napersville, IL: Cumberland House, 2006.

Fletcher, W. A., *Rebel Private Front and Rear, Experience and Observations from the Early Fifties and Through the Civil War,* Beaumont, TX: The Greer Print, 1908.

Henley, L. J., 'Lt Col. Benjamin F. Carter', *UDC Magazine,* Vol. 73, 2010.

Hood, J. B., *Advance and Retreat, Personal Experiences in the United States and Confederate State Armies,* Philadelphia, PA: Burke and McFeetridge, 1880.

Hoopes, J. W., 'The Confederate Memoir of William M. Abernathy', *Confederate Veteran Magazine*, Vol. 2, 2003.

Hunt, J. W., *Fourth Texas Infantry: Handbook of Texas Online,* Texas State Historical Association, (accessed via www.tshaonline.org/handbook/online/articles/qkf01).

Jones, A. C., 'Longstreet At Gettysburg', *Confederate Veteran,* Vol. 23, 1915.

Joselyn, M., 'For Ninety Nine years and the War, the Story of the 3rd Arkansas at Gettysburg', *Gettysburg Magazine,* Issue 14, January 1986.

Lasswell, M. (ed.), *Rags and Hope: The Memoirs Of Val C. Giles, Four Years With Hood's Brigade, Texas Infantry, 1861-1865,* New York, NY: Coward-McCann, 1961.

Lewis Publishing Company, *Memorial and Biographical History of Dallas County, Texas: Containing a history of this important section of the great state of Texas, from the earliest period of its occupancy to the present time, and biographical of its pioneers, and also of prominent citizens of today,* Dallas: 1892; *History of Texas, with a biographical history of Milam, Williamson, Bastrop, Travis and Burleson counties: containing a concise history of the state, with portraits and biographies of prominent citizens of the above named counties and personal histories of many of the early settlers and leading families,* Dallas: 1893.

Nabours, W. A., 'Active Service of a Texas Command', *Confederate Veteran,* Vol. 24, 1916.

Parker, E. R. (ed.), *Touched By Fire: Letters From Company D 5th Texas Infantry Hood's Brigade Army Of Northern Virginia,* Hillsboro, TX: Hill College Press, 2000.

Petruzzi, J. D., and Stanley, S., *The New Gettysburg Campaign Handbook July 9–July 14, 1863: Facts, Photos, And Artwork For Readers Of All Ages,* El Dorado Hills, CA: Savas Beatie, 2011.

Polk, J. M., *Memories of the Lost Cause and Ten Years in South America,* Austin, TX: J. M. Polk, 1905; *The North and South American Review,* Austin, TX: J. M. Polk, 1912.

Polley, J. B., *Hood's Texas Brigade: Its Marches, Its Battles, Its Achievements,* New York, NY: The Neale Publishing Company, 1910; *A Soldier's Letters To Charming Nellie,* New York, NY: The Neale Publishing Company, 1908.

Rumpel, C. F., *Texas Souvenir: A Collection of poems devoted to the scenery and historical events of Texas,* Austin, TX: Von Boeckmann-Jones Co., 1903.

Shuffler, R. H., (ed.), *Decimus et Ultimus Barziza: Adventures of a Prisoner of War 1863-1864,* Austin: University of Texas Press, 1964.

Simpson, H. B., *Hood's Texas Brigade: A Compendium,* Hillsboro, TX: Hill Junior College Press, 1977; *Hood's Texas Brigade: In Poetry And Song,* Hillsboro, TX: Hill Junior College Press, 1999; *Hood's Texas Brigade: In Reunion And Memory,* Hillsboro, TX: Hill Junior College Press, 1974; *Hood's Texas Brigade: Lee's Grenadier Guard,* Hillsboro, TX: Hill Junior College Press, 1970.

Springfield, B. (ed.), 'A Memorial: Henry Haywood Daniel, Confederate Soldier', in *East Texas Genealogical Society,* Vol. 2, No. 2, Summer 1978.

Stevens, J. W., *Reminiscences of The Civil War,* Hillsboro, TX: Hillsboro Mirror Print, 1902.

Todd, G. T., *First Texas Regiment,* Waco, TX: Texian Press, 1963.

United States War Department. *The War of the Rebellion: A Compilation of the Official Records of the Union and Confederate Armies,* 129 vols, Washington, D.C.; U.S. Government Printing Office, 1880-1901.

West, J. C., *A Texan In Search of a Fight—Being the Diary and Letter of a Private Soldier in Hood's Texas Brigade,* Waco, TX: J.S. Hill and Company, 1901.

White, W. T., 'First Texas Regiment at Gettysburg,' in *Confederate Veteran*, Vol. 30, 1922.

Winkler, C. M., *The Life and Character of Gen. John B. Hood. Written at request and read before Hood's Texas Brigade Association, June 27, 1885*, Austin, TX: self-published, 1887.

Yeary, M., *Reminiscences of the Boys in Gray*, Dallas, TX: Smith and Lamar, 1912.

Newspapers

Abilene (TX) Reporter-News
Alto (TX) Herald
Blytheville (AR) Courier News
Brownsville (TX) Herald
Bryan (TX) Daily Eagle and Pilot
Bryan (TX) Eagle
Clarksville (TX) Standard
Cleburne (TX) Evening News
Corsicana (TX) Daily Sun
Crockett (TX) Courier
Dallas (TX) Dallas Herald
Fayetteville (AR) Northwest Arkansas Times
Fort Worth (TX) Daily Gazette
Galveston (TX) Daily News
Galveston (TX) Weekly News
Henderson (TX) Henderson Times
Houston (TX) Daily Post
Houston (TX) The Age
Houston (TX) Tri-Weekly Telegraph
Jasper (TX) Newsboy
Little Rock (AR) Daily Gazette
McKinney (TX) Democrat
McKinney (TX) Weekly Democrat-Gazette
Mexia (TX) Weekly Herald
Orange (TX) Daily Tribune
Palacios (TX) Beacon
San Antonio (TX) Express
Tulia (TX) Herald
Waco (TX) Evening News
Waco (TX) News Tribune

Index